IMAGES
of America

SACO REVISITED

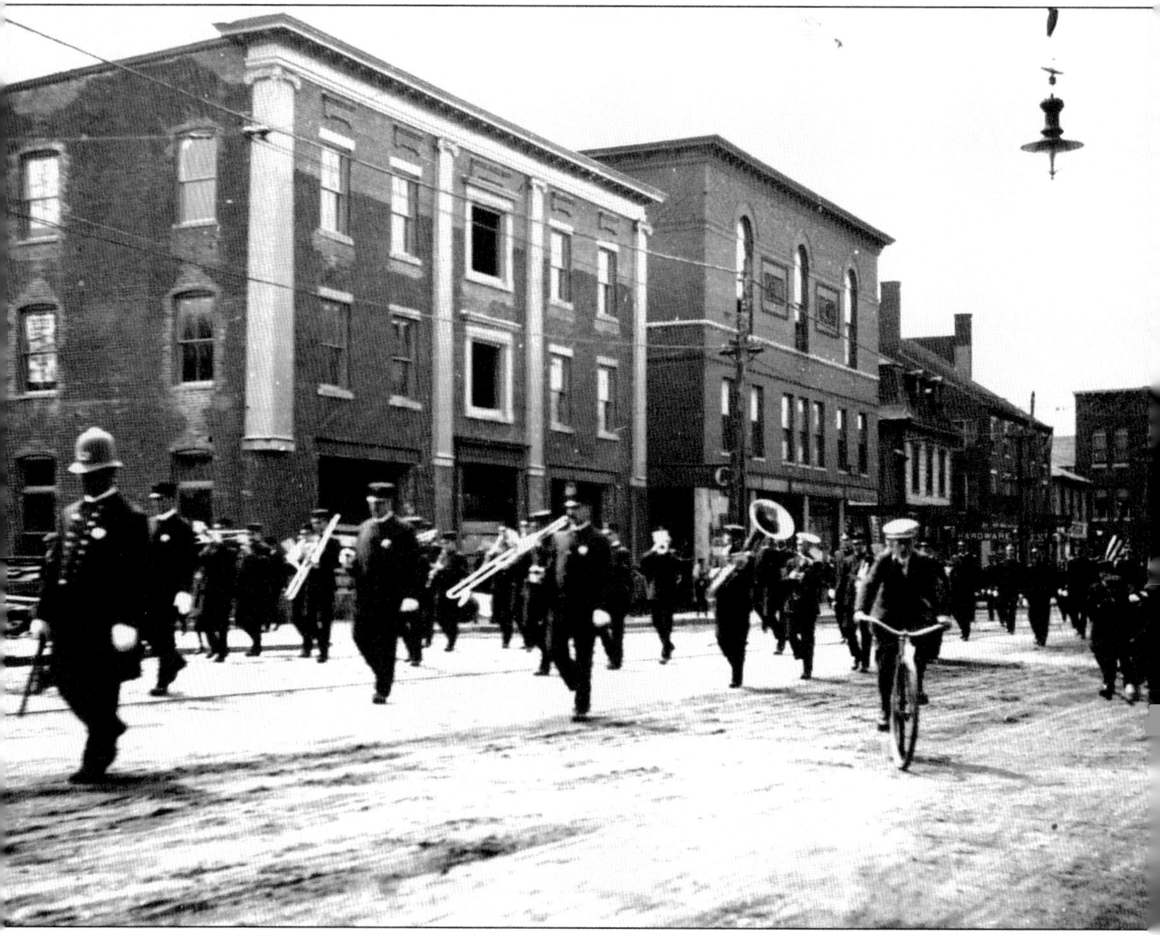

A policeman, with a band following, marches past the former Saco House hotel, which burned in a devastating fire on December 9, 1912. Much of the facade was saved when it was converted to the store for Atkinson's Furniture. The building seems to be in the process of restoration—the peaked roof is gone, two of the windows are missing their glass, and the openings on the street level appear to be boarded up. Today, while Atkinson's is gone, the building still stands, looking much like it does in this picture. (Courtesy Dyer Library and Saco Museum.)

On the cover: Please see page 15. (Courtesy Dyer Library and Saco Museum.)

IMAGES
of America

SACO REVISITED

Dyer Library and Saco Museum

ARCADIA
PUBLISHING

ISBN 978-0-7385-7213-0

Published by Arcadia Publishing
Charleston SC, Chicago IL, Portsmouth NH, San Francisco CA

Printed in the United States of America

Library of Congress Control Number: 2009928366

For all general information contact Arcadia Publishing at:
Telephone 843-853-2070
Fax 843-853-0044
E-mail sales@arcadiapublishing.com
For customer service and orders:
Toll-Free 1-888-313-2665

Visit us on the Internet at www.arcadiapublishing.com

This book is dedicated to all those who, over the years, have worked to celebrate and preserve Saco's history.

Contents

ACKNOWLEDGMENTS

The Saco Museum, originally known as the York Institute, was founded in 1866, about the same time as the earliest photographs in this book were taken. The Dyer Library was established just 15 years later, and since then the two organizations, which now operate together as the Dyer Library Association, have served as stewards of Saco's history. With the help and support of our staff, volunteers, and board of trustees, the library and museum have worked together to make this book a celebration of our collections as well as of Saco.

This book provides a definition for group effort. An army of staff and volunteers, including Fred Clark, Roy P. Fairfield, Darren French, Sallie Huot, and Camille Smalley, helped to select photographs, research and write captions, format the book, and proofread every word of text. Together we are all indebted to the scholarship of other Saco authors and historians, including John Anagnostis, Elizabeth A. DeWolfe, Jacques Downs, Tom Hardiman, Peter Scontras, Jeffrey A. Scully, and of course Roy P. Fairfield, who has literally "written the book" on Saco history many times over and who has supplied the foreword for this book. We are grateful to Hilary Zusman and Arcadia Publishing for valuing our stories and for giving us the opportunity to tell them here.

Thanks also go to the following, who have helped us to identify Saco photographs in their collections and agreed to include them in this book: Fred Clark, Jennie Aranovitch of the Congregation Etz Chaim in Biddeford, Renee DesRoberts and Dora St. Martin from the McArthur Library in Biddeford, Kevin Johnson from the Eastern Illustrating and Publishing Company Archive at the Penobscot Marine Museum, Jim and Edna Leary, John Morrill Read, Marian Stickney, and Diane and Michael Zaitlin. They are credited individually by all their photographs. Unless otherwise noted, photographs are from the collections of the Dyer Library and Saco Museum. Thanks to them and to all the photographers, collectors, and donors, known and anonymous, who have done their part to preserve these images of Saco.

Leslie Rounds, executive director
Jessica Skwire Routhier, museum director
Marie O'Brien, collections and archives manager

FOREWORD

If a picture is worth a thousand words, then assembling a host of pictures depicting a village becoming a city may serve much like a global positioning system capturing its history. Indeed Saco's pictorial history catches an area that evolved from a pinpoint on a map of the British empire to a dynamic industrial city populated by people self-conscious of their struggle to survive.

Of course, the time frame caught in this volume covers a little less than two centuries since the history of photography begins just short of the mid-19th century. However, photography grew from infancy to adulthood for the common person relatively quickly and then from the box camera era to the digital one. Hence the qualitative and the quantitative leaps and bounds of the medium enabled nearly everybody to enjoy history's pictorial bounty.

This collection reflects nearly two centuries of that phenomenon; its compilers have chosen from a vast number of images. They have struggled to find representative photographs of people engaged in agriculture, the impact of technology, the problem of keeping up with architectural changes that moved from practical needs to emerging styles, and clothing differences that run the gamut from serving as simple protection from the elements to Sunday best.

One needs merely to study the evolution of the typical southern Maine farmhouse to show how Yankee ingenuity adapted over the years. Structures connected to the main farmhouse, added progressively over time, created a customized agricultural complex that accommodated a variety of uses for different seasons. Photographs also enable one to see the increased complexity of factory working facilities, where again, architectural and industrial design took its cue from human use.

Part of my perspective on Saco's visual history inevitably relates to my own experience attending Saco schools, becoming a citizen and member of the industrial workforce, regarding it as my hometown while earning degrees and teaching in several other states, and building a summer home in this area. Writing books and monographs about the area also kept me focused on Saco but hardly homebound. In short, my eyes and memory recorded both everyday and special events. I walked the muddy, unpaved sidewalks, but I also marveled at newly laid brick ways between my in-town home and kindergarten sessions in the city hall. In fact, I counted the rows of bricks in that walk, and I tried not to step on the spaces between them. Then with my family moved to the country outskirts, I saw how increasing automobile traffic on Main Street (Route 1) forced pedestrians to walk on wintery sidewalks cleared by horse-drawn plows. I marveled at the sound of Saco's newly acquired tractor plows clanking their way through the 10-foot drifts "up-country" three miles away.

Photographs of automobile mechanics remind me of my garage-owner father and his discussions about many individuals depicted here. Not only did I grow up in that environment, but I also learned to repair some of those very cars. I swam in the river (against my parents' warnings about Squando's curse that the river would consume its quota of human beings per year), worked in the mills, attended the schools and churches, ran my first car over both mud and newly laid cobblestones on Main Street, and rode the excursion boats and trolley cars that constituted traffic. Ironically, my life barely overlapped with the closing days of horse-drawn wagons and the generations-long dependence on those means. At the age of 10, I fell off a pile of hay, since I had not quite mastered the skill of "making a load."

My experience of Saco has always been public as well as private. Involvement includes marching as a Boy Scout in parades, gathering at Laurel Hill Cemetery to honor soldiers who died in America's wars, and more recently, studying names on the current war memorial that reflect the demographical trend from old Yankee to immigrants from Scotland, Ireland, French Canada, Greece, and other parts of the world. It is a study worth the time of both natives and visitors. Also I have written dozens of letters to the editor and spoken to many social groups about a one-year Fulbright Fellowship in Greece and the romance of writing local history.

Those familiar with the ancient theory that the world is made up of four elements—earth, air, water and fire—would have no difficulty finding all those elements in Saco. Agriculture easily fulfills the earthly focus; vast acres of grass and forest contribute to that despite the ever-advancing suburbs.

Increased use of the air in the 1920s and 1930s certainly stimulated the imagination of people of all ages in and around Saco. At the first sound of an airplane, children ran into an open space to wave to the pilot. Making model airplanes became a passion. International airplane travel, especially through Old Orchard Beach after Charles A. Lindbergh conquered the Atlantic, drew hundreds of local people of all ages the moment the press and newly evolving radio announced a new pilot taking off from Old Orchard Beach's long, flat stretch. The exclamation marks of the mills' mighty brick chimneys along the river dominated our view of that air.

With Saco being bordered by water on two of its four sides and a flooding river as an ever-present threat, the development and use of water to power mills of many types has been an ever-living fact, facet, and challenge of every focus and creative imagination in each generation.

As for the fourth element, fire, Saco's citizens have experienced more than enough of that to occupy both firemen and those who practice chasing fires for curiosity's sake, probably to capture the excitement and uncertainty in the lives of Saco's citizens and the inevitably changing vistas. It would not be difficult to fill a volume such as this with photographs of fires in all states of burning, with every implication for Saco citizens' fate, future, and fatality. Yet some fires made us think of change and new ventures, architecture, and vistas. In short, these disastrous, unimaginable changes ultimately effect new viewpoints for this human community dedicated to dynamic optimism rather than negative fatalism.

Whereas the limits of photographic evolution shape the contours and tones of this book, today's technology probes the sky for a Saco that may be revisited a decade or century hence.

—Roy P. Fairfield, August 2009

Introduction

Since prehistoric times, the city of Saco has been defined by the dramatic course of the Saco River. Native Americans settled near the mouth of the river where the city center stands today, harnessing the swift, deep Saco River as a trade route and as their primary mode of transportation. When Samuel de Champlain visited in 1604, he noted that, "The Indians remain permanently in this place, and have a large wigwam surrounded by palisades on a high bluff. This place is very pleasant and as attractive a spot as one can see everywhere." Following this early period of European exploration, the long Native American name of "Shawakotoc" became transformed into "Chouacoet" and ultimately "Sawco," or Saco.

The first permanent European settlement arrived in 1631, when England's Plymouth Company granted patents for the land lying on both banks of the Saco River, and the patentees pledged to transport 50 people to their tracts "within the seven years next ensuing, to plant and inhabit there." It was not long after this that the power of the falls was first harnessed for industry. By the 18th century, gristmills and sawmills populated the shores of the Saco River, producing flour and lumber for local use, as well as for communities up the river and across the ocean.

The 19th century brought modern industrial development to Saco. Col. Thomas Cutts, an early entrepreneur, saw the potential for development in the islands that lay in the river between the two settlements now known as Saco and Biddeford. Beginning in 1759, he began to purchase portions of the land now known as Factory Island. Soon he built a home there and operated a successful nail factory and retail store. His efforts were helped along by a network of bridges and ferries that made Factory Island the fastest, most direct route across the river. By the mid-19th century, cotton mills, machine shops, iron foundries, box shops, and cigar factories, among other industrial sites, crowded in and around Factory Island. With companies like York Manufacturing, Pepperell Mills, Laconia Mills, the Saco-Lowell Shops, Garland Manufacturing, and others occupying the mill district, the sister cities of Biddeford and Saco became leaders of manufacturing in the industrial age. The need for industrial labor spurred mass immigration from Europe and Canada.

The pressures of growth and increasing needs for services led the citizens of Saco to incorporate as an independent city in 1867. The town hall, built in 1856, was rededicated as city hall, and in the ensuing years it expanded and added a bell tower. Cultural organizations and institutions of higher learning—the Dyer Library, the York Institute (now the Saco Museum), Thornton Academy, countless places of worship, Masonic and other fraternal organizations, parochial schools, and charitable foundations—were also established or greatly expanded.

It was around this time that Saco also developed as a tourist destination, with visitors from larger northeastern cities riding the Boston and Maine Railroad directly to Saco's beaches and unique summer communities. Impressive summer homes sprang up near the beaches of Camp Ellis and Ferry Beach, and Saco became a destination for summertime parades, picnics, musical performances, and other events. Inns and hotels dotted Main Street, and entertainments like roller-skating and cycling soared in popularity. The river proved to be a thoroughfare for the tourist industry as well as the manufacturing industries. It was used for swimming, fishing, canoeing, and pleasure boating, and it also provided a conduit between northern New England's two great tourist centers: Maine's coast and New Hampshire's White Mountains. Artists and photographers were also drawn to the region, creating idyllic images of scenes from the wooded riverbanks and falls to the shore.

This era of prosperity continued until the mid-1950s, when the closure of the York Manufacturing Company marked the beginning of an economic downturn in Saco. Although jobs became scarcer, manufacturing continued on Factory Island to one degree or another through the present day. The groups who emigrated here to work in the mills have also stayed, and the children, grandchildren, and great-grandchildren of mill workers have put down deep roots in the community. In recent years, the city has become revitalized as an artistic, cultural, and economic center, with creative reuses for the mill buildings, including restaurants, sports facilities, apartments, and artists' studios. The railroad is once again a hub of commerce and activity, with the wind-powered Saco Transportation Center, built in 2009, serving as a community gathering place and a locus for travel to and from Boston, Portland, and farther flung destinations. A historic preservation ordinance, established in the 1970s and strengthened in 1990, has safeguarded the landmarks of Saco, and in 1998, the downtown district earned a listing on the National Register of Historic Places, recognizing the important role that the city of Saco has played in centuries of American life.

Shortly before the dawn of the 20th century, Saco author and publisher John S. Locke spoke to a group of students about the museum he had helped to found 25 years before. "When another quarter of a century shall bring its anniversary . . . you will be making the history of York Institute. And when the present and the future shall become the past and your records are read by generations which follow you, may they find in them examples of energy, industry, philanthropy and patriotism worthy of imitation." More than 100 years later, Saco remains equally dedicated to preserving its past and strengthening its future. Accordingly, Locke's eloquent words provide the basis for this book, with each chapter examining those areas of memory and self-invention that he identified more than a century ago. In photographs and text, this book explores the ways in which Saco's unique geography and its industrial history have affected and informed city life. The energy, industry, philanthropy, and patriotism of Saco and its citizens, then and now, indeed provide a model of civic pride that is worthy of imitation.

This introduction is indebted to "A Brief History of Saco, Maine" by Tom Hardiman, part of the City of Saco's online history resources at www.sacomaine.org.

—Jessica Skwire Routhier, museum director

One

ENERGY

Saco is defined by the energy that is embodied both in its distinct geography and in its inhabitants. The ceaseless power of the wide, deep Saco River, moving swiftly over the landscape before rushing over falls and into the ocean, has set the course of the city itself. All of those who have settled here, from the Native Americans to present-day residents, navigate their daily lives around the topography of the river, its falls, its islands, and its banks. The early nonnative settlers situated their homes and businesses strategically for both proximity to and protection from the river, while in the 19th century, factories and mills were built literally over the falls in order to harness their power.

With the river's power came peril: spring freshets and floods, log jams, and unforgiving winter weather that froze ships in the harbor and brought the water powered industry to its knees. Saco residents persevered during these trials, finding innovative ways to help one another and to get around in the hazardous landscape.

Saco's citizens have always reflected the energy of the city's geography. Its early inhabitants braved long winters and spring floods to build elegant homes and, ultimately, powerful factories. Energy is embodied in another way as well—in the joyful spirit of a populace that loves a celebration and in the boundless energy of its youth, always ready for a friendly competition or a caper.

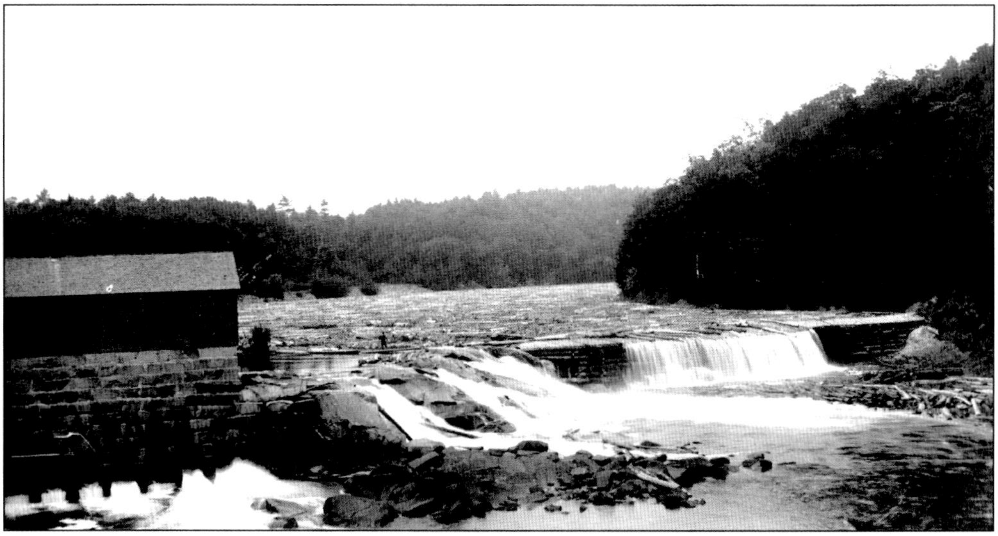

Proximity to the dense forests of inland Maine made the wide, deep Saco River essential for Maine's lumbering industry. For 300 years, the river transported massive numbers of logs, feeding the sawmills on the falls. This practice often resulted in dangerous logjams; note the man standing on the dam breaking up entangled logs.

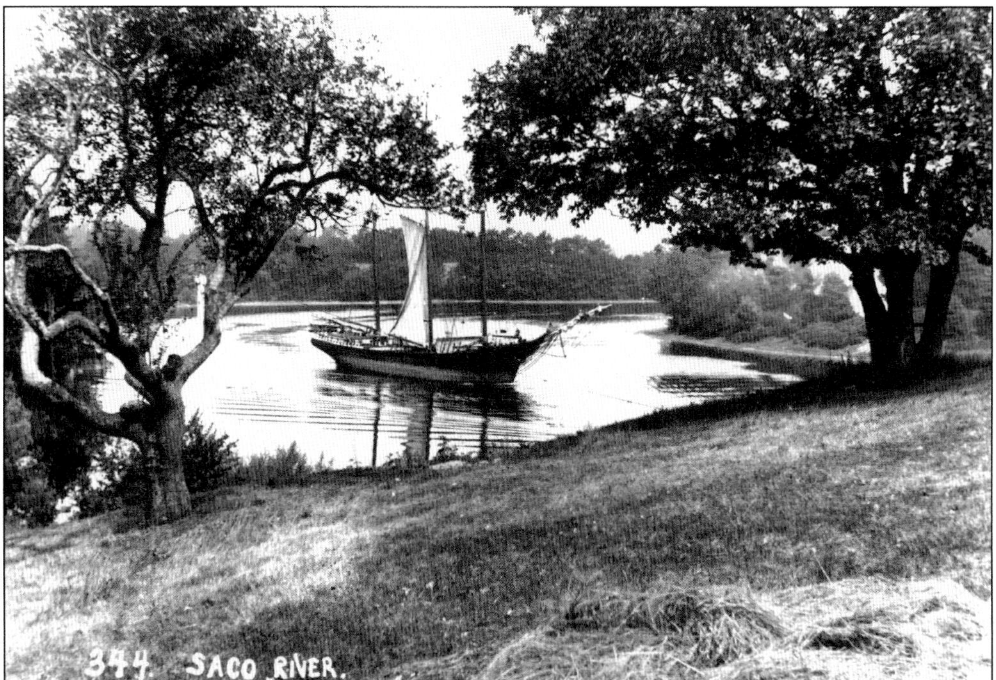

Undeveloped riverbanks far away from the town's center recall the pre-industrialized scenery of the 1600s, when a local tragedy gave birth to the myth of Squando's curse. An infant son of the Native American chief drowned when three English sailors decided to test the theory that Native American children were born with the ability to swim. Squando subsequently cursed the waters of the Saco River, so the story goes, declaring that the water would take the lives of three white men every year until they fled the area. (Courtesy McArthur Public Library.)

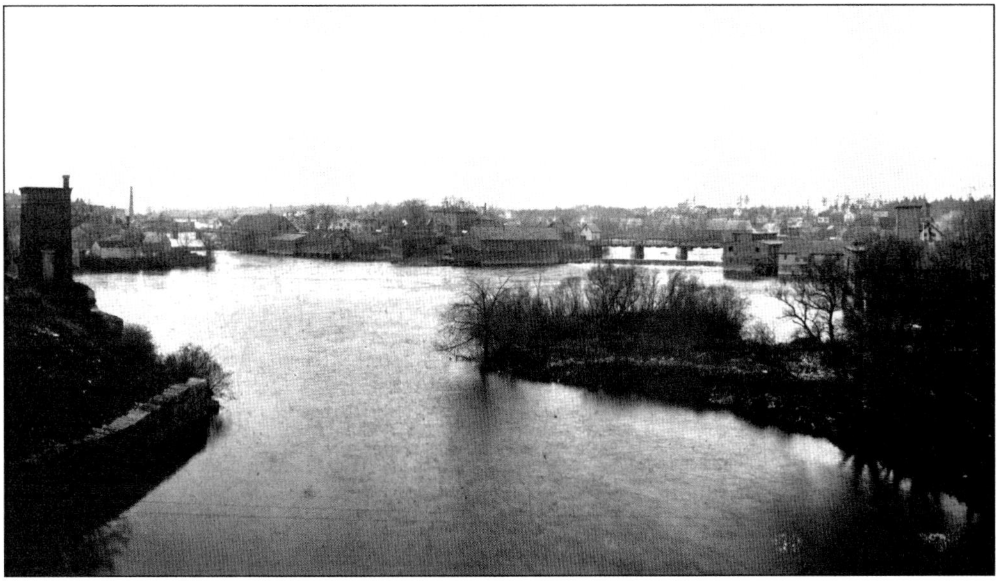

This view of the Saco River, looking toward Spring Island, shows the breadth of the river as it flows between Saco and the neighboring town of Biddeford. Visible in the center is Spring's Tavern (also called Spring Mansion), built by entrepreneur Seth Spring in 1798 and now the headquarters for Deering Lumber. The Capt. David Sawyer house is to the left, and the Elm Street bridge, flanked by gatehouses, is on the right. Saco's train station, built in 2009, now stands to the left of the stone bank.

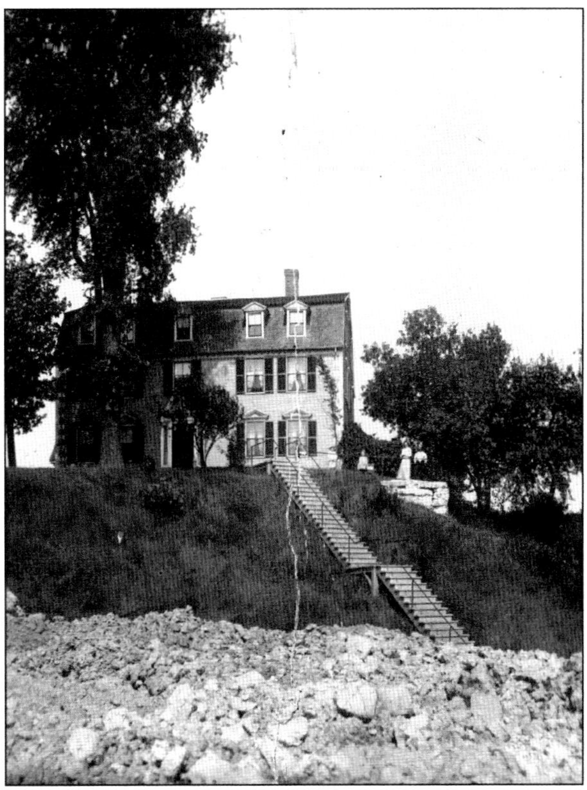

The Cutts mansion was a prominent feature on Factory Island from 1782 to about 1936, when it was taken apart to make room for a dam and later reconstructed in Saco without the second story. Gertrude Anthony paid to have the mansion dismantled and stored. Posing beside it are Grace, Ruth, Sadie, and Ernest Morrill, who resided there in the early 20th century. (Courtesy John Morrill Read.)

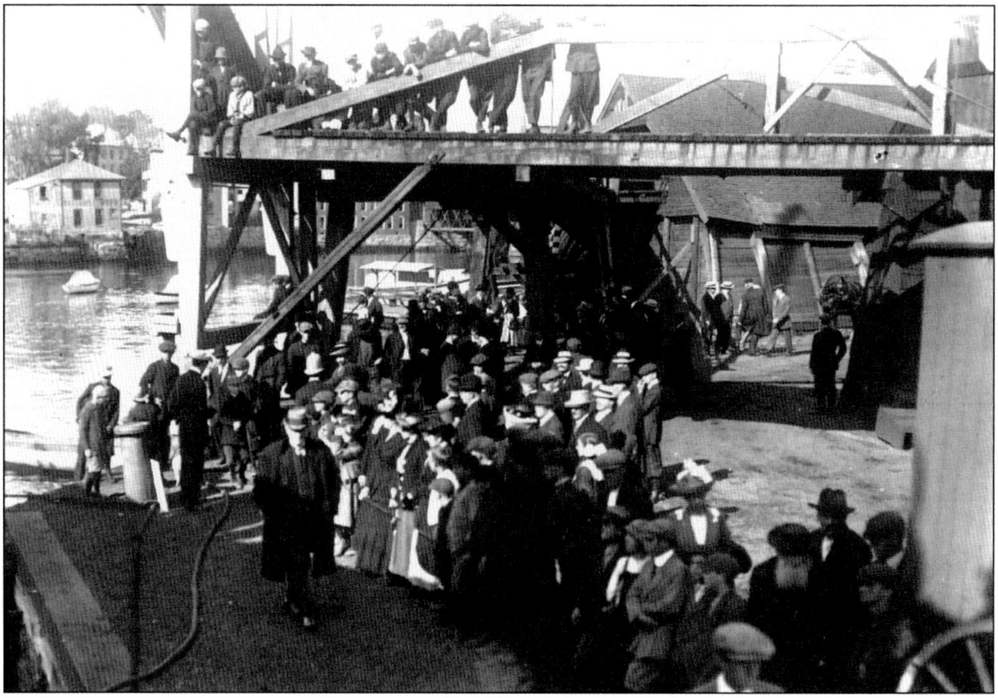

The islands in the Saco River were crucially important as the site of the mills and as the fastest route between Saco and Biddeford. From the 18th century on, a network of ferries and bridges provided access to and across the islands. Gifted local photographer Charles Moody snapped this image of families gathered to await the cross-river ferry. There were three ferries that ran to and from this Factory Island location. (Photograph by Charles Moody; courtesy McArthur Public Library.)

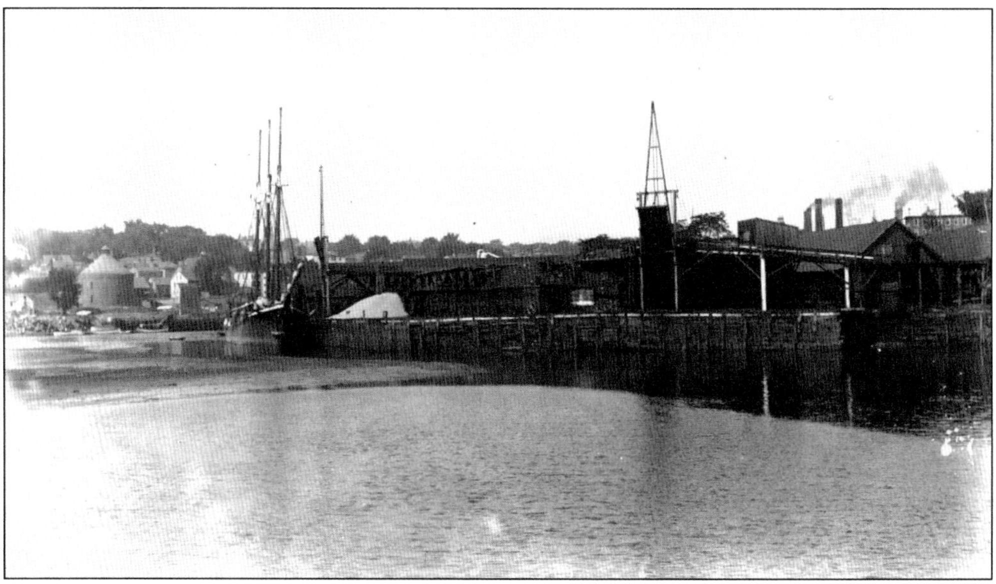

A three-masted schooner is tied up at the coal docks, where coal was unloaded and lumber and textiles were shipped out. Note the Biddeford Gas Plant, the round building to the left, which stood where the Biddeford sewage plant is now located. (Courtesy McArthur Public Library.)

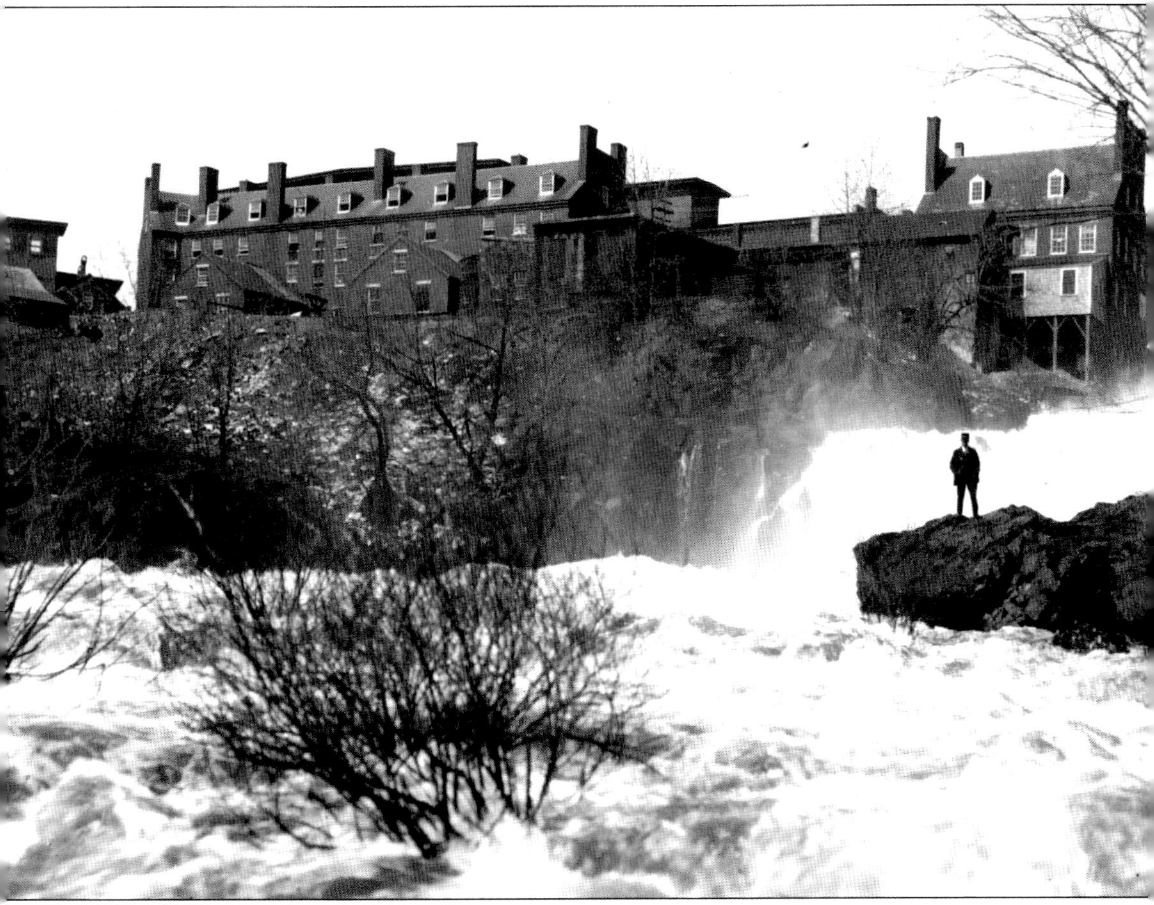

The waterpower that fueled the mills was an awesome and sometimes dangerous source of energy. This photograph, possibly taken during the flood of 1895, gives a sense of Cataract Falls's scale and strength. The building in the background housed small businesses on the ground floor and provided rooms for mill workers in the upper stories. These Main Street buildings were demolished in the second half of the 20th century.

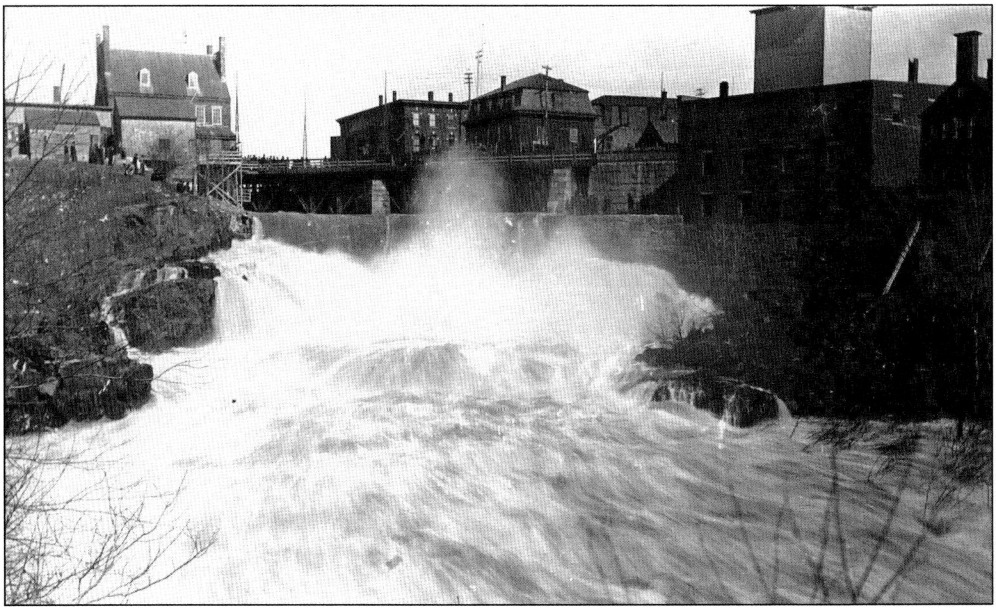

Photographed when the Saco River was running high, Cataract Falls throws a cloud of mist into the air. Notice the numerous bystanders on the riverbank and Main Street bridge. The Sweetser Block (center) still exists.

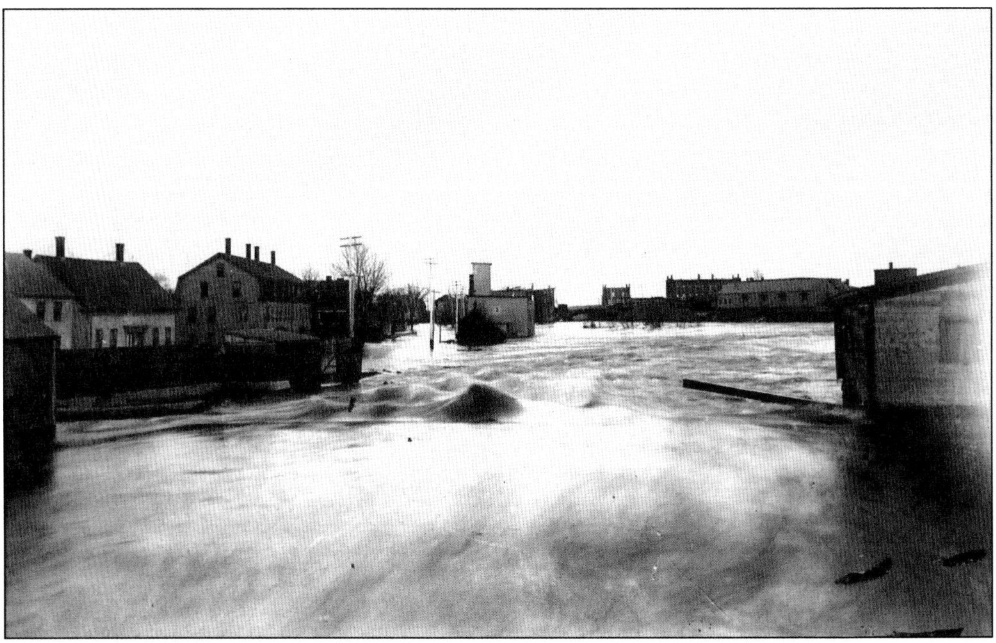

Each spring, rains and melting snow cause the Saco River to rise. Before drainage and dam improvements were made in the 20th century, these conditions frequently resulted in extensive flooding. Water Street earned its name on April 4, 1895, when this picture was taken from the Elm Street bridge. The first two houses on the left still stand, as does Garland Manufacturing (center), although it is now an apartment building.

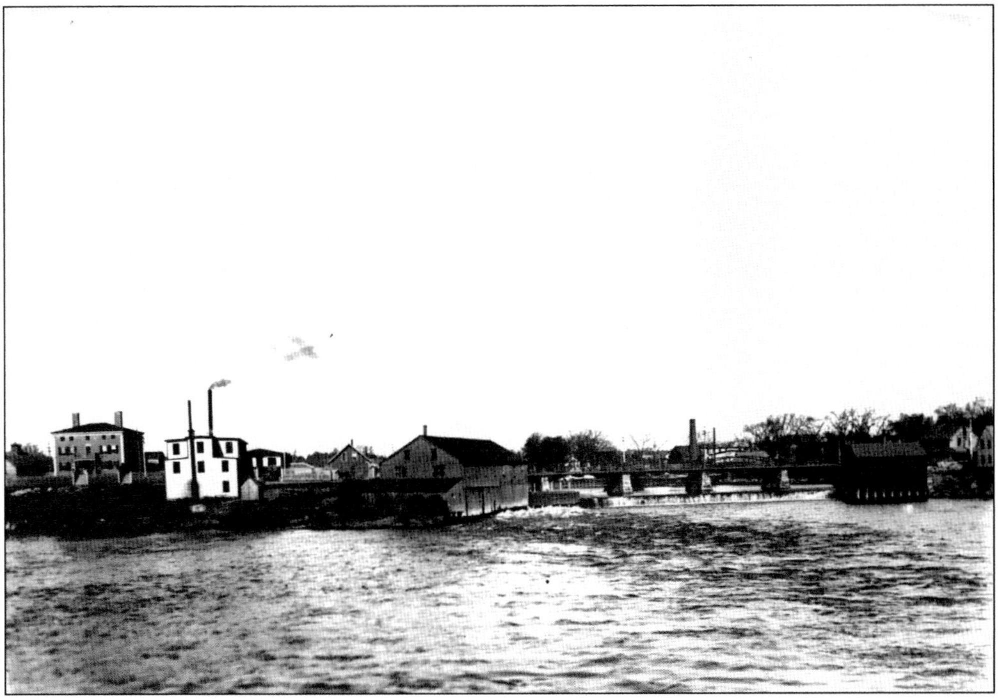

Charles Moody actively chronicled the local area in the early 20th century. Here he shows how the spring freshet of 1911 has pushed the river out of its banks again. Spring Island is on the left, and Saco is on the right. The buildings on both sides of the bridge housed gates used to control the river's flow. (Photograph by Charles Moody; courtesy McArthur Public Library.)

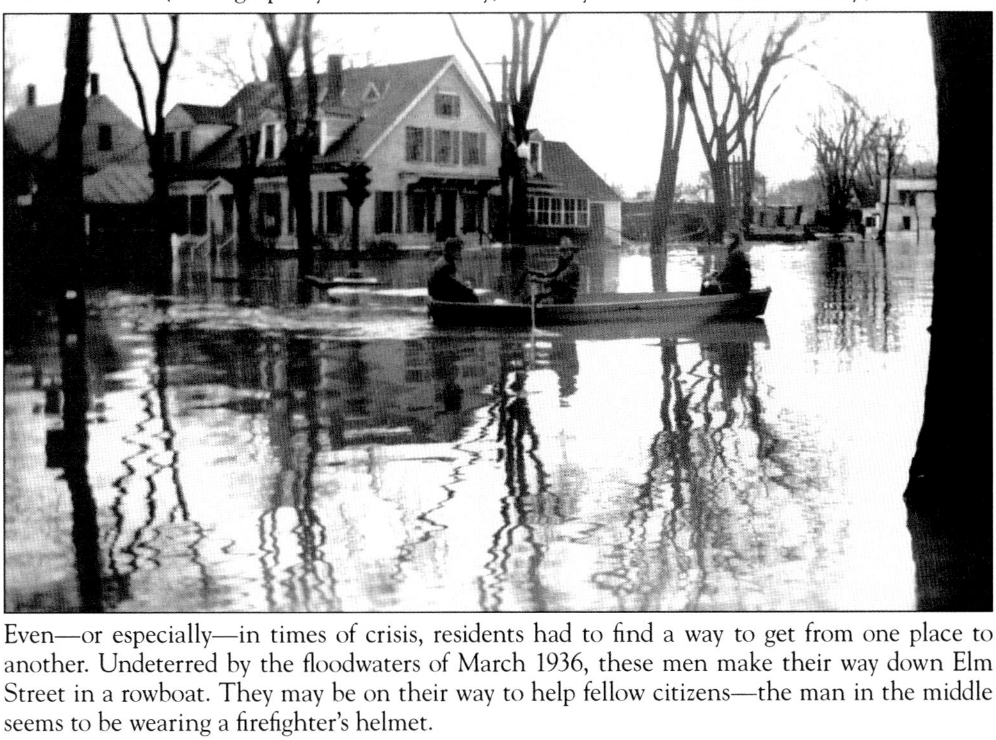

Even—or especially—in times of crisis, residents had to find a way to get from one place to another. Undeterred by the floodwaters of March 1936, these men make their way down Elm Street in a rowboat. They may be on their way to help fellow citizens—the man in the middle seems to be wearing a firefighter's helmet.

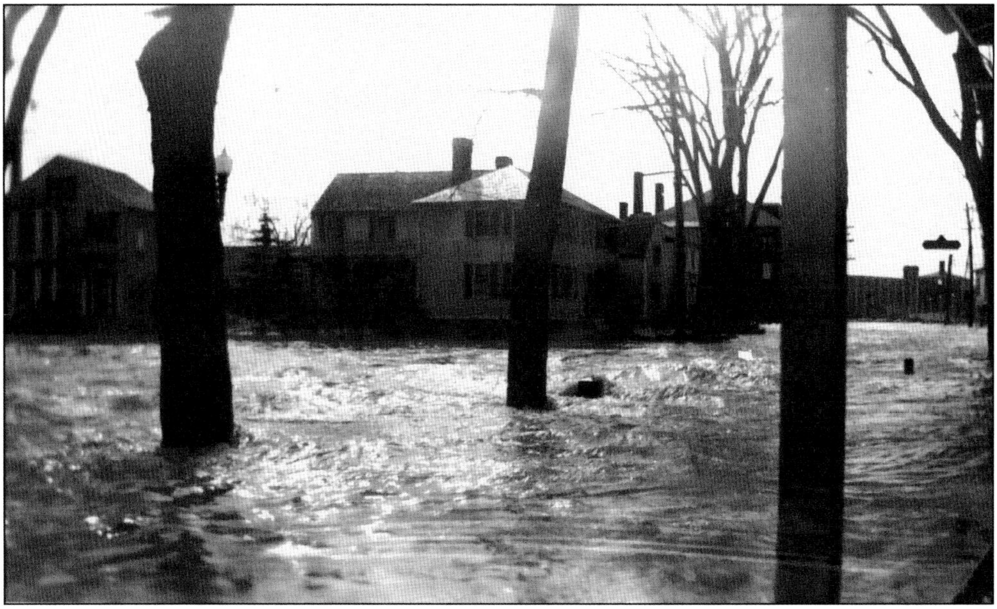

The swollen Saco River sweeps down Elm and Storer Streets during the March 1936 flood. The houses in the center still stand. After this devastating flood, Cumberland County Power and Light constructed a dam on the river near the factory district. That dam was used for power generation, but others were built upstream at the same time for flood-control purposes. Although other floods have occurred, none has matched the power and devastation of the one in 1936.

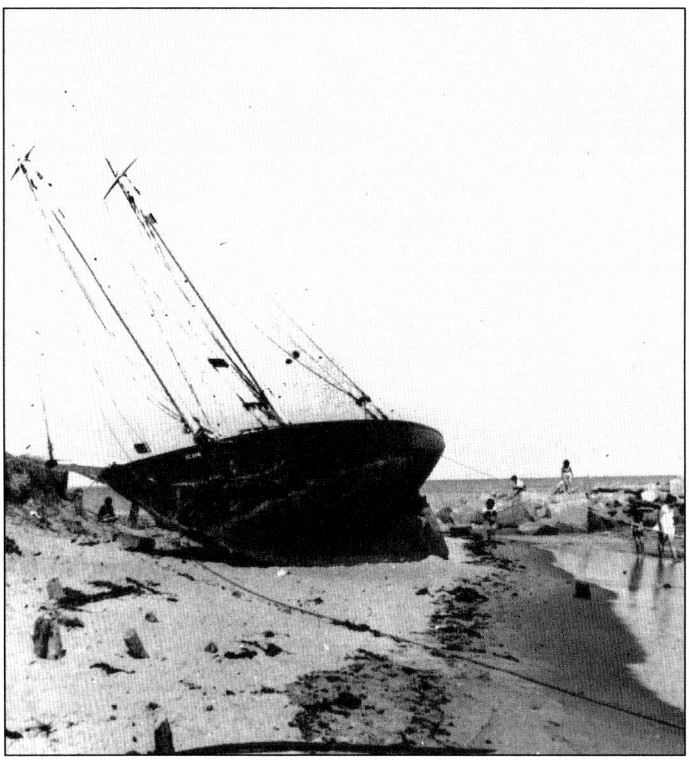

Floods were not the only danger brought by the harsh New England weather. This two-masted sailing ship was driven aground at Saco's Camp Ellis during Hurricane Carol on August 30, 1954. Camp Ellis lies at Saco's easternmost point, exposed to the brute force of the Atlantic Ocean. Beach erosion following nor'easters continues to be a concern here, and recent conversation has focused on removing or replacing the jetty installed by the U.S. Army Corps of Engineers in 1867.

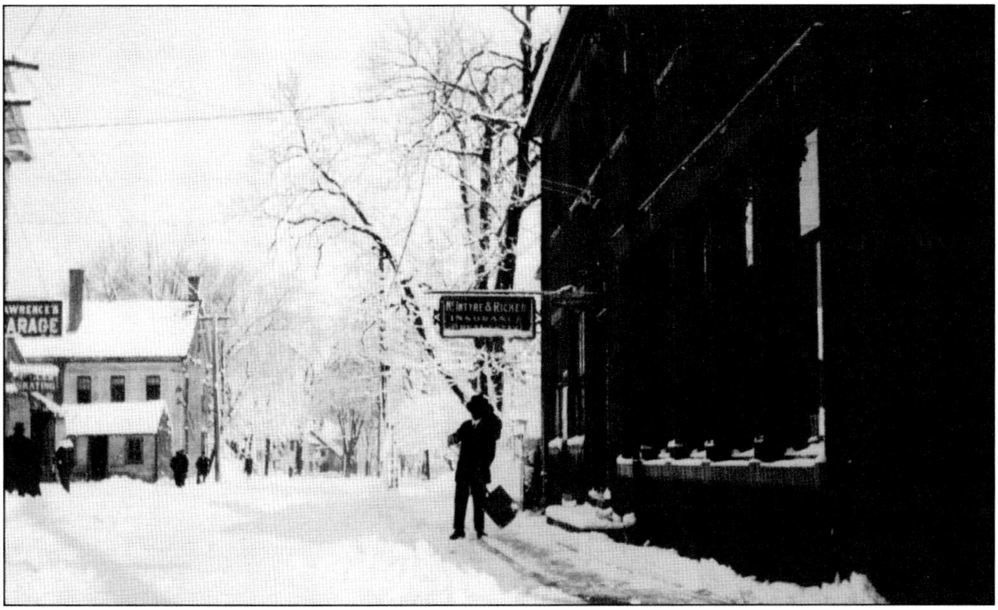

A Saco citizen shovels out in front of McIntyre and Ricker Insurance on Storer Street across from Lawrence's Garage after a big storm sometime between 1908 and 1928. No snowplows or snowblowers were used here; the only available tools were metal coal shovels or heavy wooden snow shovels.

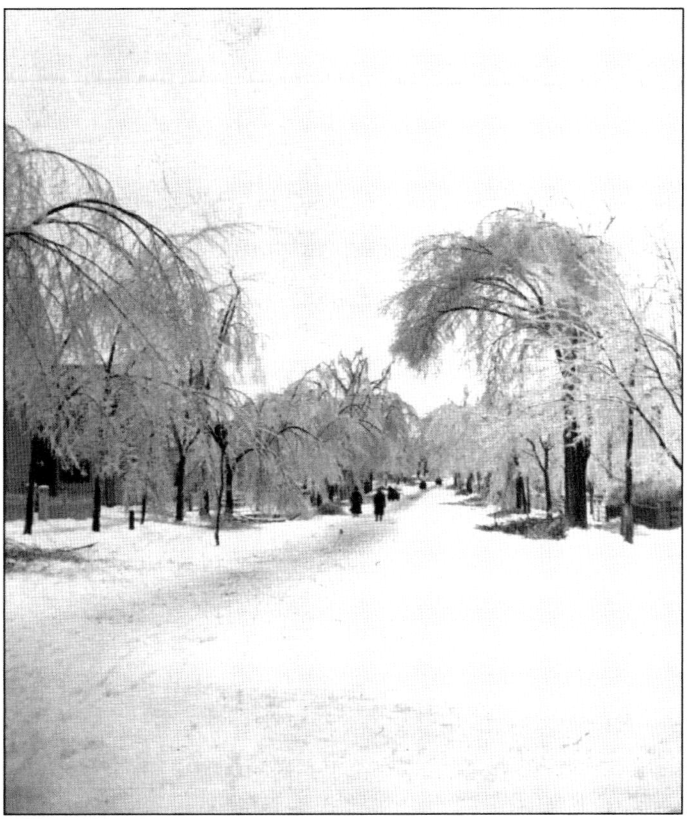

Warmer weather in January is not always welcome. Here is North Street after the epic ice storm of January 27–28, 1886, which was brought on by an unseasonable rain followed by a return to freezing temperatures. A local area newspaper called it the ice storm of the century, and severe damage was sustained by the trees, which can be seen bending under the weight of their icy burden.

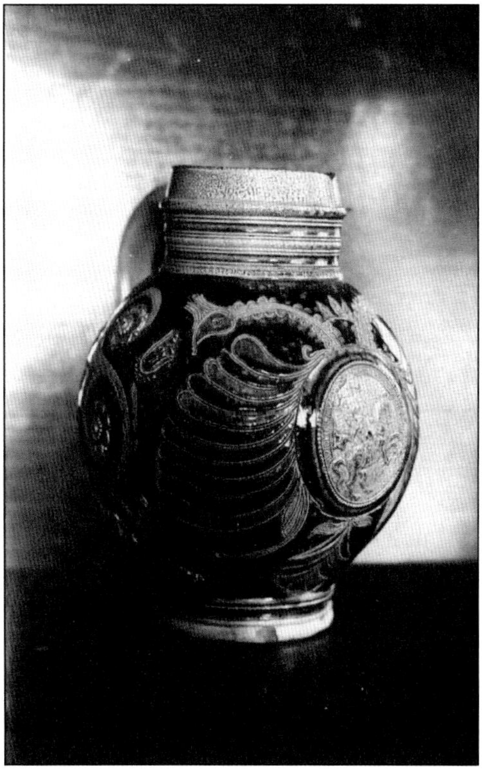

The earliest European settlers in the area had to navigate not only the river and the weather but also relations with Native American populations. Legend has it that this Westerwald jug was left in the Scamman home when the family was carried off by Native Americans in the late 17th century. When a new peace allowed them to return a year later, the jug was still on the table, untouched and still filled with beer.

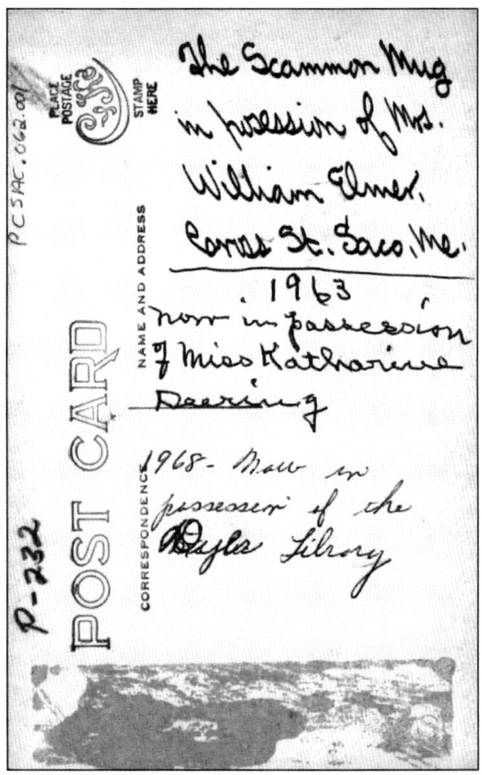

The message side of this early postcard details the Scamman jug's own history. When the postcard was made, the jug was owned by Winona Moody Elmer, wife of William Elmer. The treasured relic was passed down through the family and ultimately became a part of the Saco Museum's permanent collection.

Taking time out from hard work in the 1850s, J. Q. A. Scamman and Julia Augusta Adelaide Cutts pose for this daguerreotype, which was later turned into a postcard. Notice his asymmetrical tie and her large-plaid dress, both very popular fashions at the time.

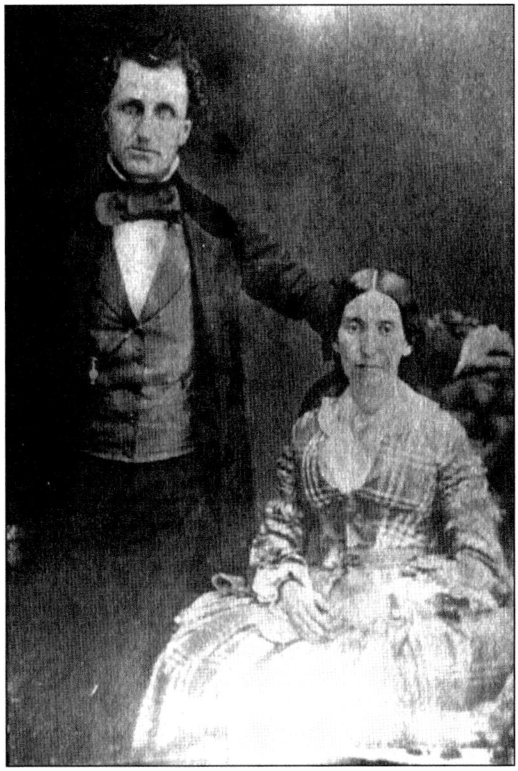

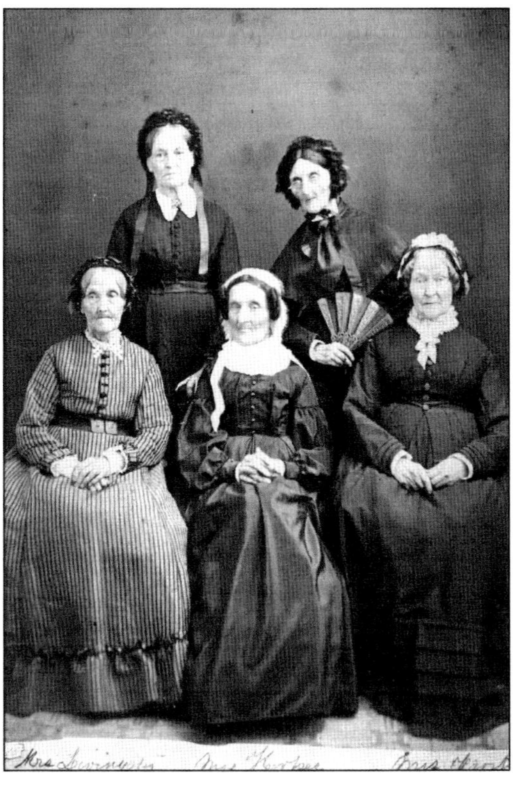

These careworn women endured the hard life of 19th-century Maine, and their countenances demonstrate both strain and steadfastness. Photographed shortly after the Civil War, these are the daughters of Richard Foxwell Cutts. From left to right are (first row) Sarah Livingston (1793–1890), Elizabeth Hooper (1787–1882), and Mary Louisa Frost (b. 1789); (second row) Caroline Webster (1801–1882) and Marianne Parks (1796–1870s).

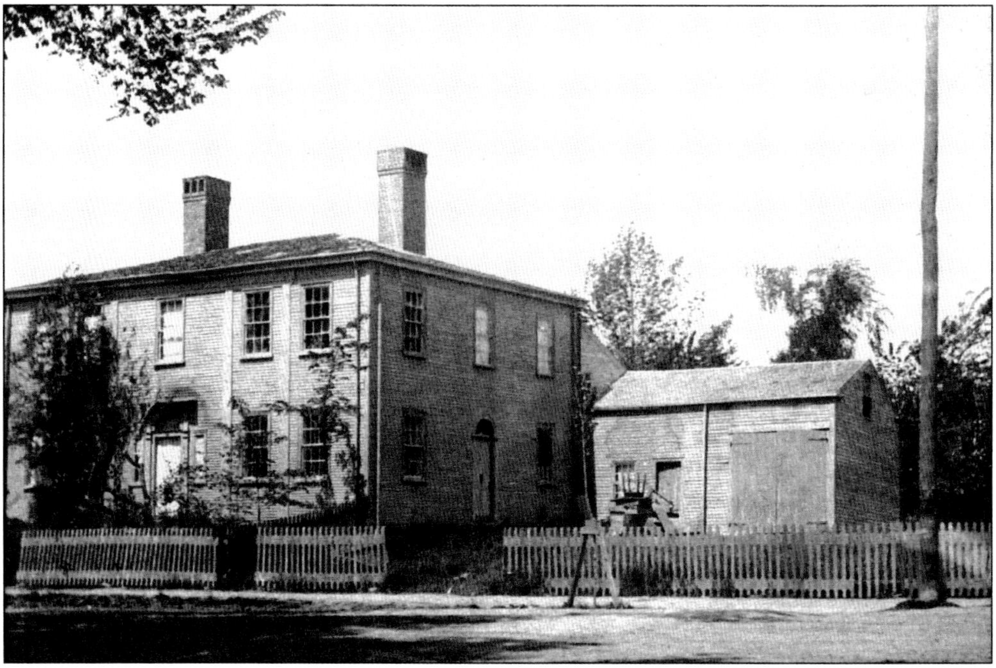

Thomas Cutts had this attractive home built at 350 Main Street for his daughter Eunice and her husband, Dr. Samuel Nye, to entice them back from Boston around the time of the War of 1812. Two of the Nye's unwed daughters lived in poverty here until their deaths around 1890. Later the house was moved to Clark Street, where it became an apartment building. York Manufacturing Company built a home for their agent on the Main Street lot.

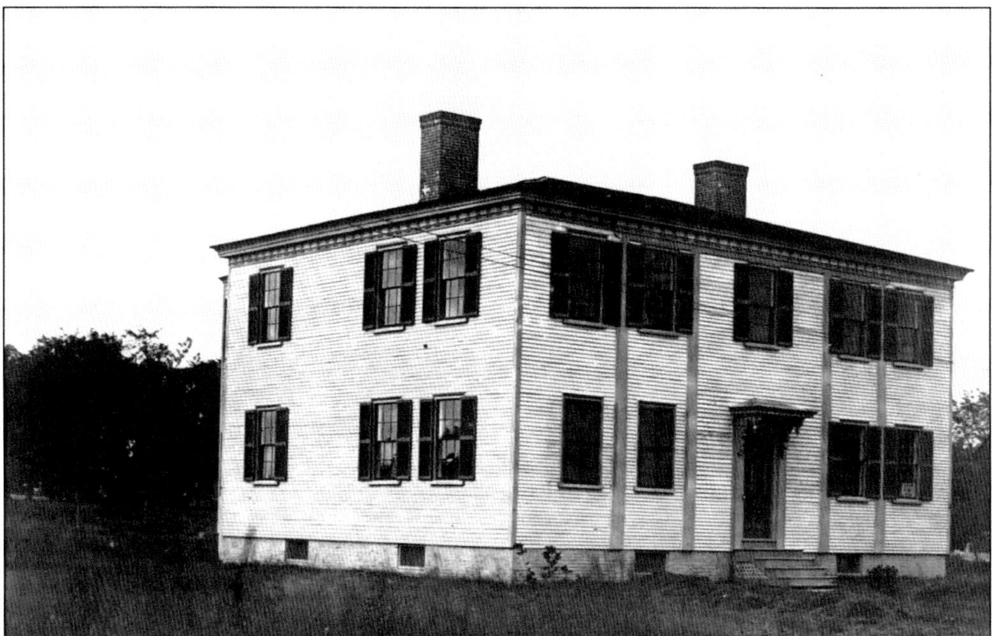

No other houses have yet been built on Clark Street in this view of the Nye home shortly after its move there.

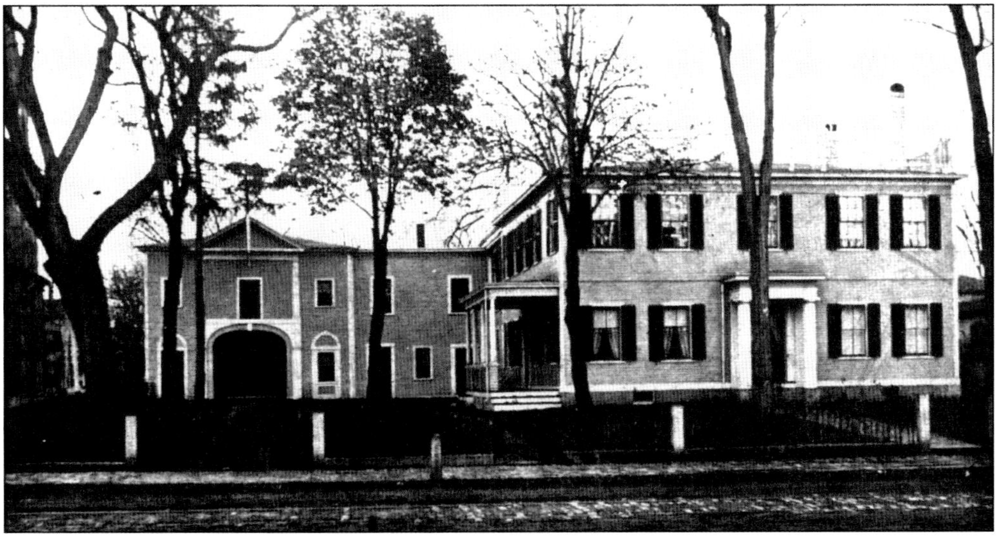

John Haley was an enthusiastic if somewhat opinionated Saco historian. He commented on this Main Street house: "This house was built by Jonathan Tucker, an old time merchant of Saco. Who, like so many others in Saco, were so anxious to outdo the others [that they] nearly ruined themselves. The[y] built not for their time but for future generations. The exact date of building this house is only approximately known, but Mr. Tucker was occupying it in 1822, and his daughter Ann Jenks Tucker was born in that year. Since then it has passed thro [*sic*] several hands, Samuel Bradley, Warren Rice, John Berry. It was converted into a movie show, and lastly into the Catholic Church which also owns the Gen King mansion for a parsonage. This latter was built sometime previous to 1817. General King [a member of Maine's famous King family] died in 1817." For more on the Tucker/Berry house, see pages 59 and 114.

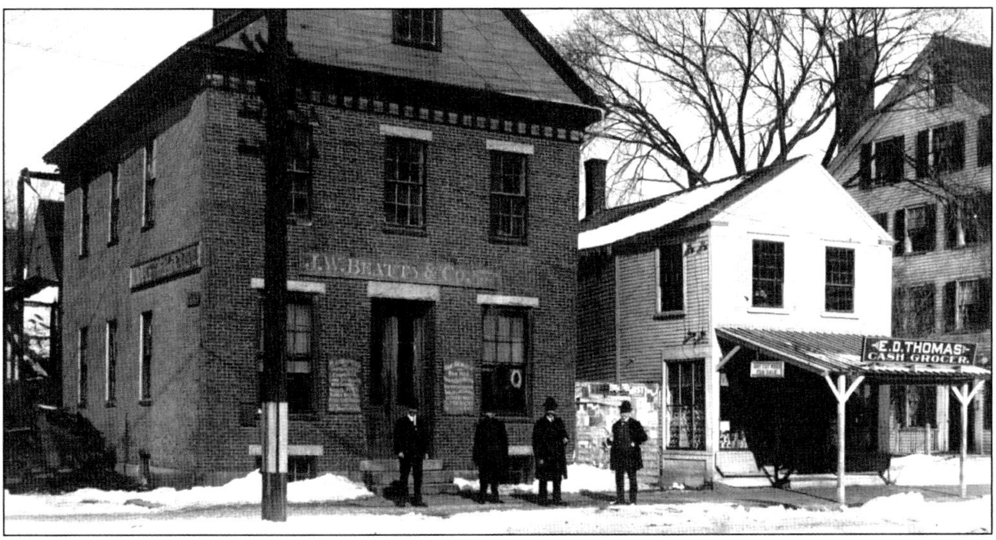

The corner of Main and Pleasant Streets, where old-timers often gathered to tell humorous, sometimes off-color stories, was known as Joker's Corner. The three buildings from left to right are J. W. Beatty's Company, which made leather belts for machinery in the mills; E. D. Thomas's Cash Grocer; and the Hotel Wallace, where Saco and Biddeford Savings Bank now stands. Legend has it that the area was called Joker's Corner because of the practical jokes men liked to play on unsuspecting Saco citizens there.

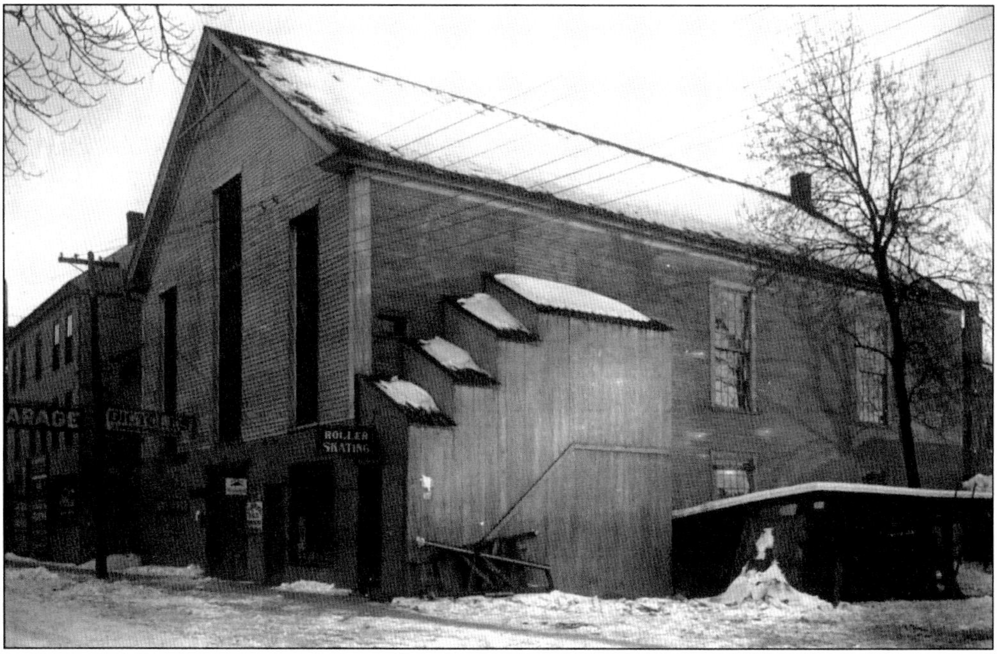

Roller-skating became increasingly popular in Saco by the end of the 19th century. City hall was used as an arena until an old church on Storer Street was converted into a roller rink, complete with rock-maple floor, blue-figured curtains, and Japanese and Chinese lanterns.

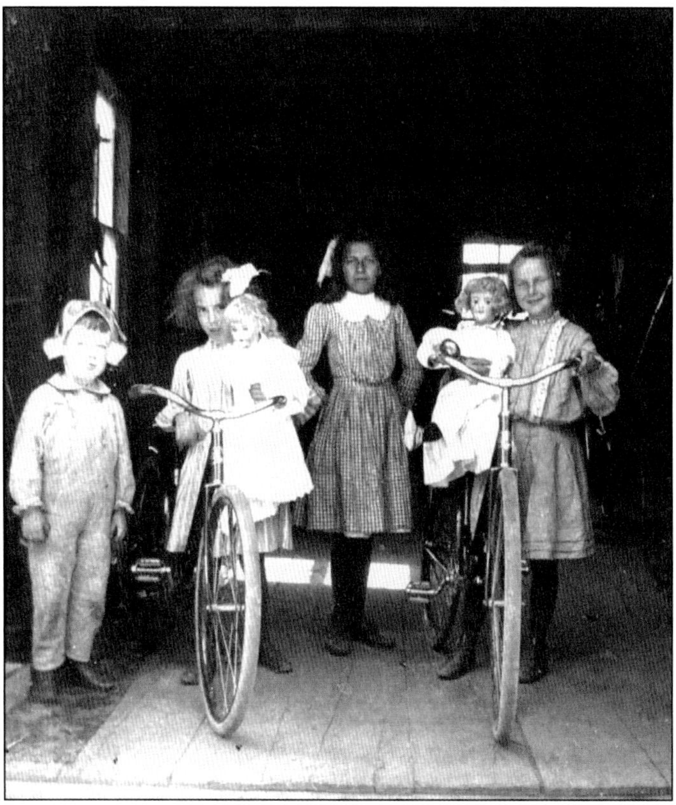

Out for a ride with their dolls, these children demonstrate the energy that would later power them on to interesting careers. From left to right, Lowell Norton of Vernon Street earned a doctorate degree and became a labor economist and lecturer at Harvard University; Lucy Hill Thornton became an elementary school principal in Malden, Massachusetts; Marie Lawrence attended Gray's Business School in Portland; and Helen Lawrence was a graduate of Thornton Academy in 1914 and Tufts University in 1943.

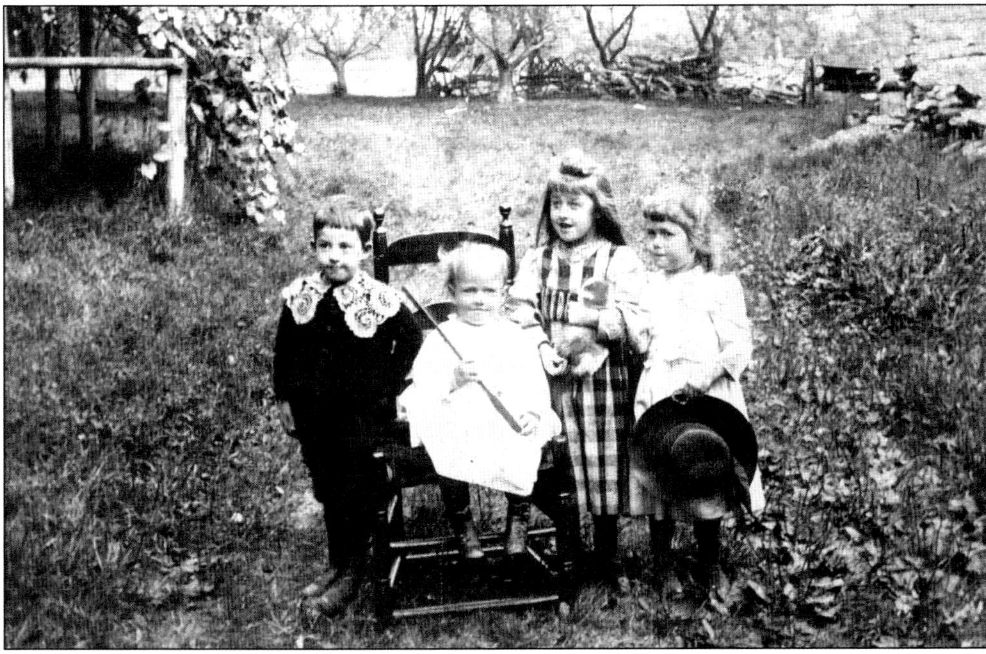

Few photographs of the 19th century fully capture the lively, active spirits of young children. Photographed here in front of their Portland Road homestead are three members of the Chapin family and a visiting friend. From left to right are William Harper Chapin (1890–1921), Dormer Malcom Chapin (1893–1904), Lillian Chapin, and Alma Pillsbury. Lillian is clearly holding some type of unhappy, live animal, which may account for the surprised look on her face. In the background of the photograph, barely visible, are several pieces of farm equipment or wagons.

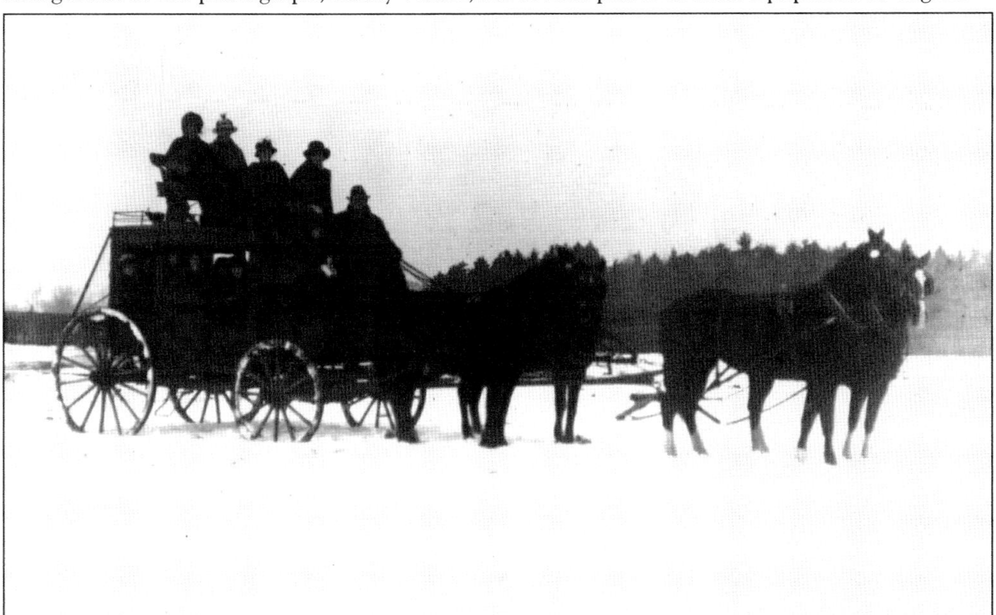

Out for a joyride on a snowy day, these Thornton Academy students seem to be trying to determine how many people could fit into this horse-drawn carriage. In spite of the overcrowding, the ladies have managed to hold onto their fashionable headgear. (Courtesy McArthur Public Library.)

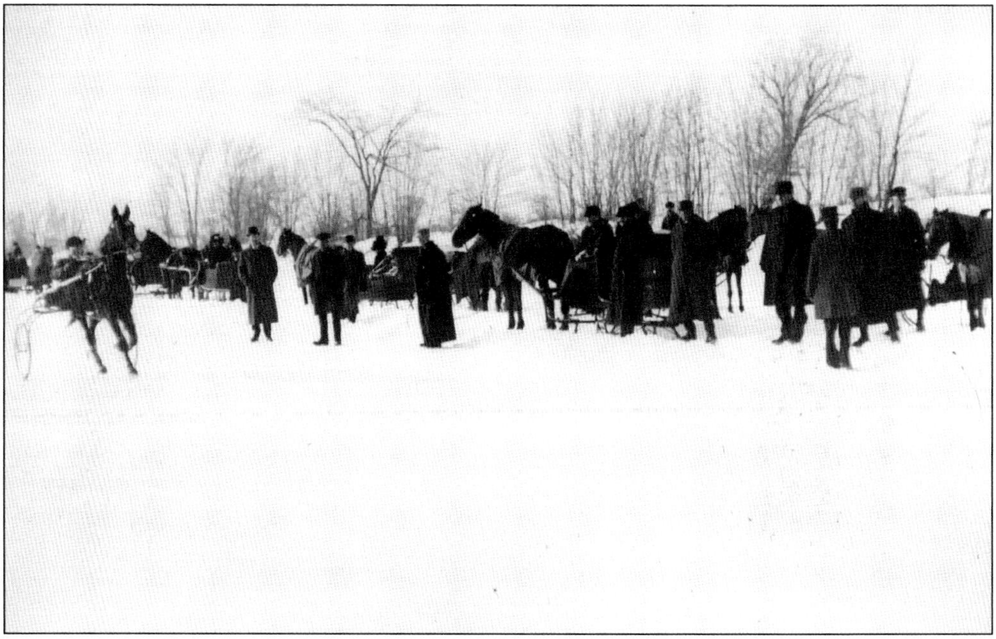

Warmly dressed townspeople gather on the ice of the Saco River at Long Reach to watch a horse race in this photograph by Charles Moody. Long, wide, and level, it must have been the perfect spot for a race—unless the ice broke. (Photograph by Charles Moody; courtesy McArthur Public Library.)

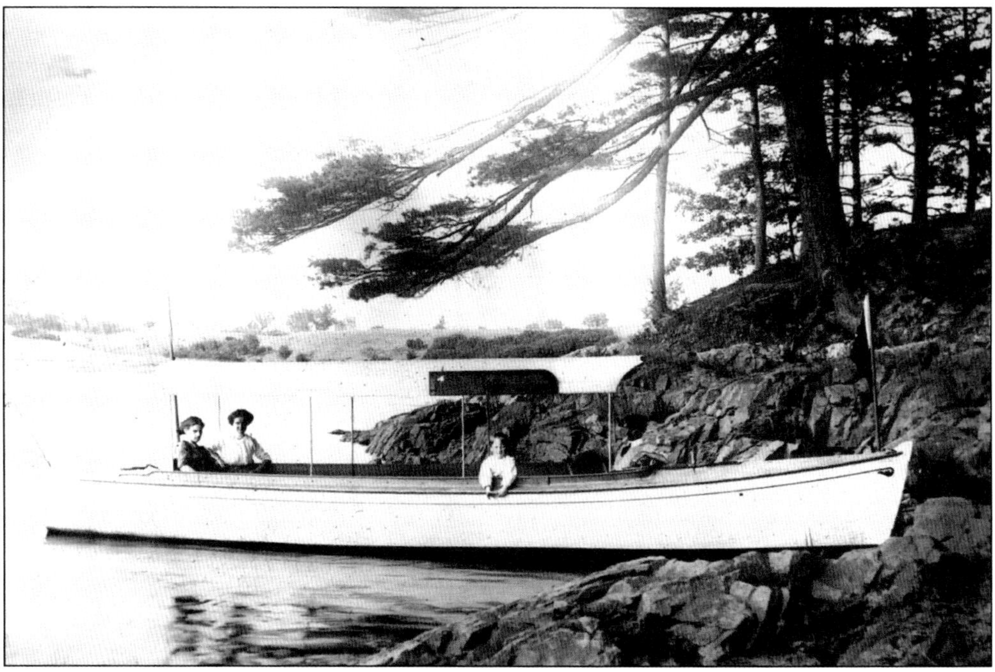

Pleasure boating became more popular in the 20th century, as tourism became one of Saco's main industries. Harry P. Chadbourne, commodore of the Saco Yacht Club, owned the launch *Yakima* seen in this view from about 1914. (Courtesy McArthur Public Library.)

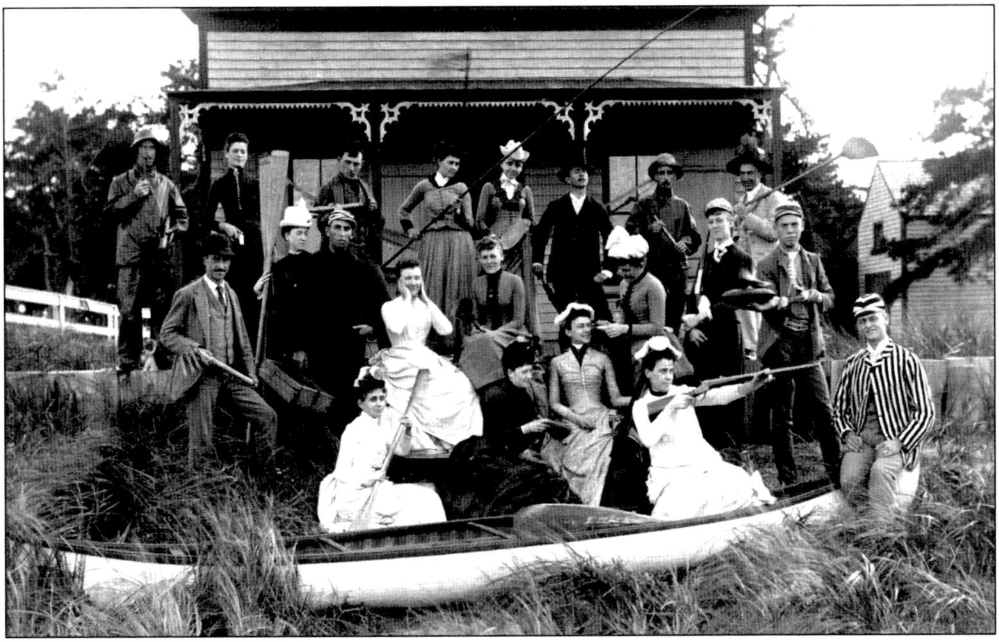

Seen here on August 22, 1888, is a late summer picnic at the Pines, the Unitarian campground at Ferry Beach. In an interesting fisherman's costume, J. Vaughn Dennett, a philanthropist and future president of the York Institute who was known for his eccentric outfits, poses in the back row on the far left. In a notation written on the back of the photograph, Dennett describes himself as "a lazy chap."

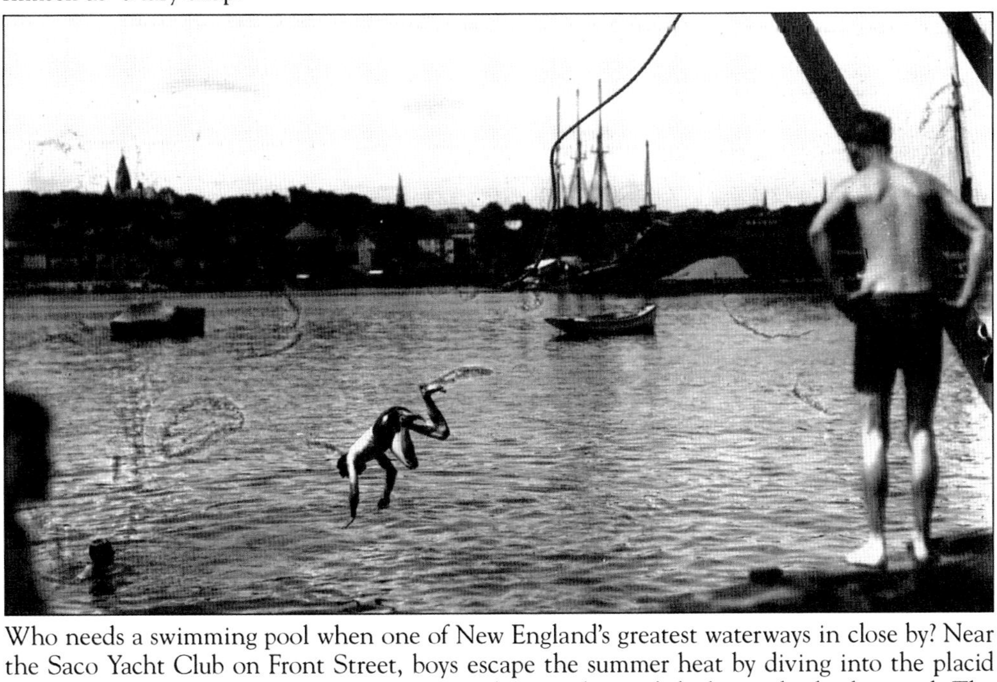

Who needs a swimming pool when one of New England's greatest waterways in close by? Near the Saco Yacht Club on Front Street, boys escape the summer heat by diving into the placid river in 1914. A three-masted schooner is tied up at the coal docks in the background. The steeple of St. Andre's Church is to the left. (Photograph by Charles Moody; courtesy McArthur Public Library.)

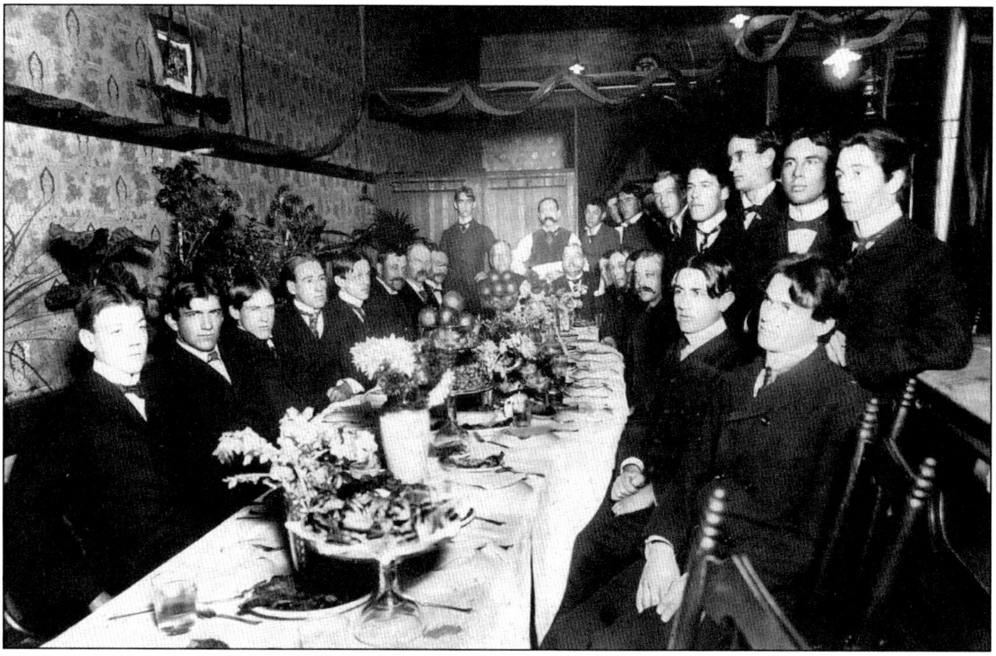

Gathered for a banquet are the young men of the York County Wheelmen, who would be referred to today as bicyclists. Until well into the 1920s, they preferred to ride large-wheeled "bonebreaker" bicycles. Notice the early lightbulbs in the ceiling fixtures.

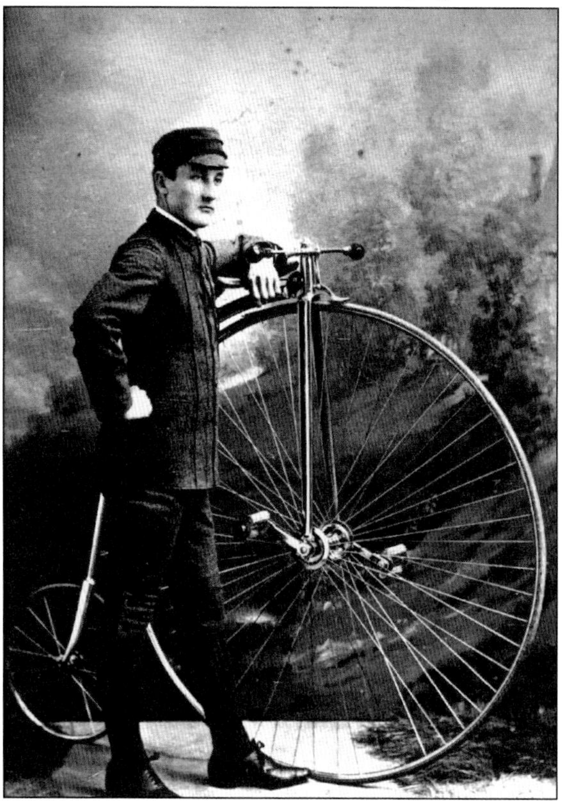

Abram L. T. Cummings (1865–1951) poses with his "bonebreaker" bicycle in 1888. His tight-fitting costume represented the most advanced and stylish athletic wear of the day. (Courtesy McArthur Public Library.)

Two

INDUSTRY

For more than a century, Saco was known as a national center of industry. Between the early 1800s and the 1950s, the city—along with Biddeford just across the river—flourished, as textile, metal, leather, and weaving industries took root. A huge complex of brick mill buildings sprang up to accommodate the complex machinery and thousands of workers required.

The York Manufacturing Company opened its first mill building in 1832; it ran eight mills by the dawn of the 20th century. The Laconia Mills (established in 1844) and Pepperell Mills (established in 1850), visible across the river in Biddeford, made the combined area one of the largest cotton milling complexes in the country, employing as many as 9,000 people. The success of the cotton mills brought related industries to Saco: the Saco-Lowell Shops manufactured opening, carding, and weaving machinery, and Garland Manufacturing made loom harnesses and other leather products. With so many workers and business owners establishing households and buying goods, Saco's Main Street became a bustling thoroughfare of storefronts.

Along with industry came danger: fires and other accidents were common in the thickly populated city center. A booming population also correlated to an increase in crime. Despite this, the tourism industry also began to develop in the 19th century, with city dwellers from the south and sun-seekers from the north drawn to Saco and the surrounding area for its pristine beaches and fun-filled attractions. Trains and trolleys made traveling to and around the area easy and affordable for all.

Another industry taking root in the 19th century and continuing to this day is the arts. Saco's unique combination of industrial and picturesque landscapes, along with the energy and bustle of city life, have provided inspiration for painters and photographers for more than 200 years.

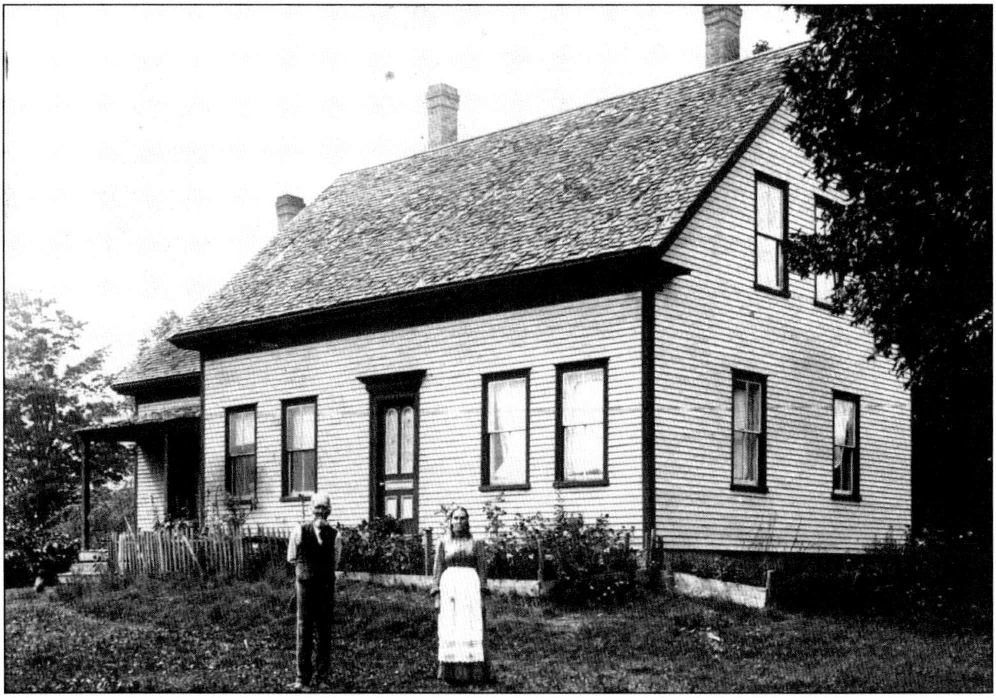

Even as industry expanded in Saco, the old agrarian ways of making a living persisted, although farms were pushed farther and farther to the outskirts of the city. Here Amos and Mary Rice Libby pose in front of their McKenney Road high-post cape in the early 1890s. (Courtesy John Morrill Read.)

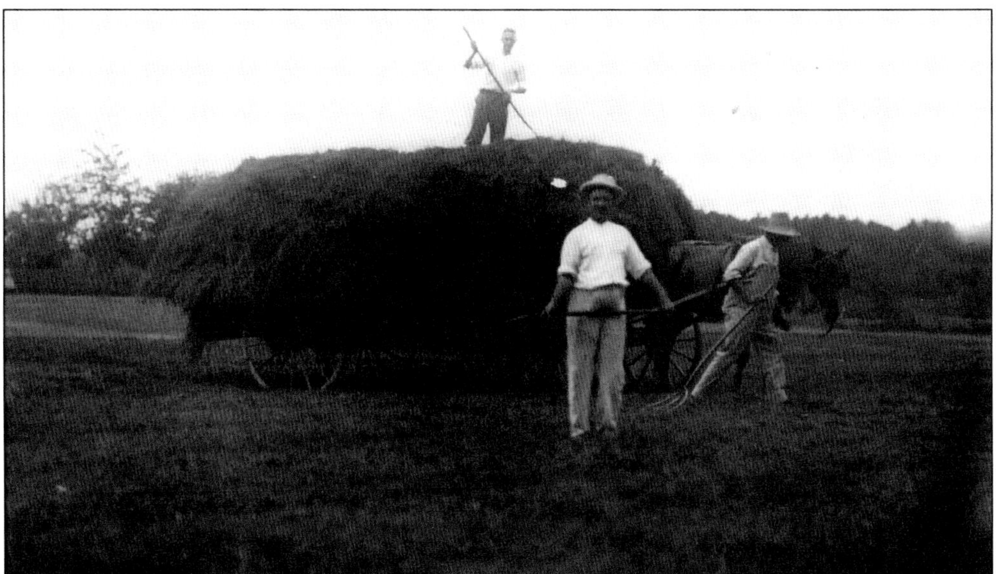

This Charles Moody photograph captures farmers in the timeless activity of stacking hay on a cart in preparation for taking it into the barn. The weary horse appears to already have dragged plenty a load. Arranging such a large pile of hay by hand is a lost art. (Photograph by Charles Moody; courtesy McArthur Public Library.)

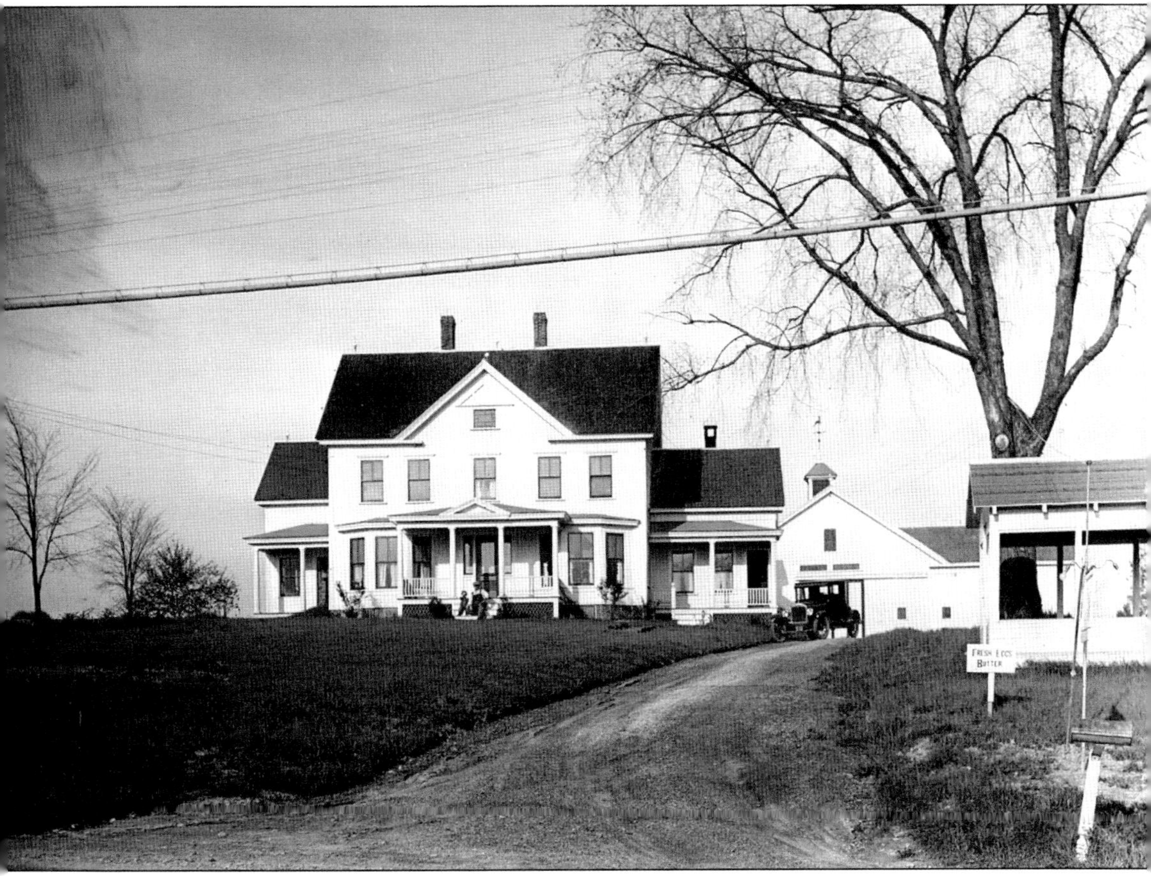

The additive nature of farmhouse architecture is evident in this rural Saco homestead. Barns, outbuildings, and additional residential wings have been added to the main central building, which appears to date to the 1830s or 1840s. The practice, which is characteristic of vernacular architecture in southern Maine, allowed for different uses in different seasons; food storage sheds and summer kitchens were often among these additions. To the right, a simply constructed farm stand offers goods for sale to passing motorists. (Courtesy Penobscot Marine Museum.)

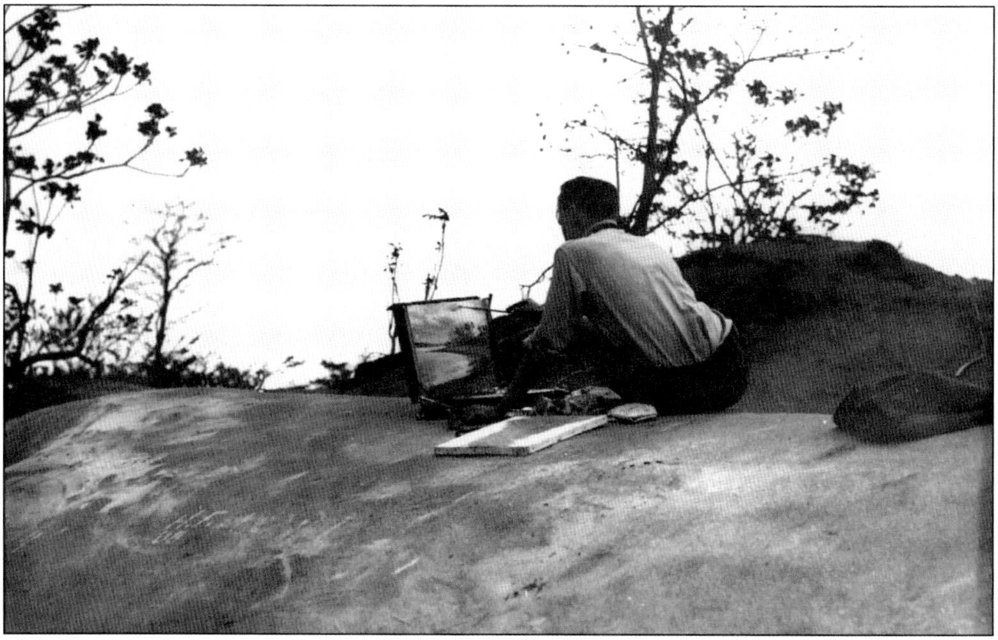

The Saco River, visible in this artist's painting, has long been a popular subject for local painters. The Saco Museum's collection includes Saco River scenes by native artists Gibeon Elden Bradbury, William Stoodley Gookin, and Charles Henry Granger, among others. This photograph of an unidentified painter was taken around 1914 by Charles Moody. (Photograph by Charles Moody; courtesy McArthur Public Library.)

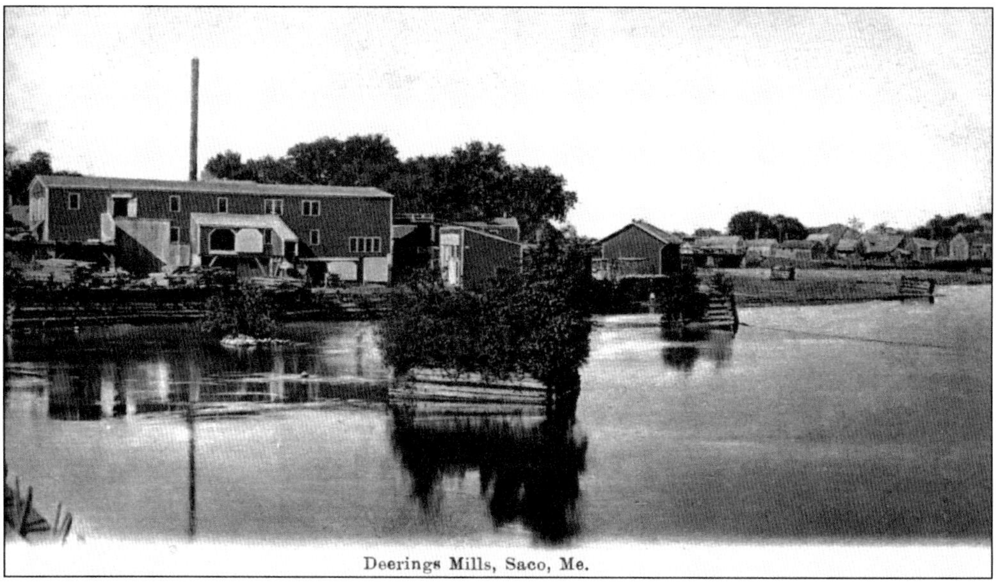

Saco's Factory Island has been a lynchpin for the logging and lumbering industry since John Davis built the area's first water-powered sawmill there in 1653. Deering Lumber, founded in 1866 and still in operation today, now occupies approximately the same spot. In this picture, a massive collection of logs, barely visible to the right, is chained up in close proximity to the Deering sawmill, awaiting processing. The crudely constructed "islands" in the river served to break up log jams.

This early view of Cataract Falls, taken in 1869, gives a sense of how precariously the factory buildings straddled the falls in order to take advantage of the power produced by the rushing waters. The tiny figures in the foreground give a sense of human scale to the scene.

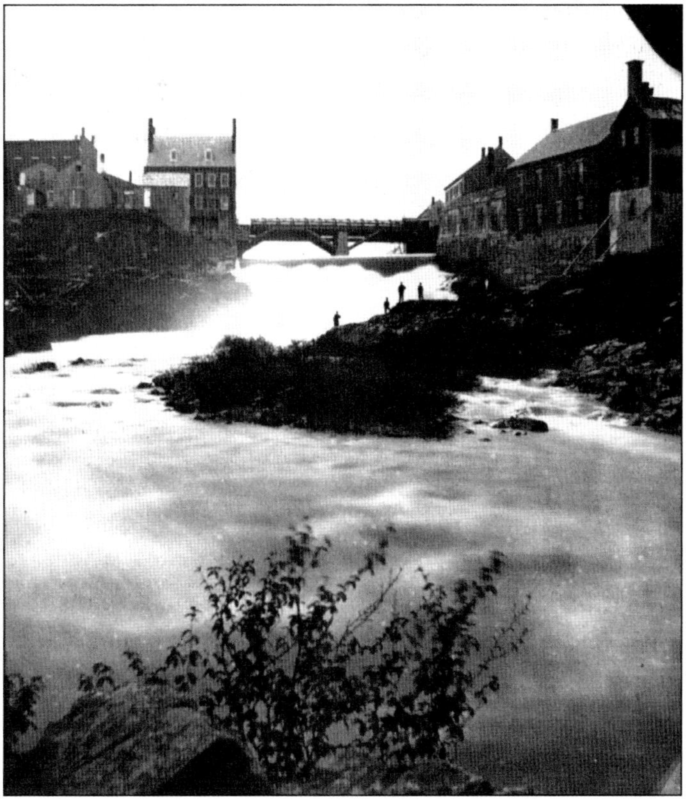

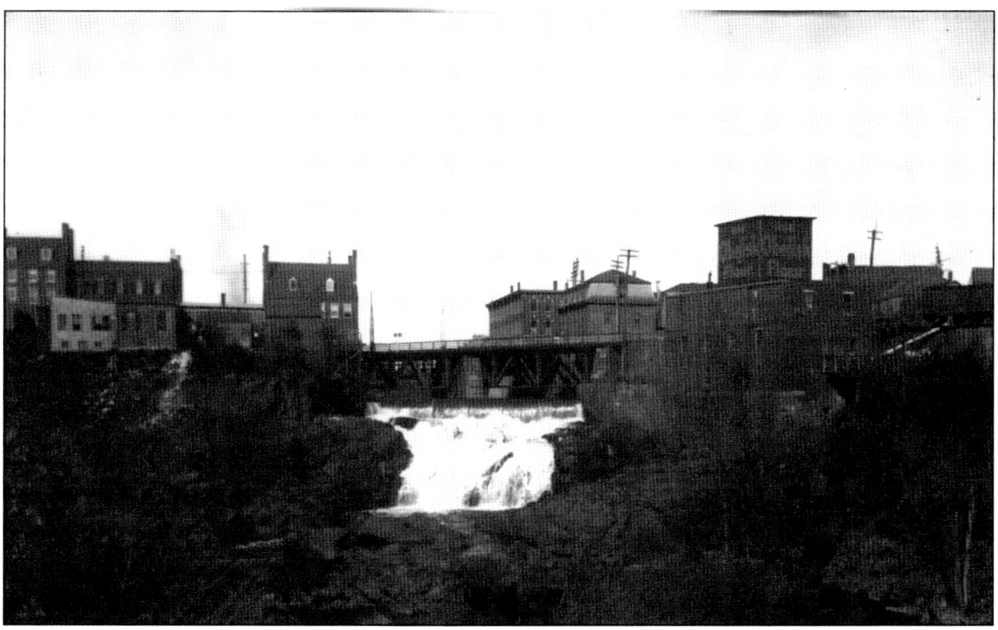

This photograph depicts Cataract Falls and the old gristmill (right) on the original Pepperell mill site in the early 1900s. The gristmill, which ground wheat into flour, contained four runs of stones, two bolting machines, and a corn and plaster mill. It was the last of its kind to survive on the Saco River until it was torn down in 1917.

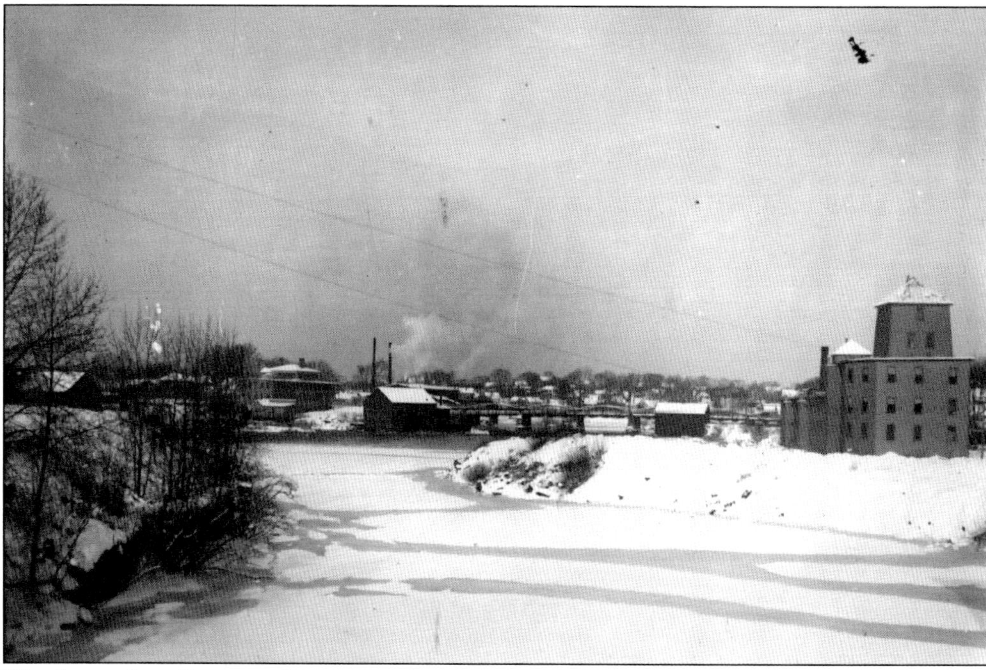

The frozen Saco River in the winter of 1912 is seen from Factory Island looking north toward Spring Island and the Elm Street bridge. On the right is Garland Manufacturing Company, which began producing water buffalo hide loom harnesses in Saco in 1887. The company is still in operation and still uses water buffalo hide to produce mallets and soft-faced hammers. (Courtesy McArthur Public Library.)

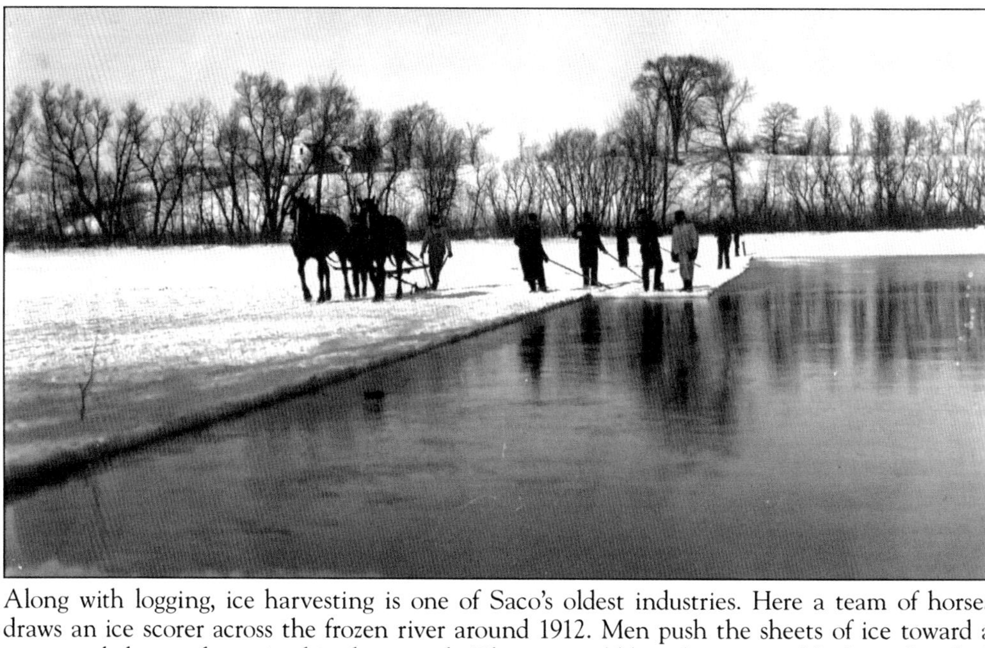

Along with logging, ice harvesting is one of Saco's oldest industries. Here a team of horses draws an ice scorer across the frozen river around 1912. Men push the sheets of ice toward a conveyor belt, not shown in this photograph. The ice would later be cut into blocks and packed in sawdust, either to be shipped to more southern climates or to be stored in a local icehouse and delivered to homes throughout the year. (Courtesy McArthur Public Library.)

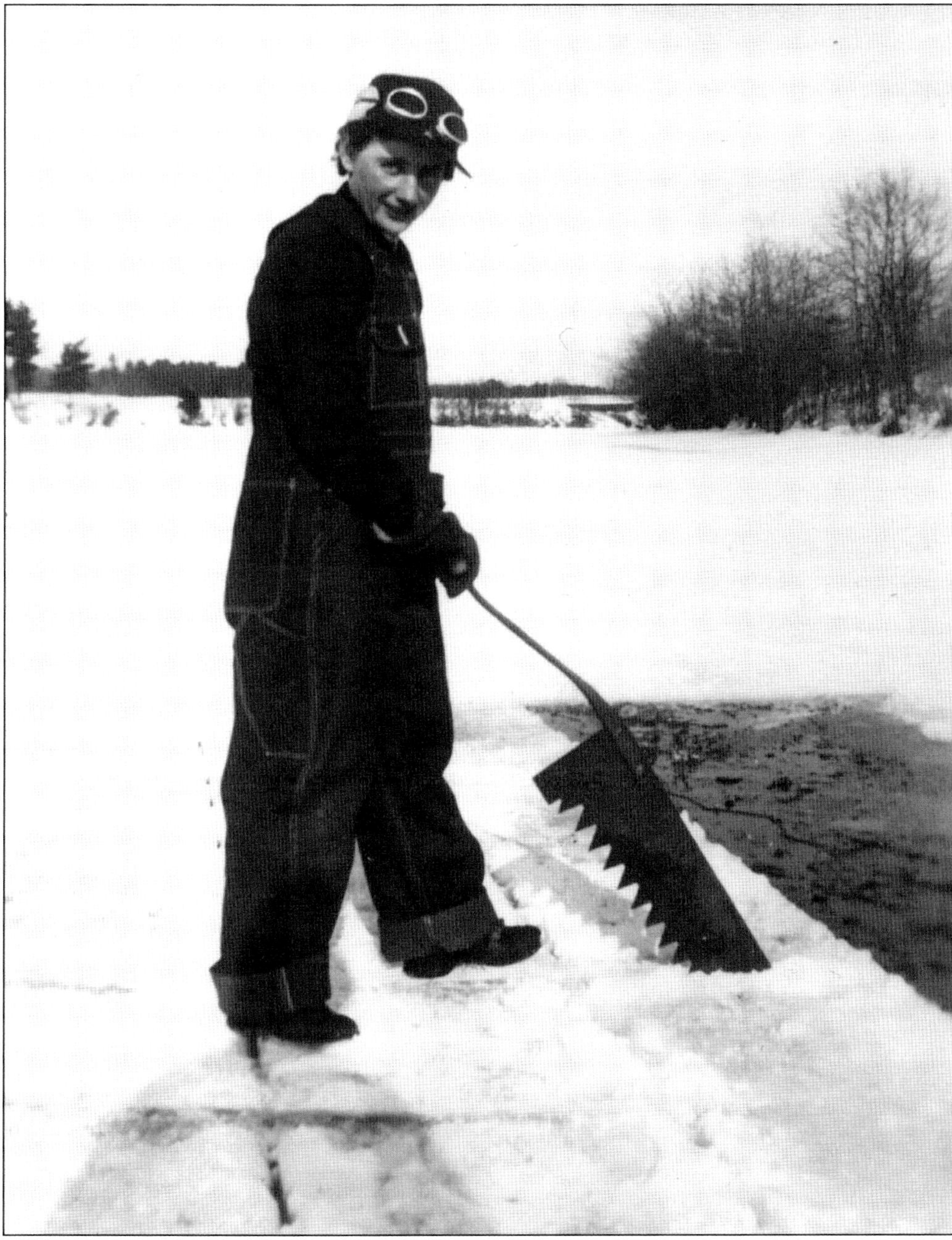

In 1943, Angelina (Angie) Tardif Beland cuts the ice in smaller blocks after the horse-drawn scorer has passed by. The Tardif family harvested ice for cooling milk and other needs on their Saco farm until the 1970s, long after modern refrigeration had made the practice obsolete and caused most locals to give it up. This photograph and the saw that Beland is holding were given to the Saco Museum by the Tardif family in 2001, along with several other photographs and tools related to ice harvesting on the their farm.

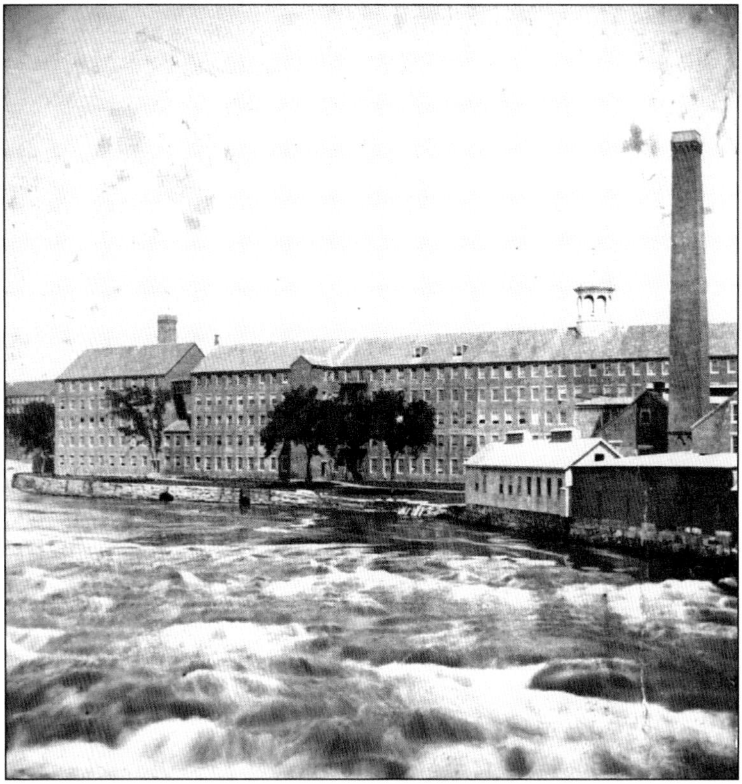

In this stereo view from around 1875, the Saco River runs high next to the York mills. The York Manufacturing Company was built on Saco Island in 1831, after another textile mill had burned down. York made cotton goods and in 1839 was operating three mills with 1,000 workers. In 1930, York Manufacturing was sold to New England Industries and became known as the York Division of Bates Manufacturing. In 1958, the factory was shut down.

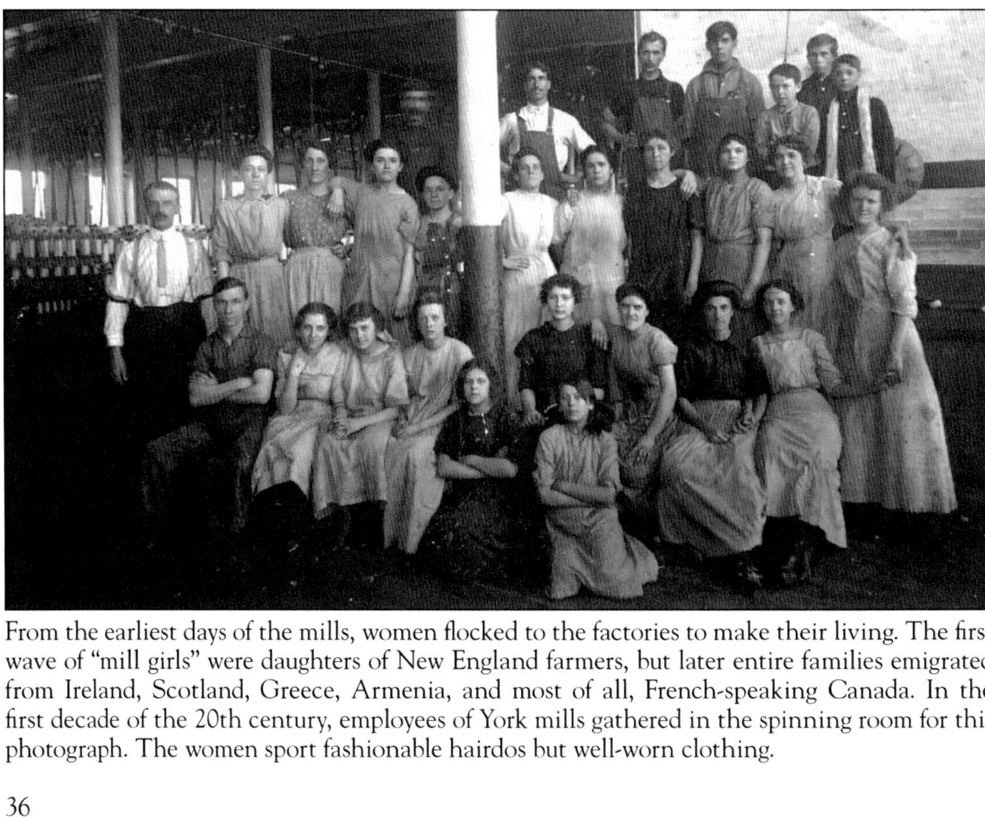

From the earliest days of the mills, women flocked to the factories to make their living. The first wave of "mill girls" were daughters of New England farmers, but later entire families emigrated from Ireland, Scotland, Greece, Armenia, and most of all, French-speaking Canada. In the first decade of the 20th century, employees of York mills gathered in the spinning room for this photograph. The women sport fashionable hairdos but well-worn clothing.

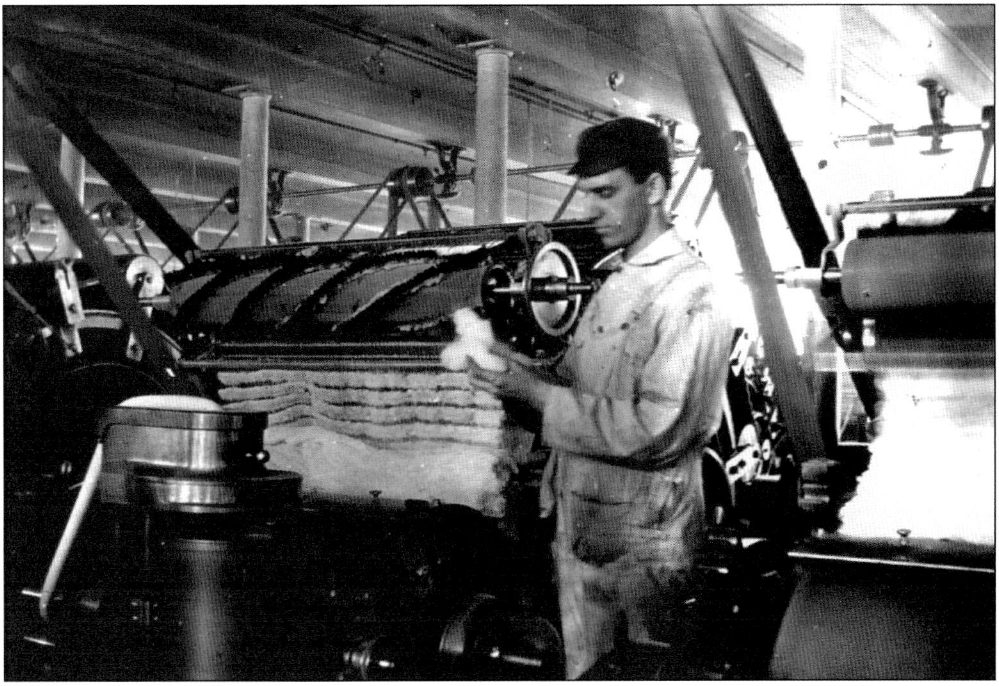

Hartley Little Lord tends a carding machine at York mills sometime between 1892 and 1902. Note the haze of cotton dust in the light of the windows on the right. Many workers chewed tobacco to try to avoid inhaling the dust.

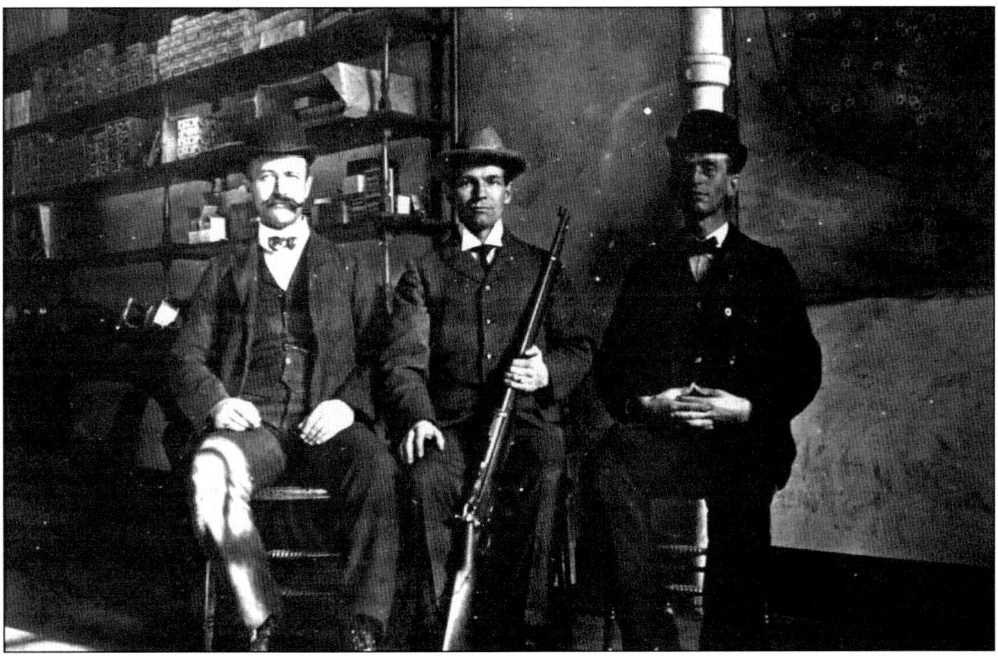

The rapid industrialization of downtown Saco led to a population boom and an increase in crime. Mill agents relied upon a strong local police force to keep order, but they also employed their own enforcers. Mill agent E. L. Morrill, who lived in the Cutts mansion on Factory Island, and his security staff pose in front of their well-used target. (Courtesy John Morrill Read.)

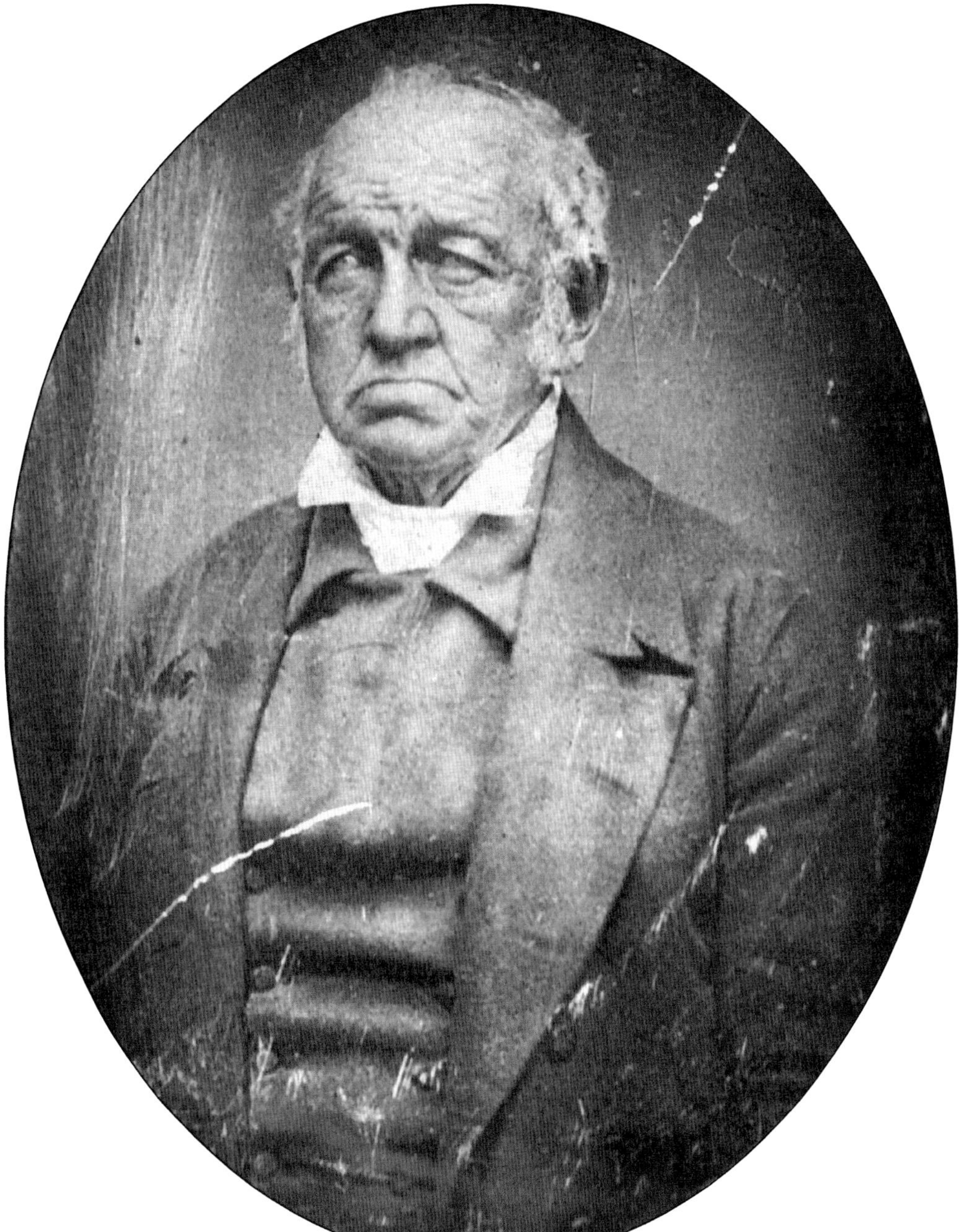

The 1850 discovery of the body of young factory worker Berengera Caswell, also known as "Mary Bean," caused widespread panic and became the subject of nationally distributed sensationalistic novels, as detailed in Elizabeth A. De Wolfe's 2007 book *The Murder of Mary Bean and Other Stories*. Tristram Jordan, pictured here, served on the jury hearing the case of Dr. James Smith, who was accused of her murder. This photograph, taken from a daguerreotype, was found in a redware pot by a Jordan descendant in the 1970s.

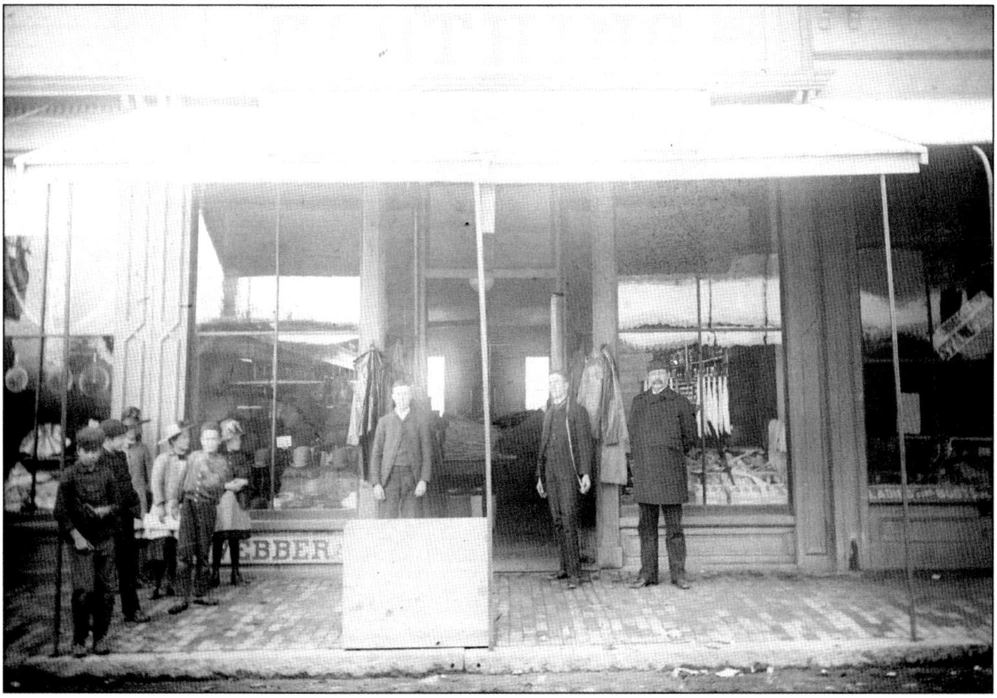

A group gathers in front of Webber Men's and Boy's Clothing in the 1880s on Factory Island. Notice the tailor with the tape measure hanging around his neck waiting to measure the next customer. The muddy street is far from being free of trash.

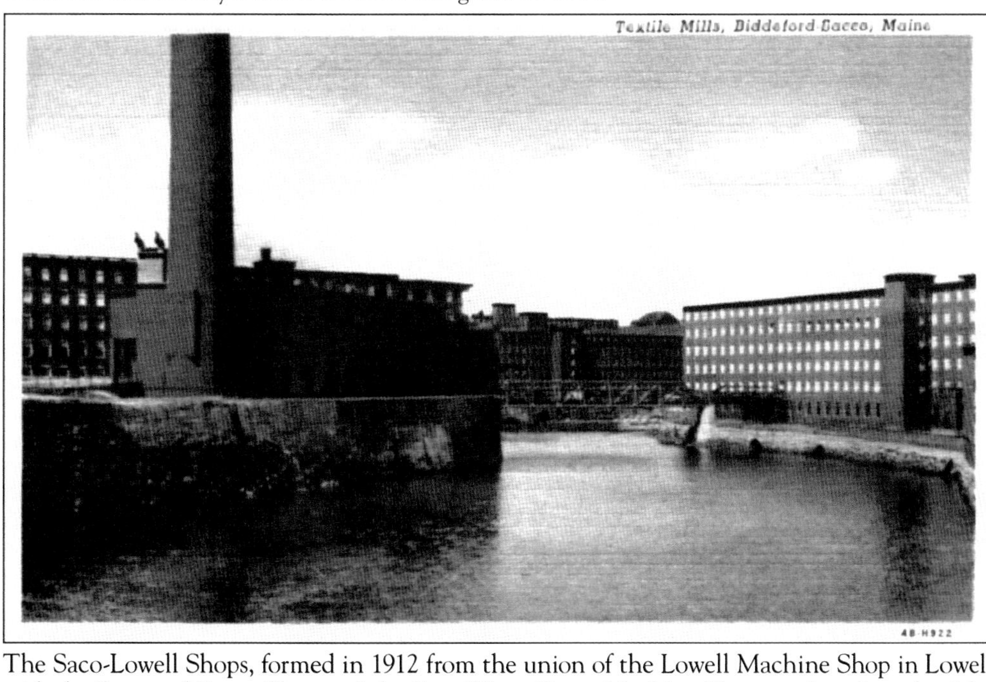

The Saco-Lowell Shops, formed in 1912 from the union of the Lowell Machine Shop in Lowell with the Saco and Pettee Shop and the Saco Water Power Machine Shop, produced much of the machinery made in the mills. The manufacturing and tourism industries overlapped in popular postcards, like this one, of Saco's mill district from the early 20th century.

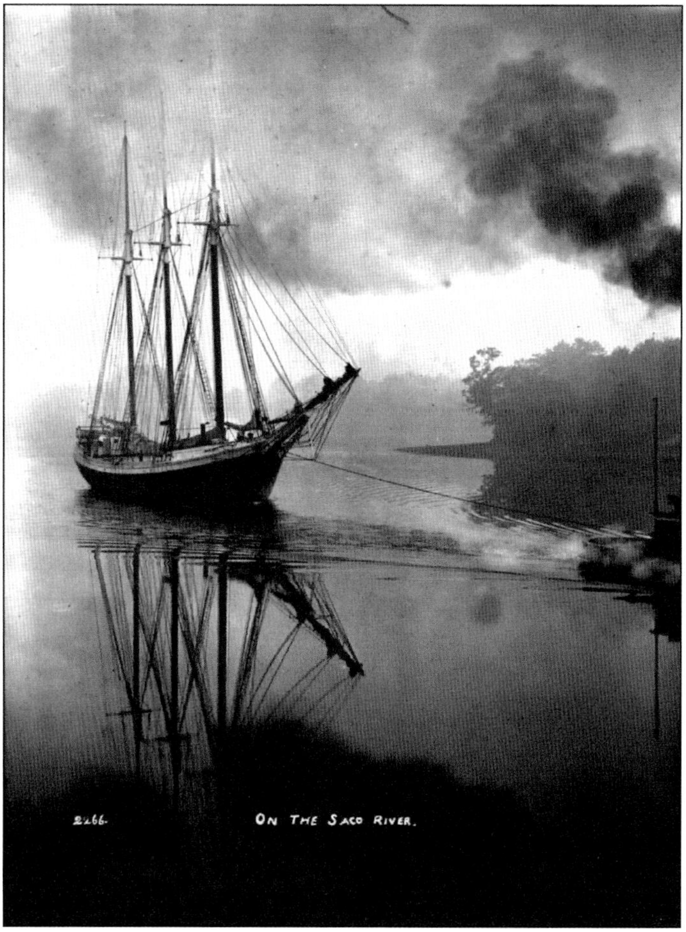

Mariners seldom attempted the twists and turns of the Saco River by sail, preferring instead the safety of a tug once these hardworking riverboats became available. (Courtesy McArthur Public Library.)

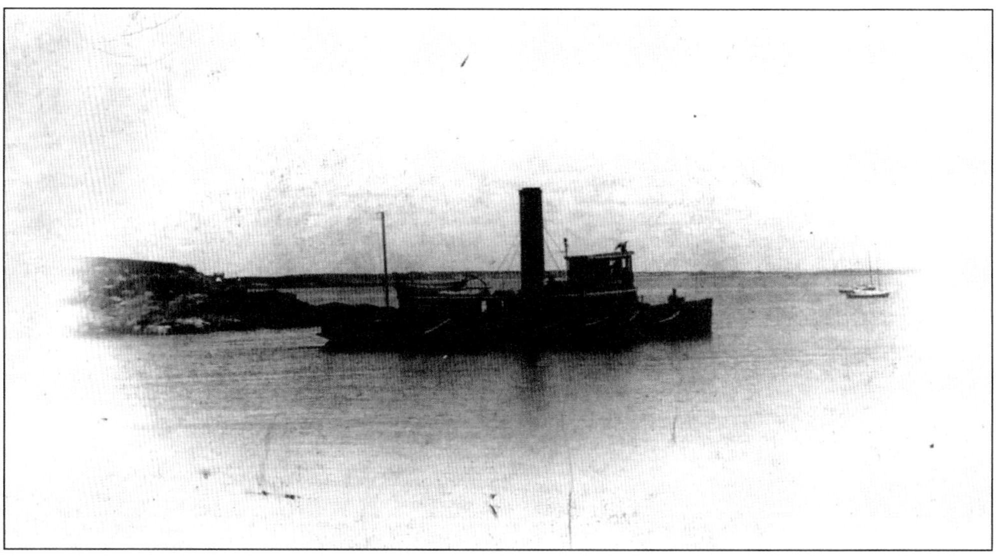

A working steam tugboat, probably the *Joe Baker*, patrols the Saco River around 1890. It guided both steam- and wind-powered oceangoing vessels up the busy commercial river.

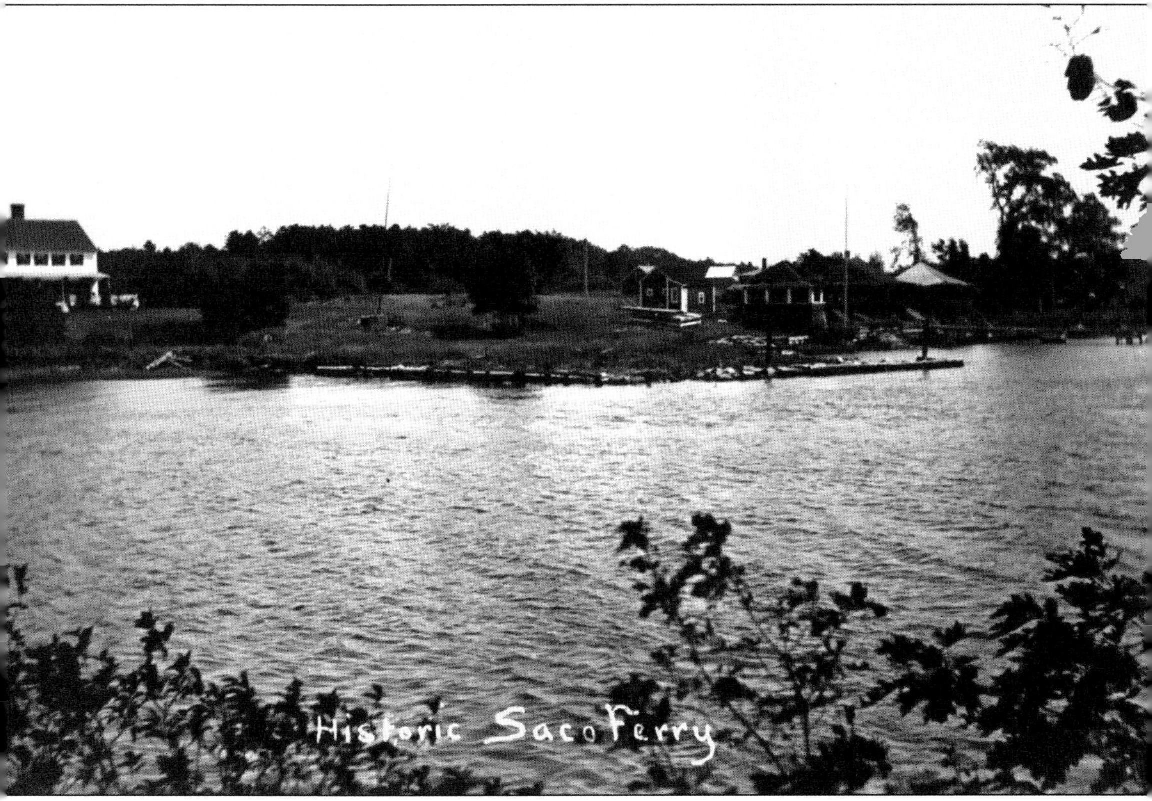

This was the site of the historic Saco ferry that crossed from Biddeford to Ferry Lane in Saco. The ferry's first voyage was in 1717, supplanting an earlier ferry that had operated since 1654. Still another ferry operated upriver at the falls by 1750, although bridges built in 1760 and 1767 soon became the preferred mode of getting from one riverbank to another. Although ferries operated through the 19th and into the 20th centuries, they were eventually adapted more toward the tourism industry (see page 14). A ferry that took a mill worker to Factory Island might then proceed to the wealthy summer community of Biddeford Pool.

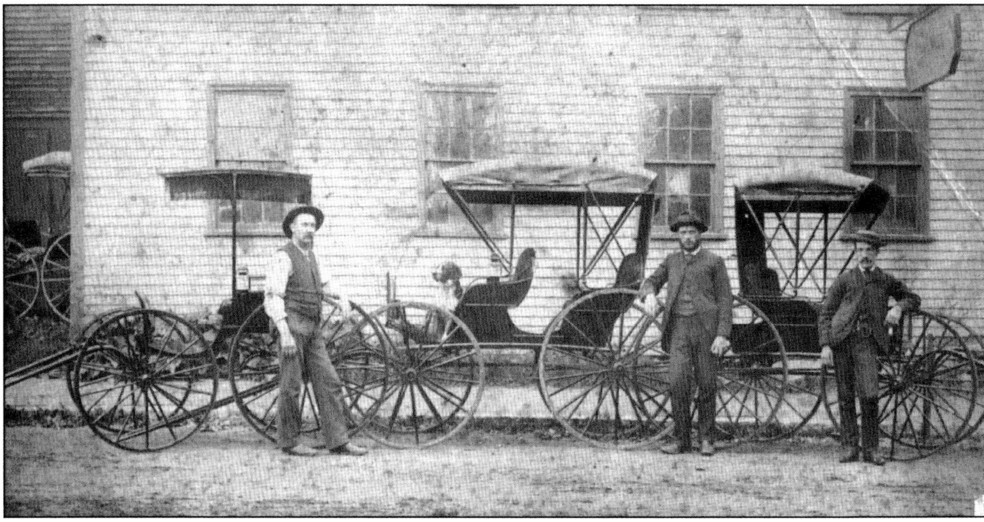

Walter L. Knight, seen here in 1896, operated as a carriage dealer on Thornton Avenue for a brief period of time in the mid-1890s after painting carriages for a living. He offered "fine, medium and low-priced carriages in all the leading styles." He returned to carriage painting by 1900, first on Water Street and then on Main Street. (Courtesy McArthur Public Library.)

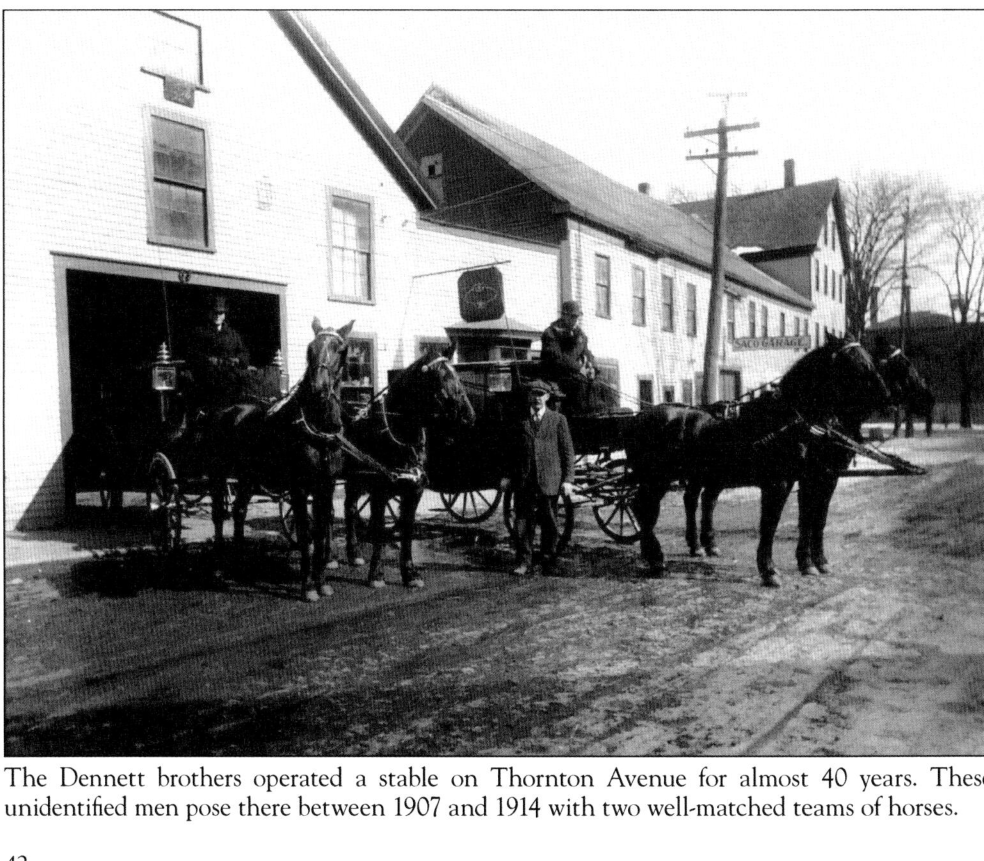

The Dennett brothers operated a stable on Thornton Avenue for almost 40 years. These unidentified men pose there between 1907 and 1914 with two well-matched teams of horses.

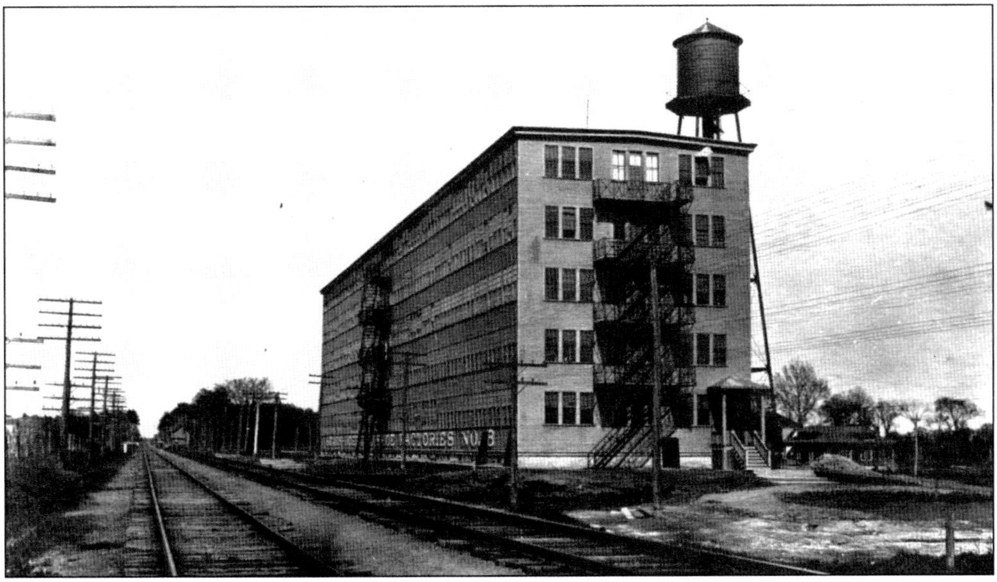

Next to the Eastern Railroad stands the Sears Roebuck Shoe Factory No. 8 on Park Street, constructed in 1915 and now converted to condominiums.

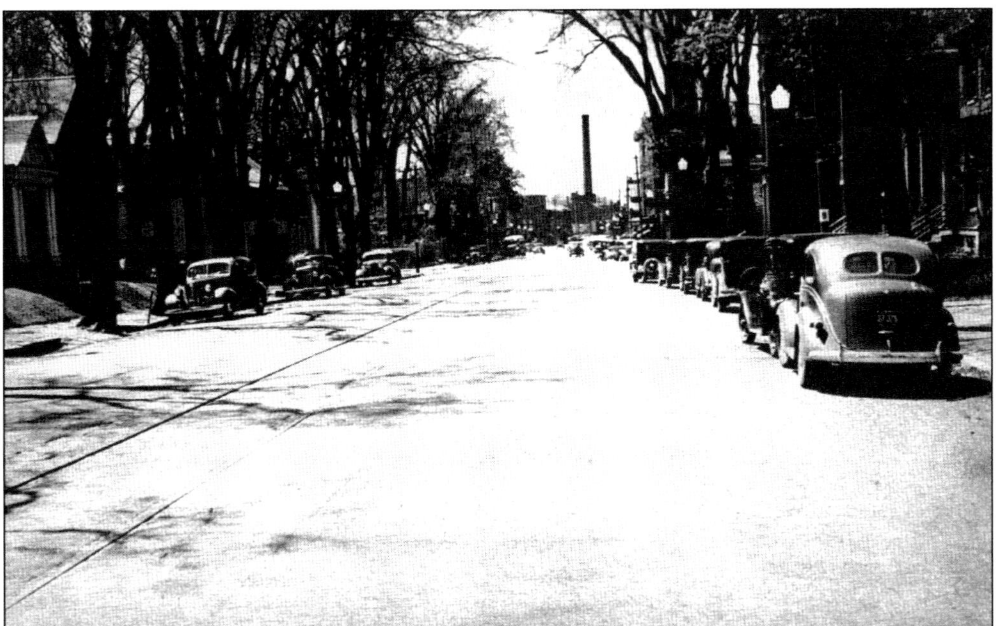

The tracks of the Saco and Biddeford Railroad trolley point toward the Pepperell Mill smokestack, standing like a giant exclamation point over Saco's Main Street, looking toward Biddeford with city hall on the right. Graceful elm trees, now gone, shade this summery scene.

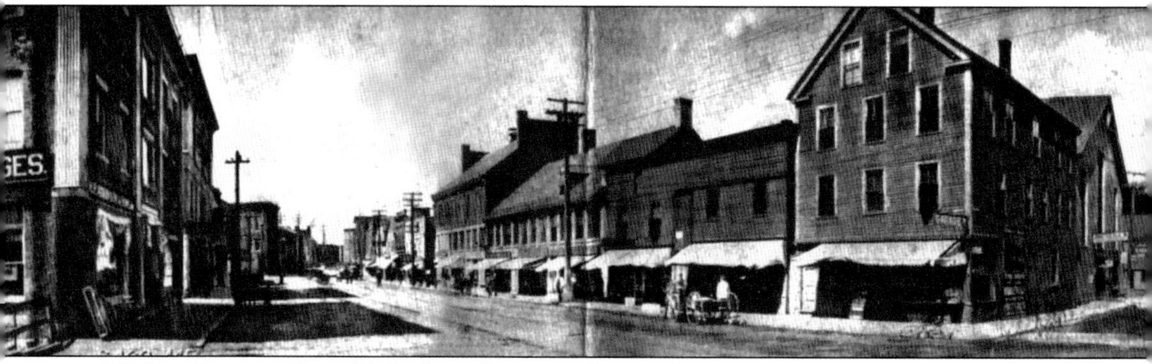

With industry well established on the river, the southern end of Saco's Main Street became a bustling center of commerce, with grocers, cigar stores, butchers, jewelers, banks, lawyers, dress shops, tailors, photographers, and more occupying storefronts on both sides. Constantly expanding industry meant that the addresses on Main Street had to be renumbered several times

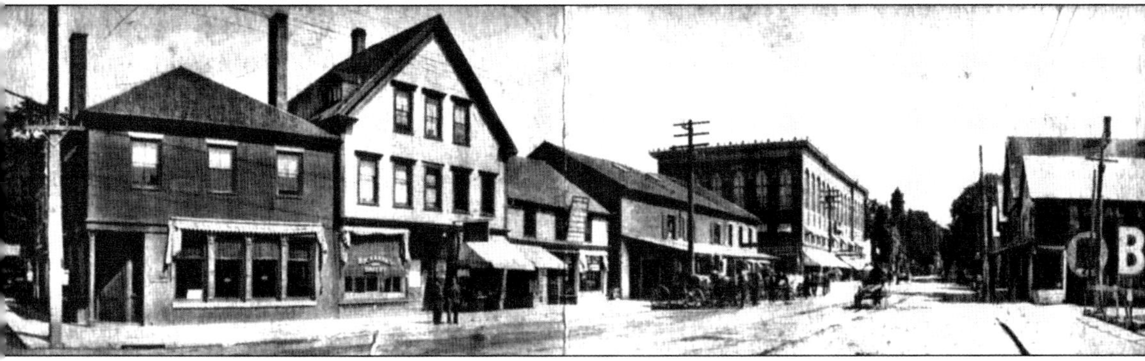

in the 19th and 20th centuries in order to allow for new businesses that had opened up. This panoramic photograph of Main Street was printed in a booklet-form design, meant as a souvenir or keepsake. By the late 19th and early 20th centuries, the commercial hubbub of Main Street was both a point of pride for Saco citizens and a draw for tourists.

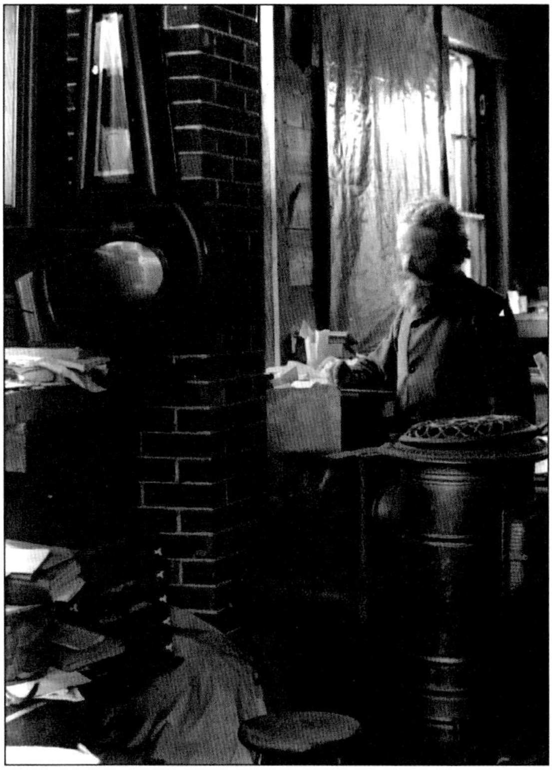

Charles O. Gerrish (1834–1896), shown here in 1888, operated a jewelry shop at 21 Pepperell Square. The store was in a building called "the Screwdriver" because of its narrowness and extremely sharp pitched roof. (Courtesy McArthur Public Library.)

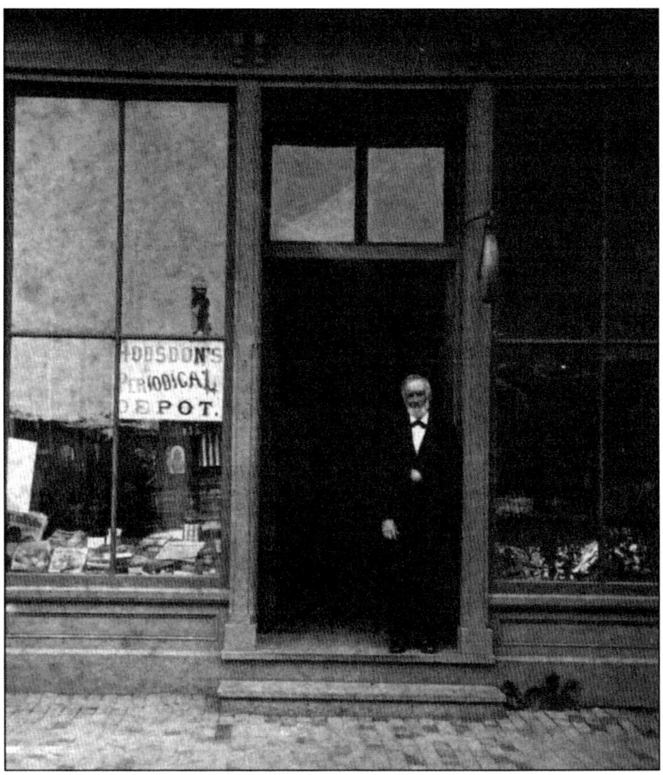

Prior to the mid-1870s, Lewis Hodsdon operated a book and periodicals store in Pepperell Square. He later moved his shop to Main Street and continued to operate it up until his death in 1886.

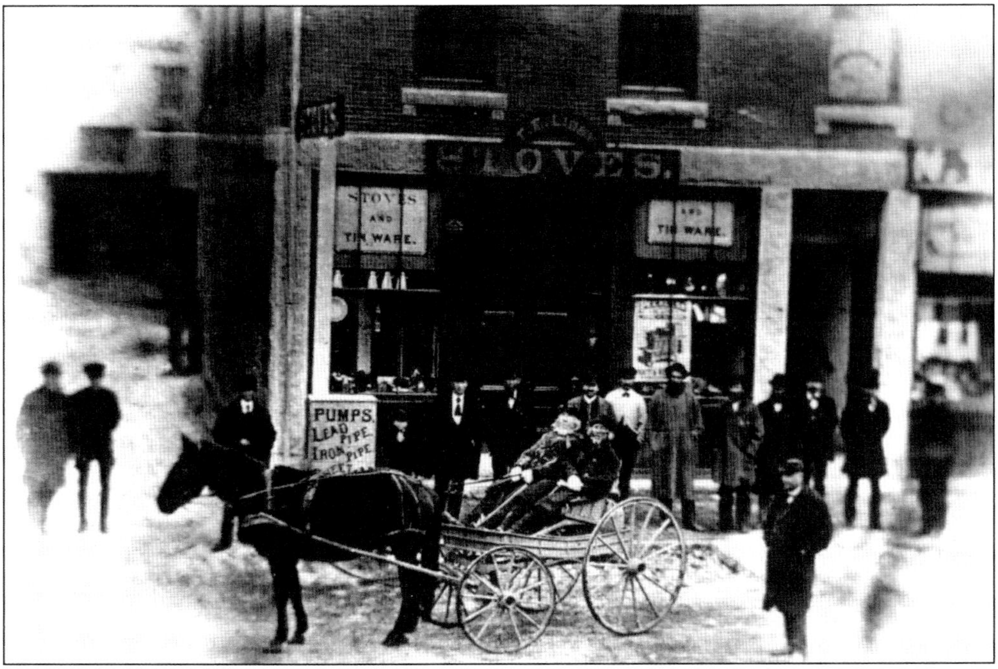

The Simpson Road is named after these two aged gentleman, Joshua Simpson (born 1788) and Eben Simpson (born 1791), who pose on the corner of Main Street and Pepperell Square in 1870. Their father, Benjamin Simpson, had participated in the Boston Tea Party in 1773. (Courtesy McArthur Public Library.)

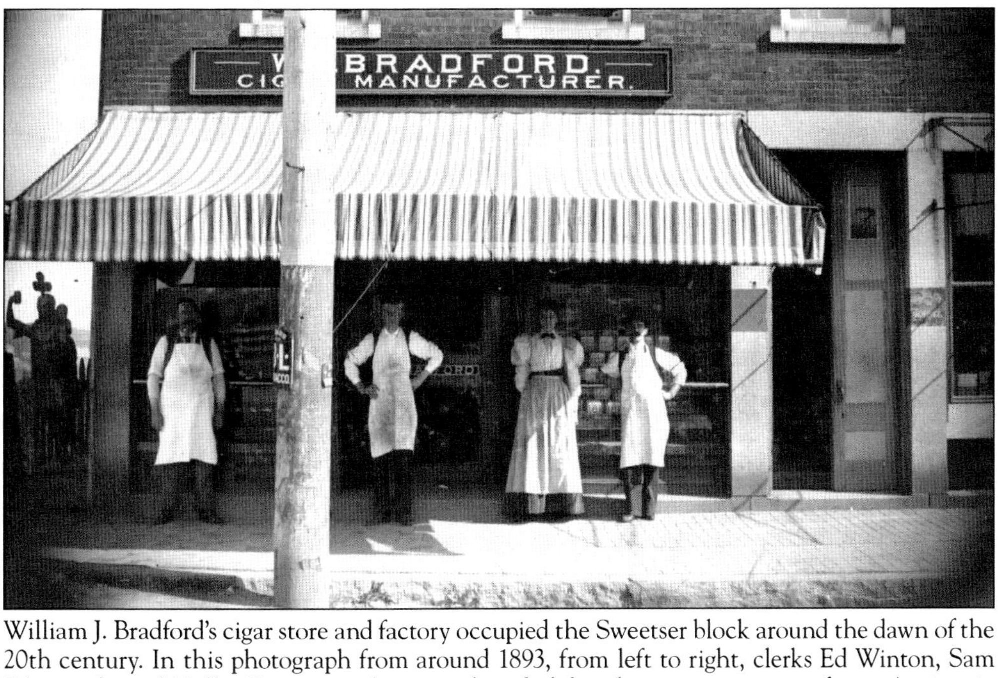

William J. Bradford's cigar store and factory occupied the Sweetser block around the dawn of the 20th century. In this photograph from around 1893, from left to right, clerks Ed Winton, Sam Edgecomb, and Nellie Founge, with an unidentified fourth person, pose out front. An iconic cigar store Indian—apparently a woman with a baby, evocative of Squando's wife and infant son—is just visible in shadow to the left, with the river beyond. (Courtesy Fred Clark.)

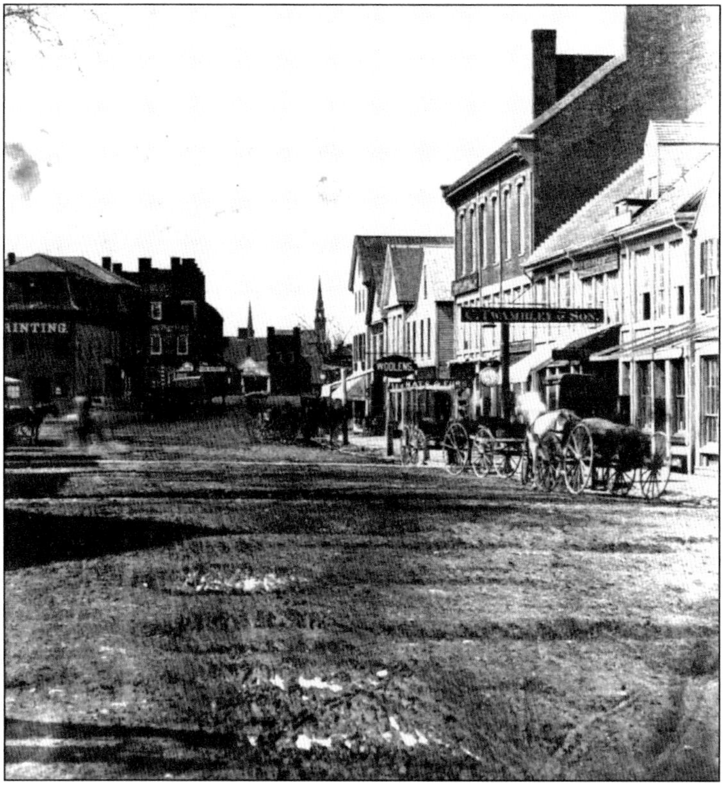

A wide variety of horse-drawn vehicles are parked along the rutted Saco Main Street in 1870, looking south toward Biddeford. C. Twambley and Son, operated by Charles Twambley (1812–1884) in partnership with his son Rufus P. (1837–1906), was located at 84 Main Street. The 1875 business directory lists C. Twambley and Son in four categories: crockery and glass, hardware, silver and plated ware, and watchmakers. (Courtesy McArthur Public Library.)

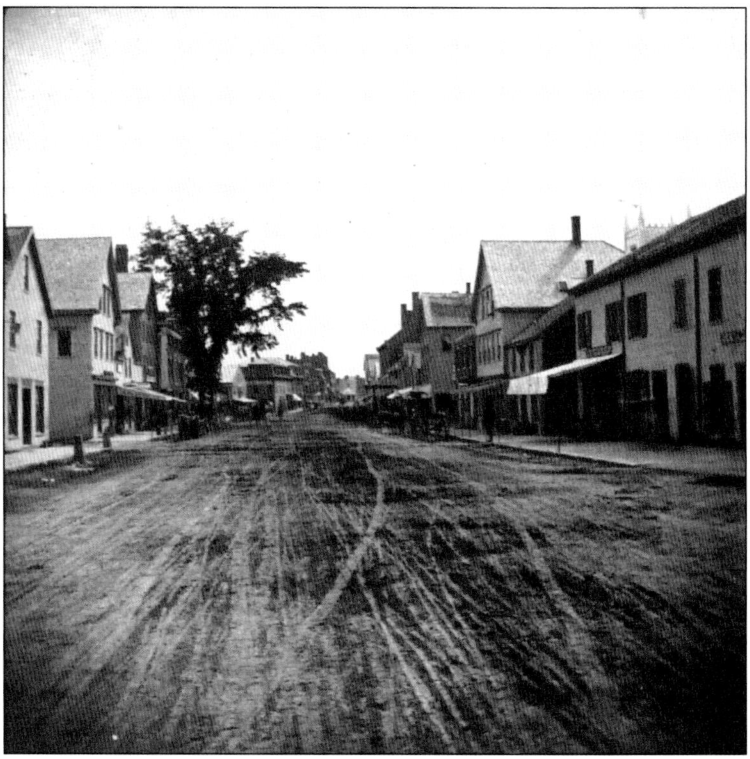

The ruts from many wagon wheels lace unpaved Main Street about 1870. Horses were tied up at hitching posts lining the streets.

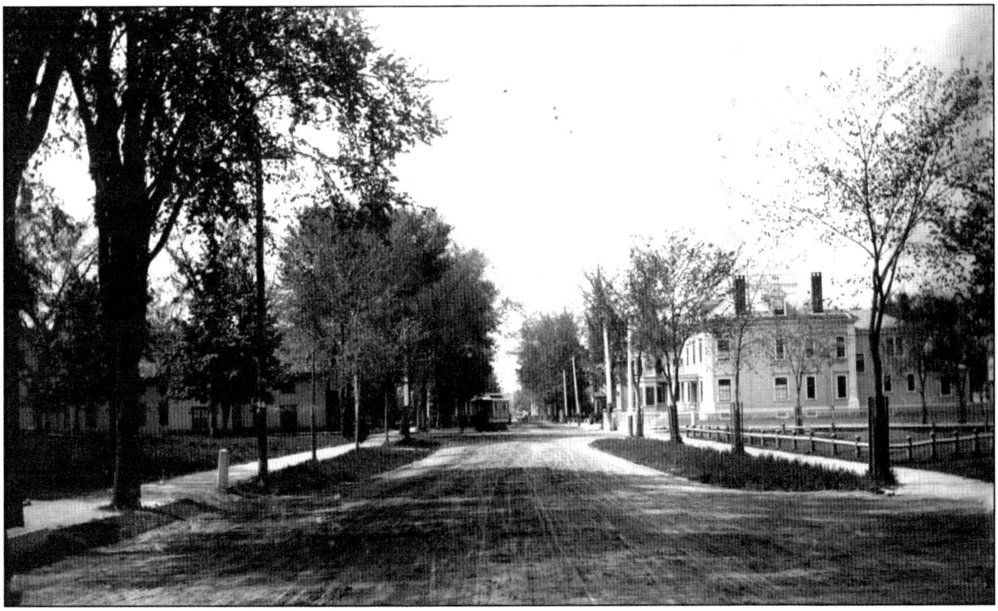

Looking south on Main Street with North Street to the right, this late-19th-century view shows that the road is still yet unpaved. Additional elm trees have been recently planted on both sides. In the 1970s and 1980s, these lovely and mature trees would be lost to Dutch elm disease. The future site of Eastman Park is on the right.

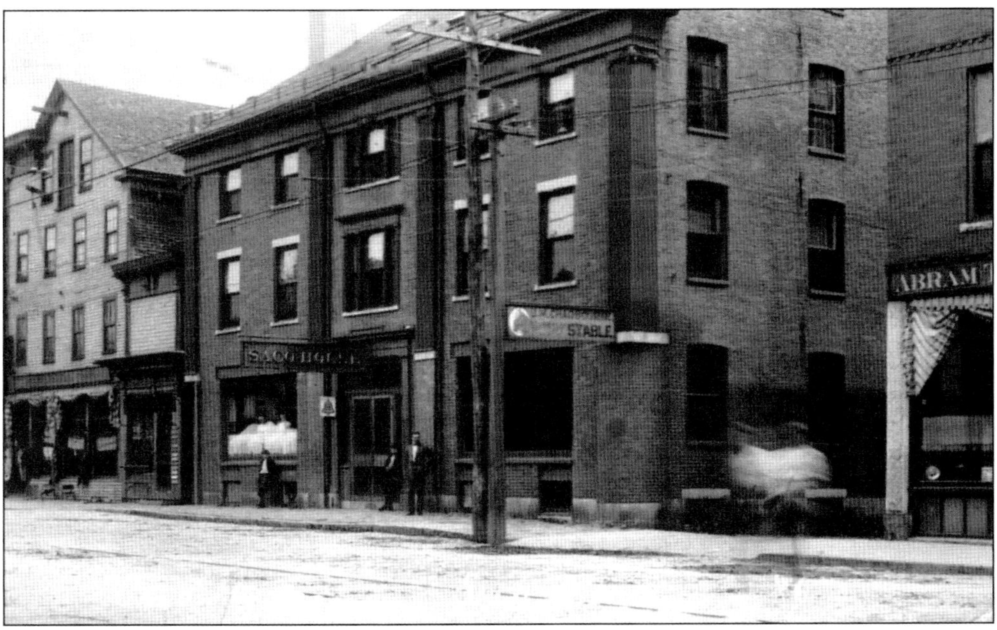

James M. Chadbourne and his son Edward M. briefly operated a stable at 205 Main Street. Prior to that, James was a farmer on the Ferry Road. Their sign is visible on the corner of the Saco House hotel. Abram T. Lord and Son sold furnaces and ranges at 20 Main Street. They promised in their 1911 advertisement "jobbing of all kinds promptly attended to." Patriotic bunting adorns a shop farther down on Main Street. Judging by the sign, a public telephone was available at the Saco House hotel.

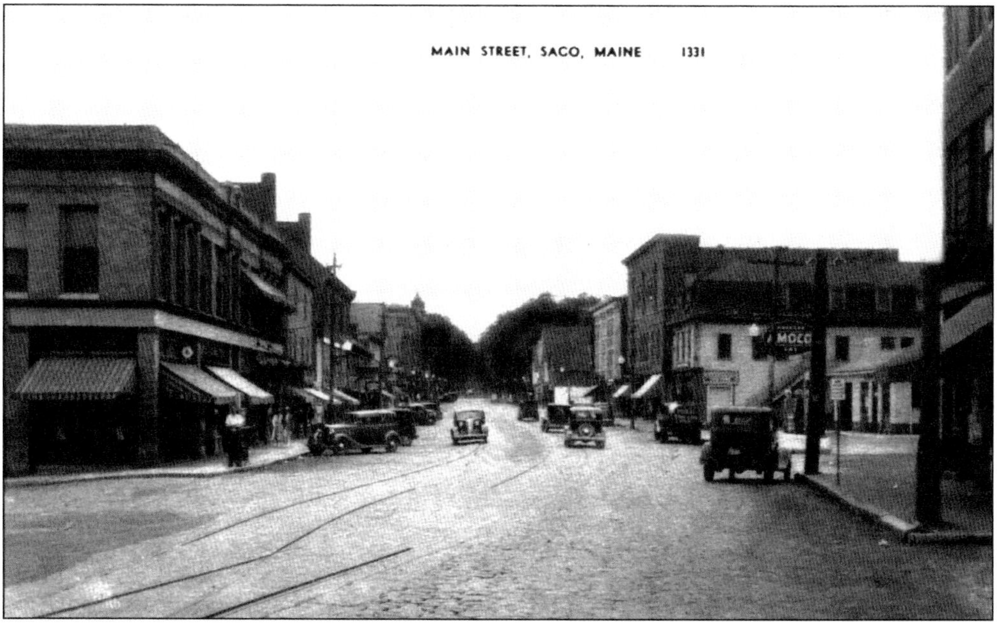

The Main Street site of this mid-1930s Amoco gasoline station represents changes in commerce in Saco over the years. A century earlier, a store belonging to shipping magnate James B. Thornton stood here and advertised "European and West India Goods." Today the landmark Rapid Ray's Diner caters to automobile and pedestrian traffic on the same spot.

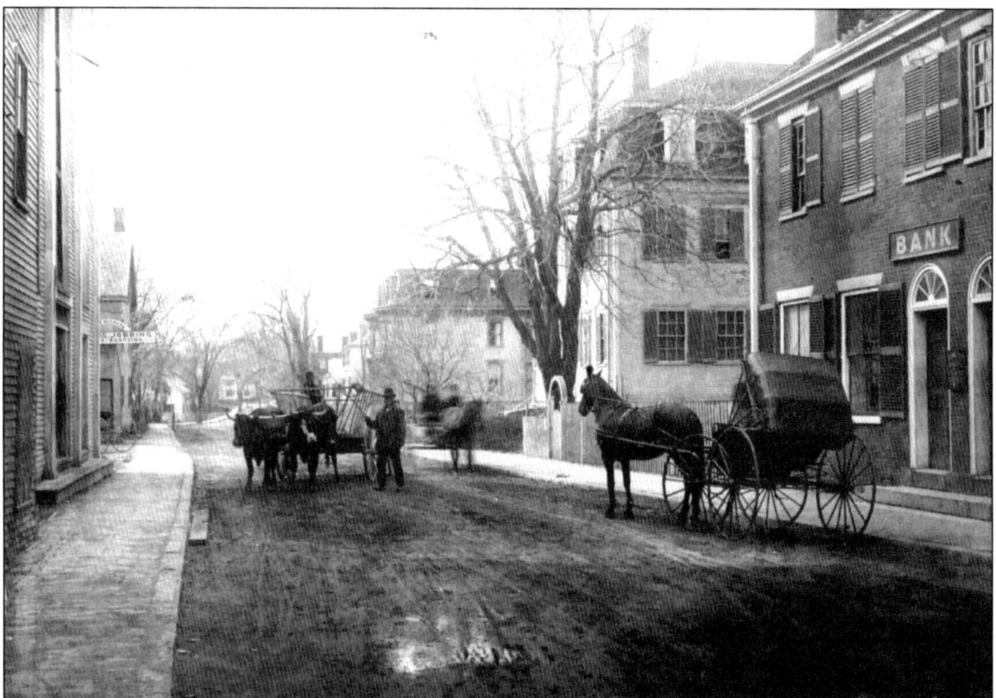

"Uncle" Hiram Hill, driving his team of oxen west on Storer Street from Main Street, stands beside the livery stable of Charles C. Fenderson across from the Saco Savings Bank, about 1890.

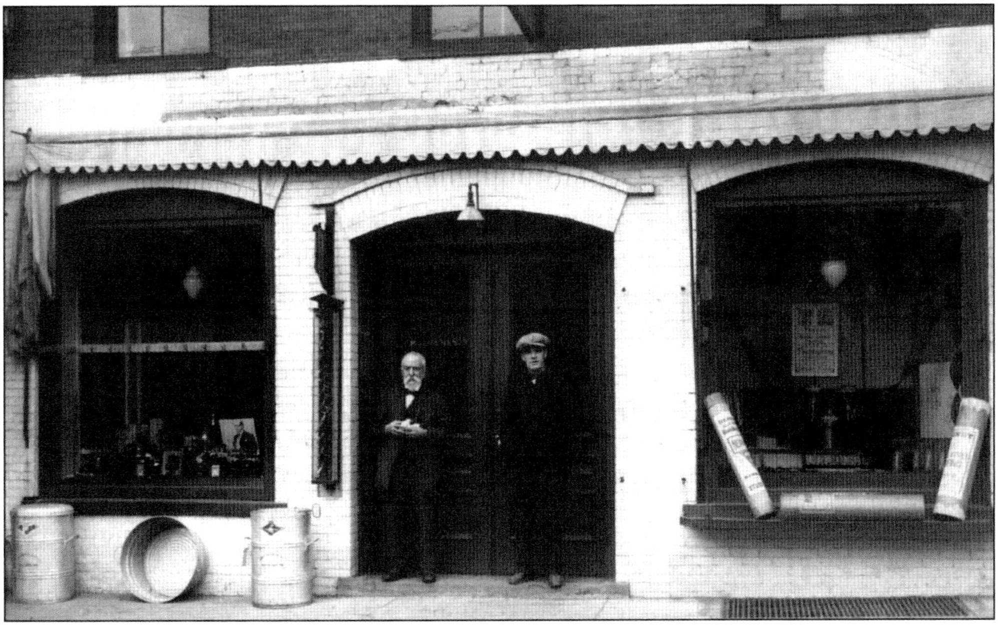

Lyman Beecher Milliken, named for the father of Harriet Beecher Stowe, poses in front of his 84 Main Street watch and jewelry store around 1880.

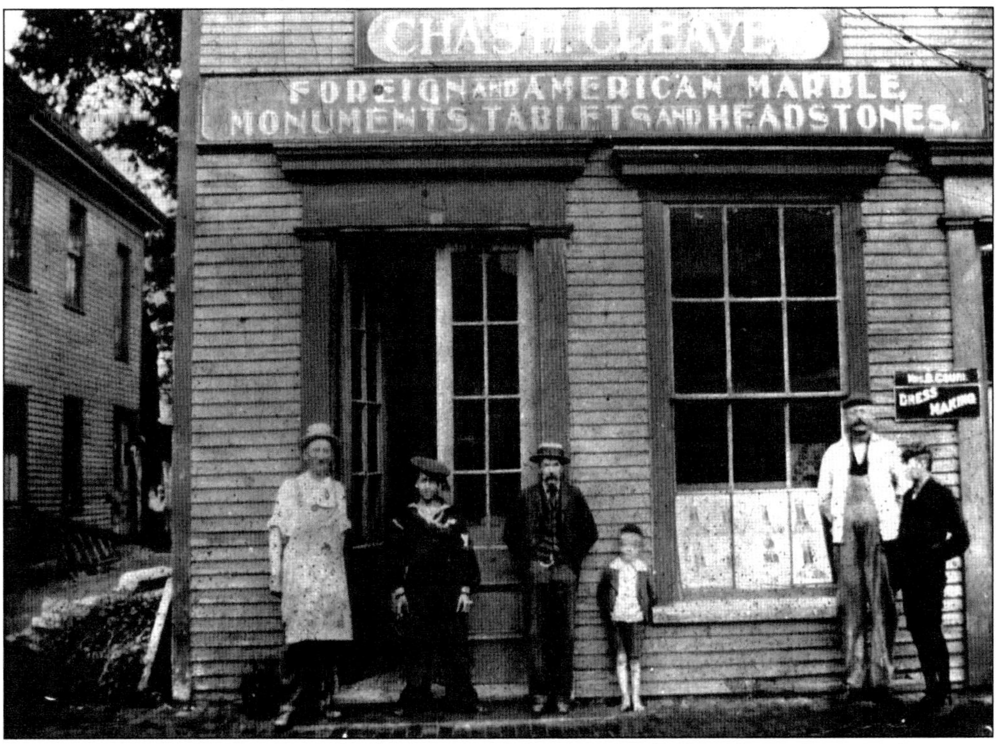

First a marble worker at this establishment, around 1882, Charles H. Cleaves became the owner of the Saco Marble Works. He was known as the "angel carver" for his distinctive and artistic headstones. The business was located at 133 Main Street. This photograph dates from the late 19th century. (Courtesy McArthur Public Library.)

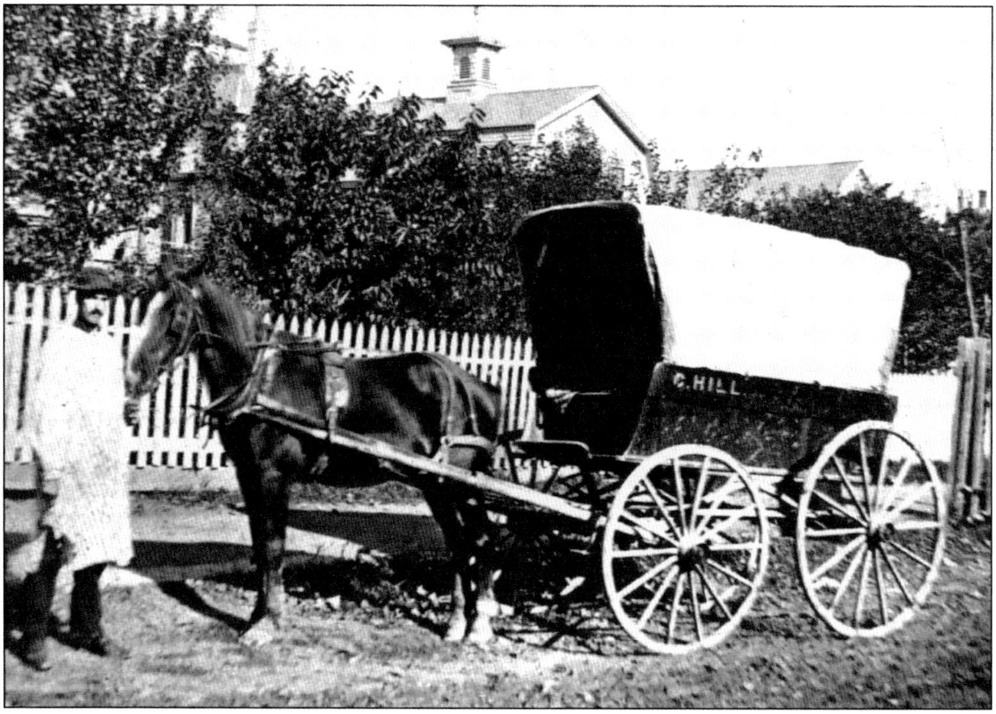

Photographed in about 1870, Charles Hill briefly operated a provision shop at 73 Main Street and made deliveries. Like many working men of the 19th century, he wears a long smock to protect his clothing.

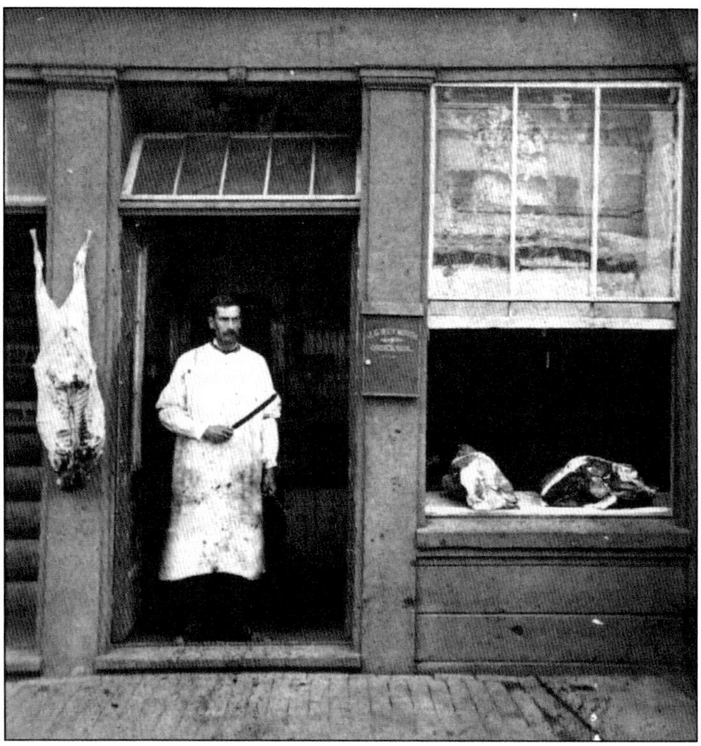

Although he operated a butcher shop out of his home at 171 Main Street for many years, Joseph G. Weymouth did not open the store shown here at 73 Main Street until 1882. In addition to selling beef, pork, lard, ham, sausage, and tripe at wholesale prices, he also offered neat's-foot oil, used to soften leather. Shoppers could leave requests in the box by his door, an important feature in the days before telephones. The Weymouth family operated a slaughterhouse well into the 20th century.

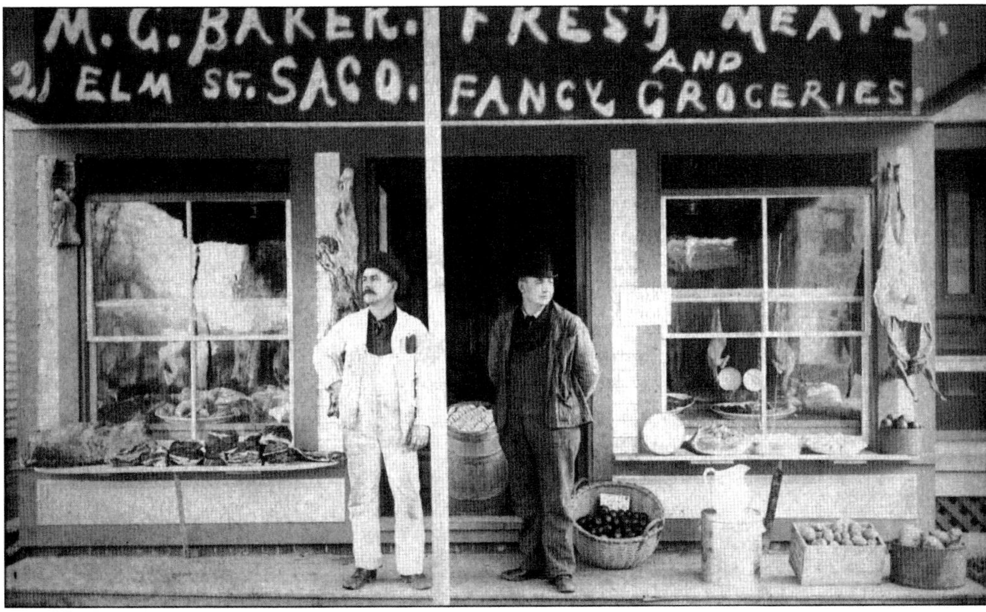

According to advertisements in the city directories, Maurice C. Baker only briefly operated as a "Dealer in Beef, Pork, Sausage, Ham, Mutton, Lamb, and Veal, also Fancy Groceries and Country Produce" on Elm Street, from about 1894 to 1896. By 1900, he had moved his home to Franklin Street and was selling provisions on North Street. That his produce had come from the country shows a changed local view of Saco: it had become an urban area and was no longer a source of farm products.

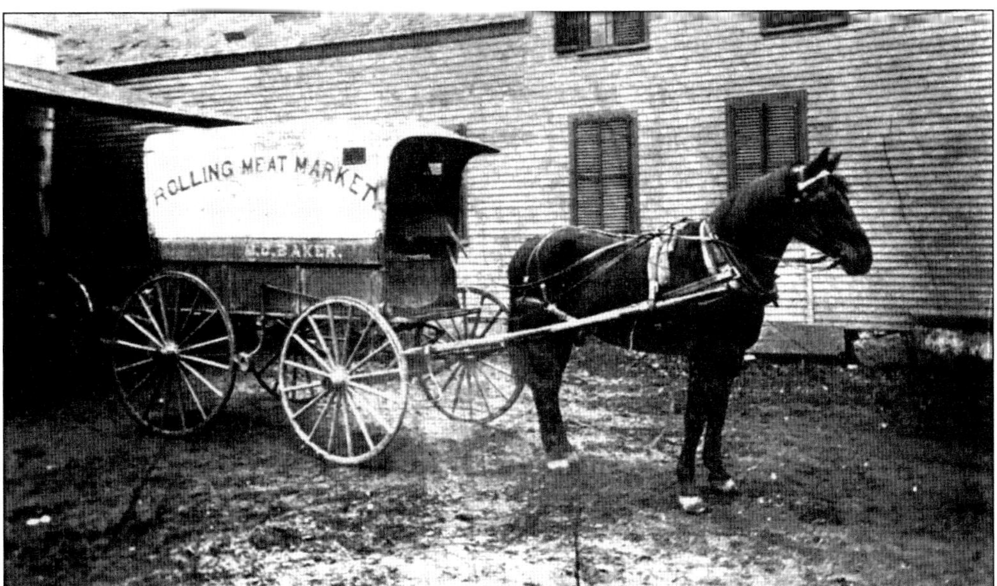

Baker is seen here, barely visible, in his "rolling meat market." This photograph was used both as an advertisement and as a signal for the driver to stop with a delivery. The back reads, "All people who buy their meats at the Rolling Meat Market can enjoy a good dinner . . . If you wish to prove above statement, place this card in your window, and we will call on you as frequently as you desire."

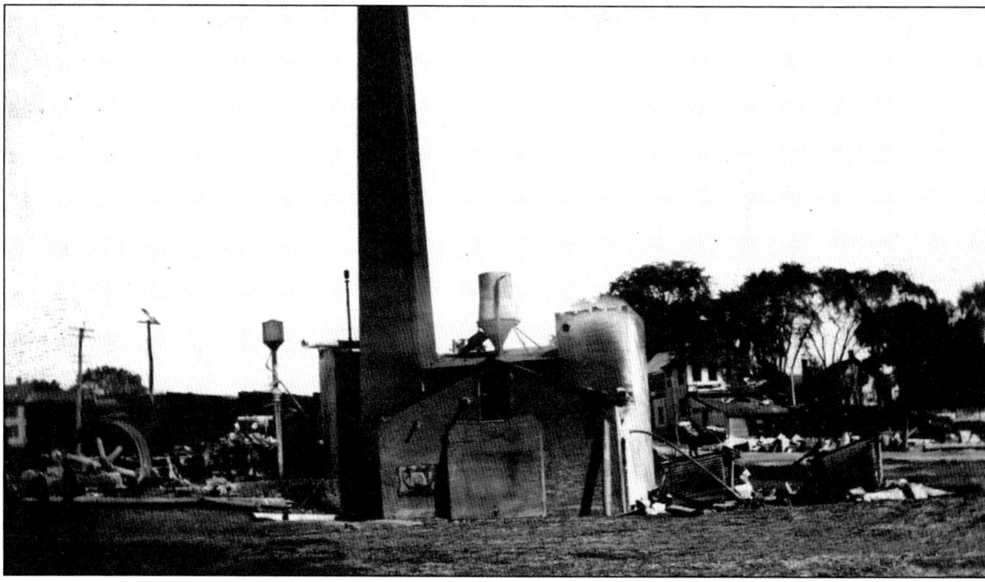

The Somesville fire on September 15, 1908, was one of the most destructive fires in Saco's history. Somesville was a section of Saco on the bank of the Saco River across the Somes Bridge from Spring's Island. The cause seems to have been someone smoking in the Diamond Match Company's lumberyard. The fire burned over 15 acres. Little remains of Crossman's Box Shop—which had turned nine million feet of pine into containers annually—except a giant machinery wheel to the left and the square brick chimney.

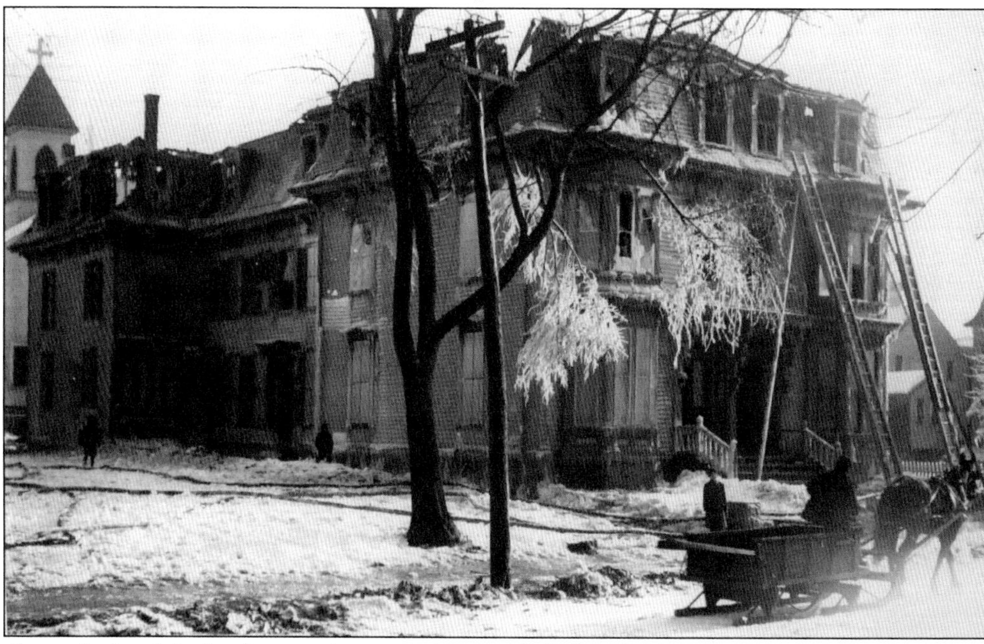

George L. Sands had only recently moved from Biddeford to this impressive home on Storer Street before a fire destroyed it on February 14, 1912. The fire was an additional burden for his wife, Jennie, since he had passed away just 13 days before. Firemen's hoses and ladders are still visible in this photograph of the fire-devastated house with the water used to fight the fire frozen on the branches of the tree out front. (Photograph by Charles Moody; courtesy McArthur Public Library.)

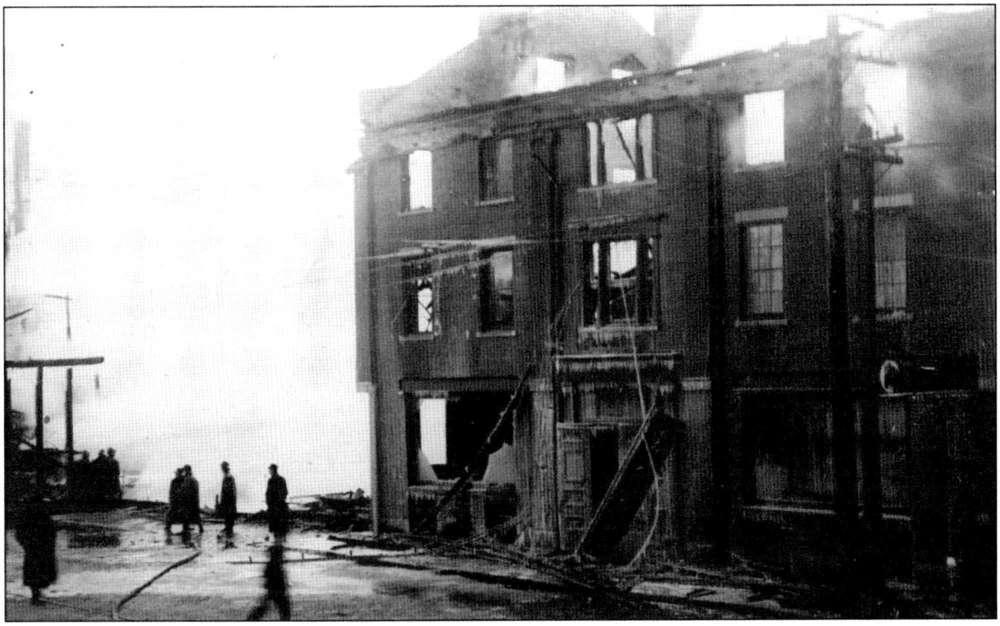

The Saco House hotel, operated by L. P. True, stood at 117 Main Street until it was destroyed by a disastrous fire on December 9, 1912. The remains of the Saco House were rebuilt with a flat roof to house the Atkinson Furniture Company.

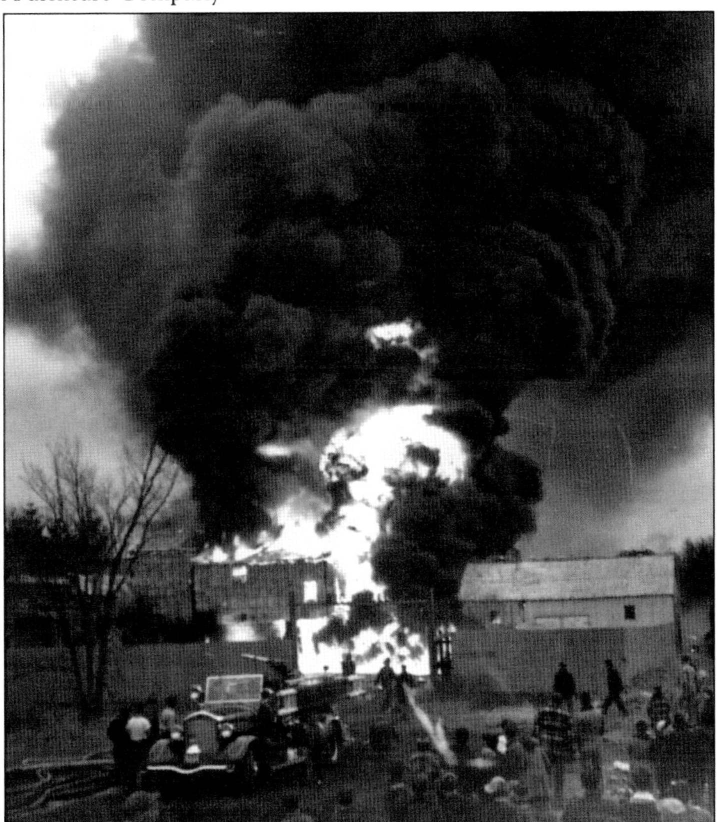

A fire rages out of control at the Mutual Oil storage facility on North Street on March 13, 1953. Over 30,000 gallons of heating oil and gasoline were blown up and burned off. Saco firemen can be seen racing to the fire from their truck.

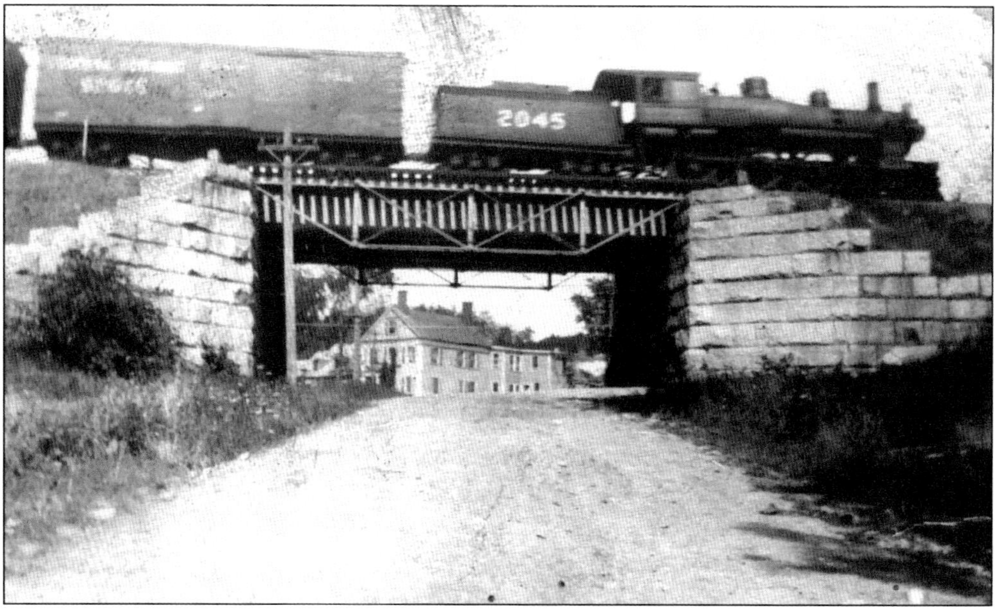

The railroad came to Saco in 1842 with the Portland, Saco and Portsmouth Railroad, which ran west of town. After the company merged with the Boston and Maine Railroad in 1887, the tracks ran straight through the factory district and across the river through Pepperell Square. This steam train crosses the Common Street overpass around 1917. The home seen through the bridge's opening still stands.

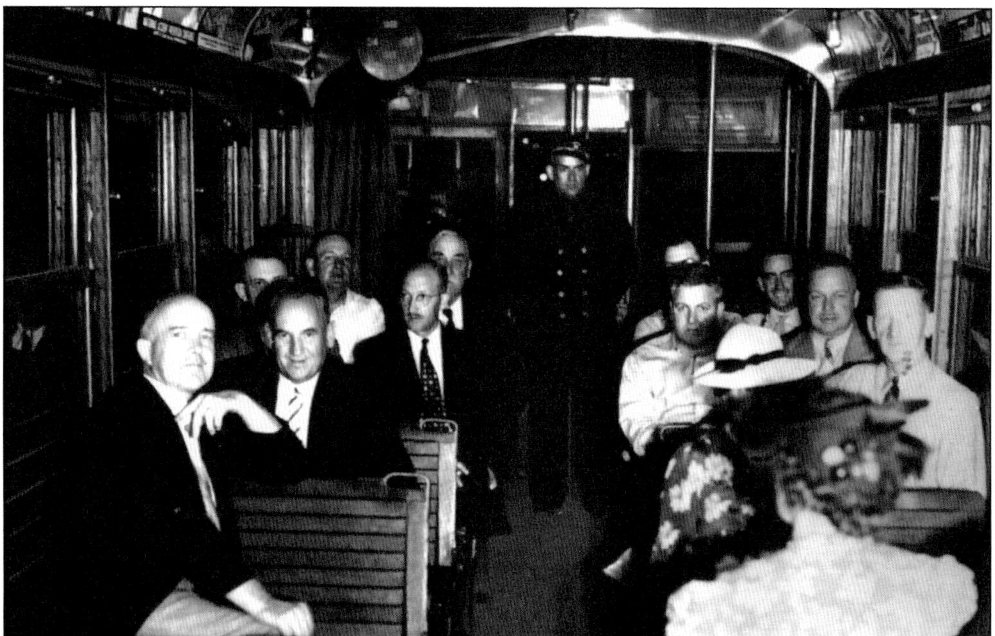

The Saco and Biddeford Railroad, actually a trolley line, was the area's primary means of public transportation from July 4, 1888, to July 5, 1939. Here Saco mayor Louis Brock (second seat on the left) takes a ceremonial last ride over the line in car No. 616. City clerk Bob Alexander is seated just in front of him.

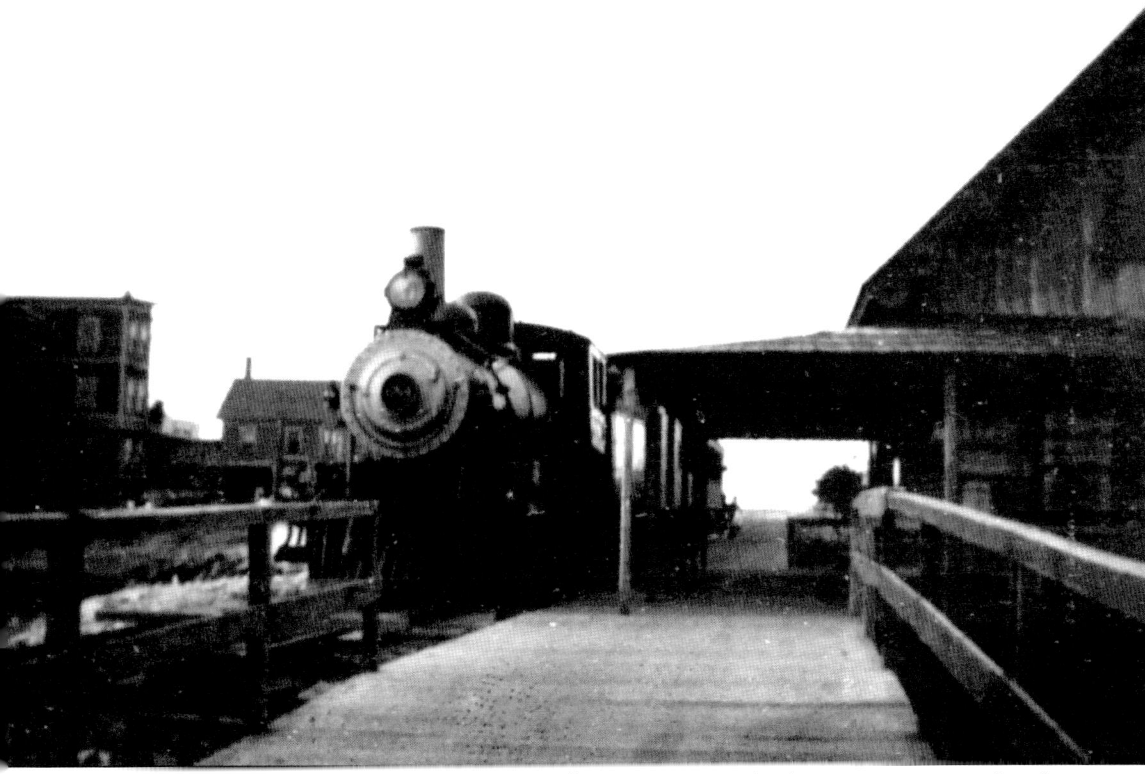

The "dummy railroad" is pictured here at Camp Ellis in August 1915. This narrow-gauge railroad operated from June 26, 1880, to September 5, 1923. It ran forward in one direction and backwards in the other, shuttling tourists between Old Orchard Beach and Camp Ellis, Saco's popular beachfront area.

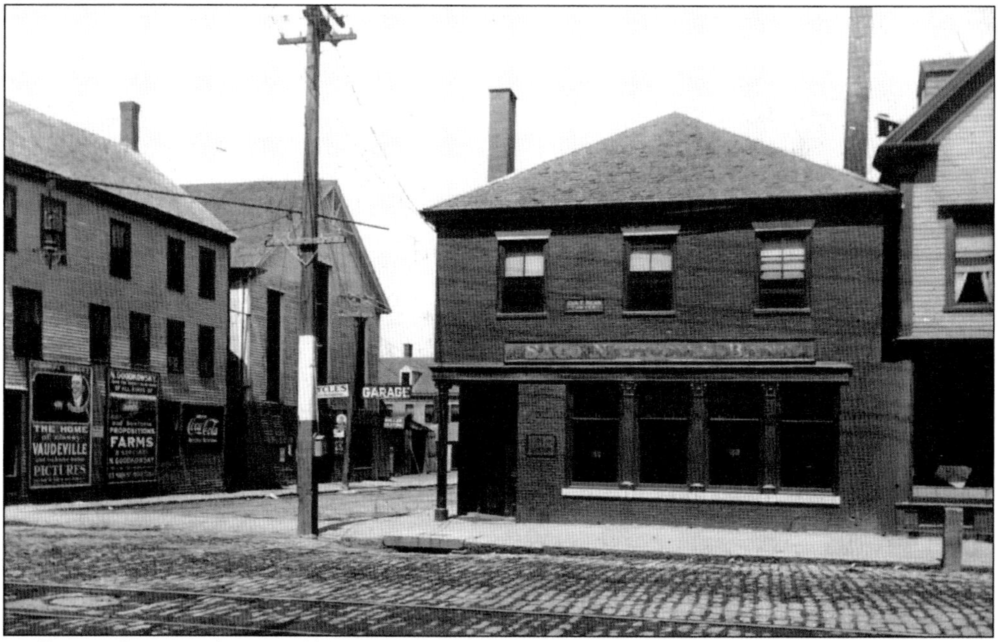

Trolley tracks extend over cobblestone-paved Storer Street on the corner of Main Street in this photograph from the 1920s. Residents could enjoy an ice-cold Coke while visiting the "home of classy vaudeville." "Wheelman" Jack Lawrence's garage and bicycle shop, the first ones in Saco, are visible nearby at 3 Storer Street.

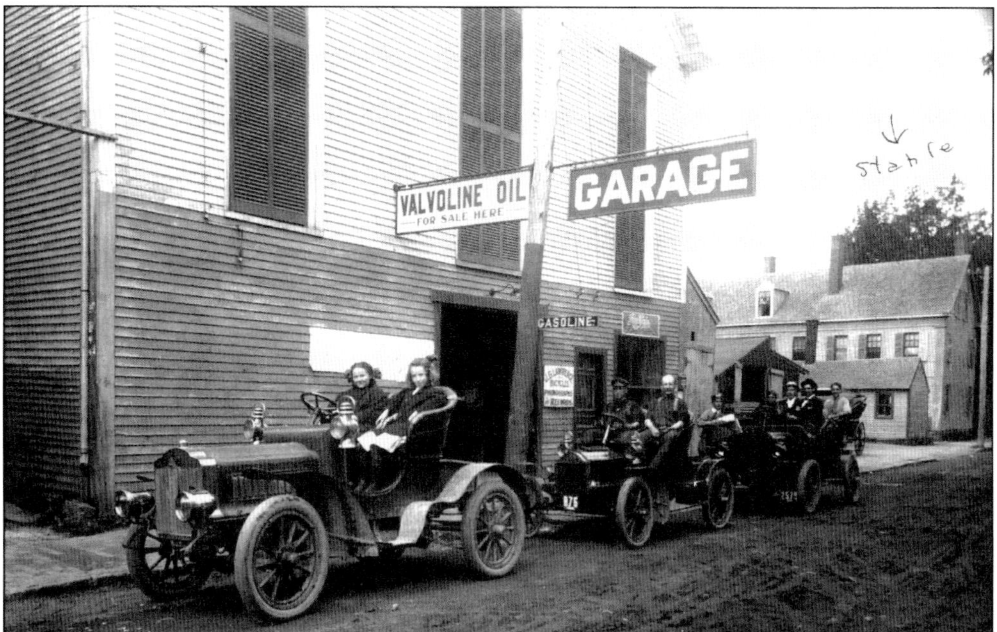

Pictured outside of Lawrence's garage in 1910 are three early automobiles: a three-cylinder Thomas, a single-cylinder Oldsmobile, and a Winton. Helen Lawrence, age 11, is the driver of the Thomas; a note accompanying the photograph says that she was still driving 69 years later at the age of 81.

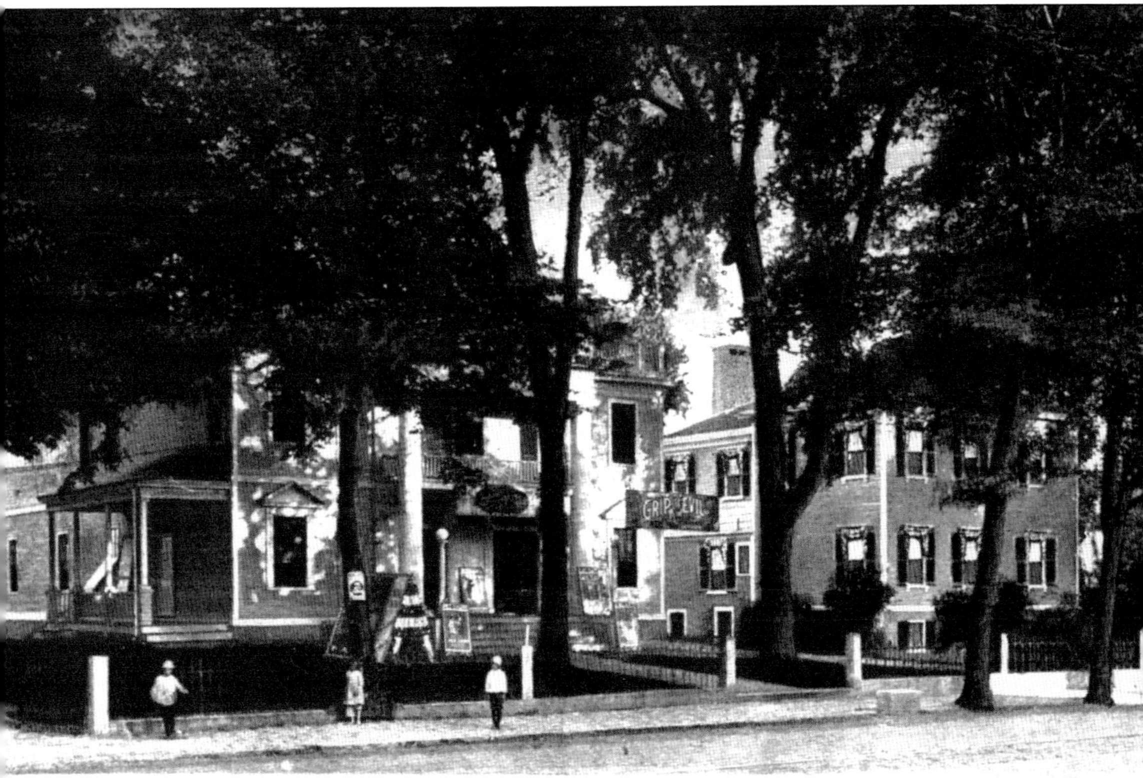

ERA HOUSE AND PAROCHIAL RESIDENCE, SACO, ME.

The production at the opera house on Main Street is *The Grip of Evil.* Although called the opera house, it was primarily used as a moving picture theater. Jonathan Tucker originally constructed the building around 1810 and ran a successful business with Daniel Cleaves there. After a financial reversal in the 1840s, Tucker was forced to sell to the Honorable Francis Warren Rice, a former newspaperman who ran a general store on the corner of Pepperell Square and Main Street. A successful Biddeford druggist, John Berry, owned it next and sold it to the Maine Amusement Company in 1915. They extensively renovated it, creating a huge interior space that seated 700 to 800 people. Although tickets sold for just 25¢, 35¢, and 50¢, the theater closed less than two years after the grand opening on January 24, 1916. Most Holy Trinity Catholic Church used the adjoining property as a rectory and later purchased the defunct theater and converted it into a church. It was then torn down to make way for the present structure. For more on the Tucker/Berry house, see pages 23 and 114.

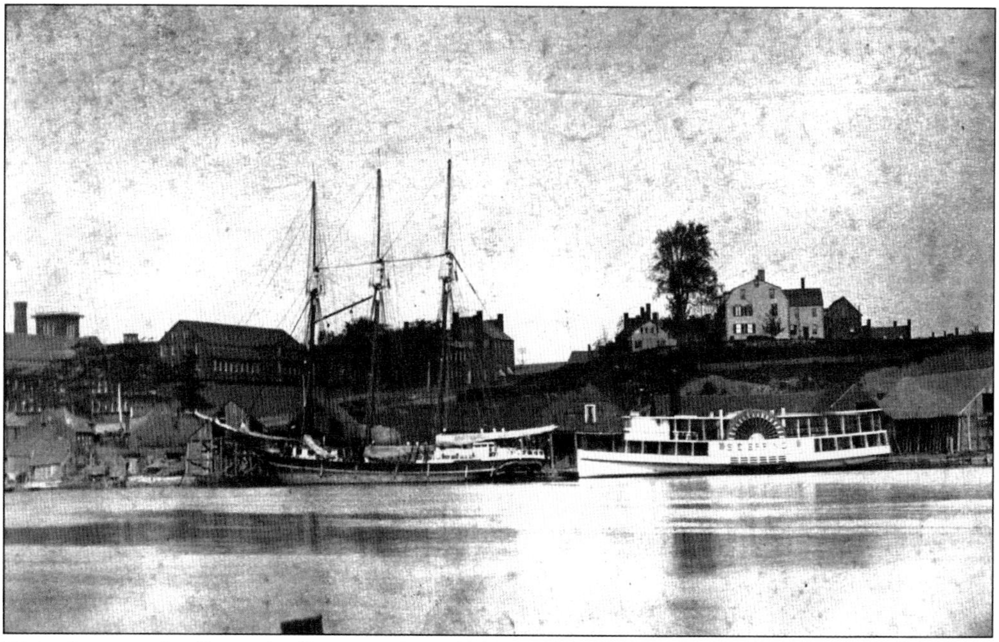

This photograph effectively illustrates how the manufacturing and tourist industries existed side by side in Saco. These boats, including a three-masted schooner and the steamboat *S. E. Spring*, are shown moored at a wharf on the lower side of Factory Island. The *S. E. Spring* side-wheeler steamer was an excursion boat built in Portland's East Deering neighborhood in 1881. From the 1880s on, it operated on the Saco River between Factory Island, Camp Ellis, and Biddeford Pool.

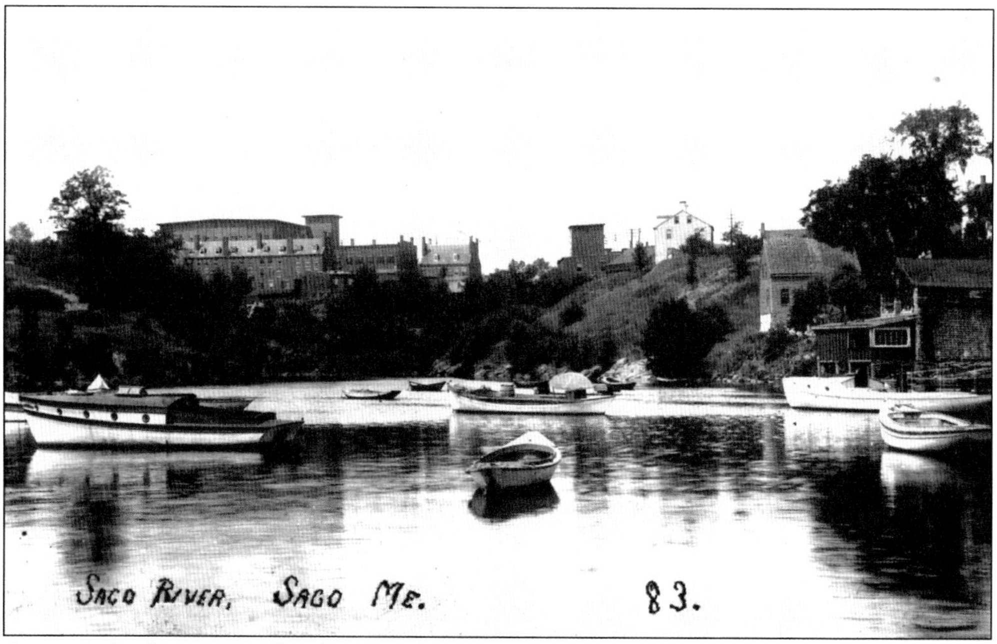

Again the background is all industry and the foreground is all tourism in this postcard produced around 1910 by the Eastern Illustrating and Publishing Company of Belfast. On the far right, the site of the Saco Yacht Club nestles in the shadow of the larger industrial buildings.

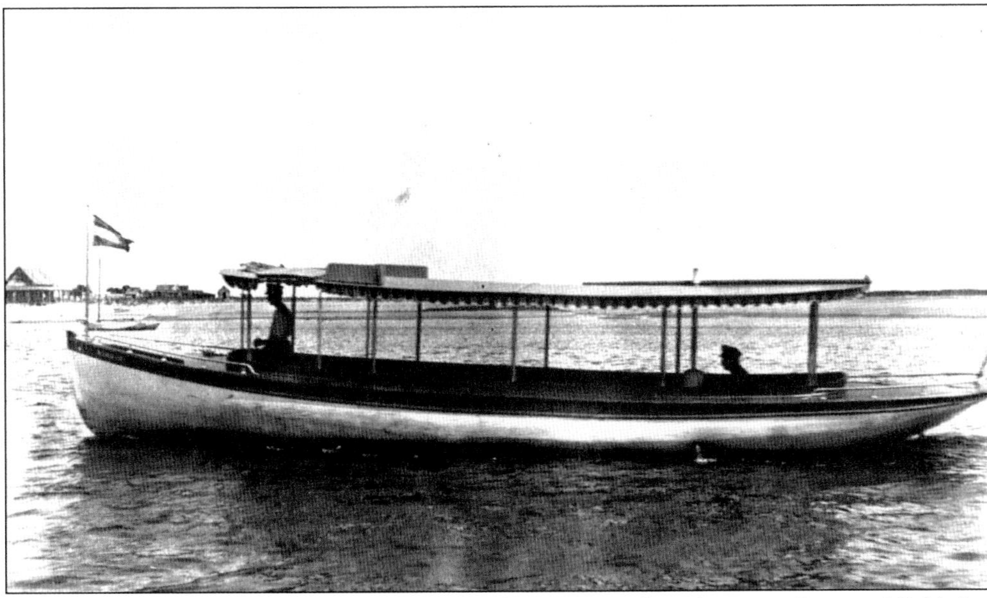

For most of the 1920s, Edwin M. Piper operated a passenger boat between Saco and Biddeford Pool. Here he shows off the clean lines of the *Nimrod* near Camp Ellis. He lived on Bartlett Street in Saco.

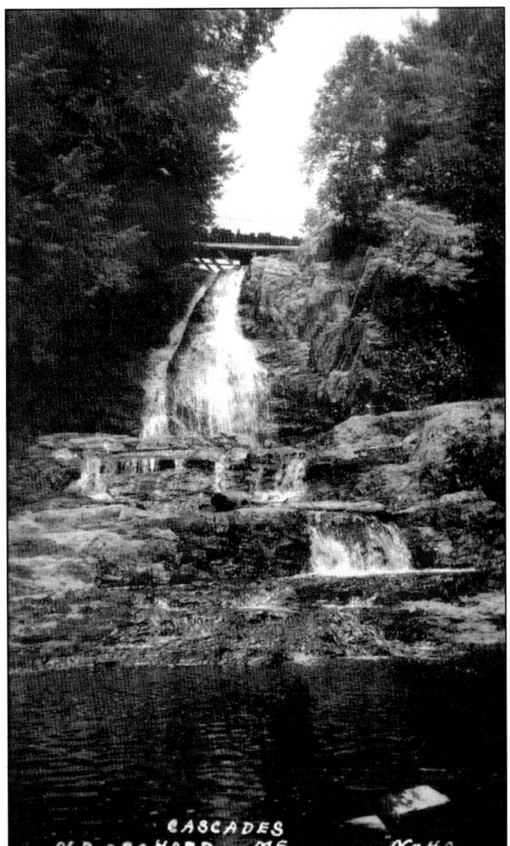

Although the postcard says Old Orchard, the Cascades, or Cascade Falls, are in Saco. A popular gathering place for tourists, the area once included a dam, now gone, which created a small pond that was used for boating. The state of Maine kept a caged bear near the falls for the amusement of picnickers. On the reverse side, this postcard says, "Weather is beautiful today, am enjoying myself immensely." Although the area is quiet today, there is a steady trickle of visitors thanks to the efforts of Saco Bay Trails.

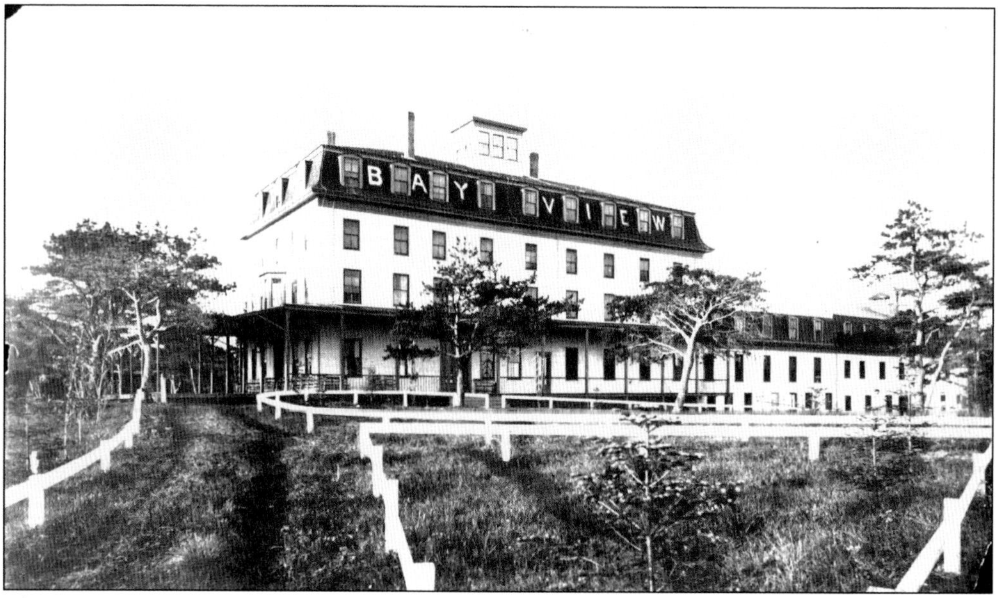

The Bay View Hotel was located on the oceanfront between Kinney Shores and Ferry Beach. It was built in the early 1870s and enjoyed by high society members and summer visitors. It was operated first by Oscar F. Page and later by Emma Manson, the widow of James Manson, and her son Albert. Emma married Abiathar W. Leavitt around 1904, and she died in 1909 at age 79. In 1948, the hotel was purchased by the Servants of the Immaculate Heart for use as a convent and inn.

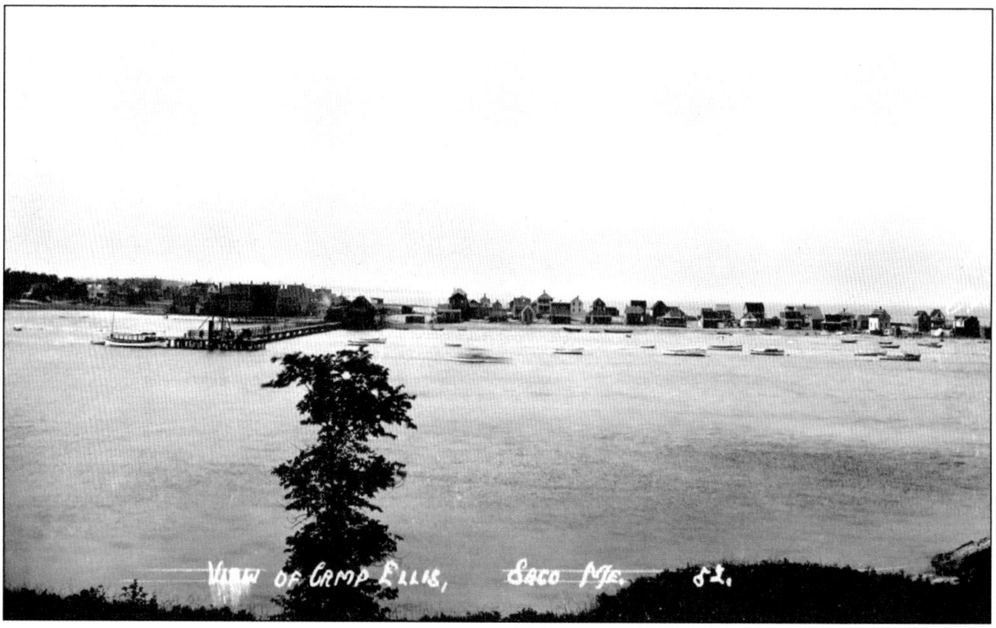

This postcard view, produced by Eastern Illustrating and Publishing Company of Belfast, shows the narrow spit of land that comprises Camp Ellis. Many of these homes have since been damaged or destroyed by beach erosion, for which some citizens blame the jetty built by the U.S. Army Corps of Engineers in 1867. Visible just left of center is the dummy railroad station and adjacent dock, which was well used by fishermen and tourists. (Courtesy Penobscot Marine Museum.)

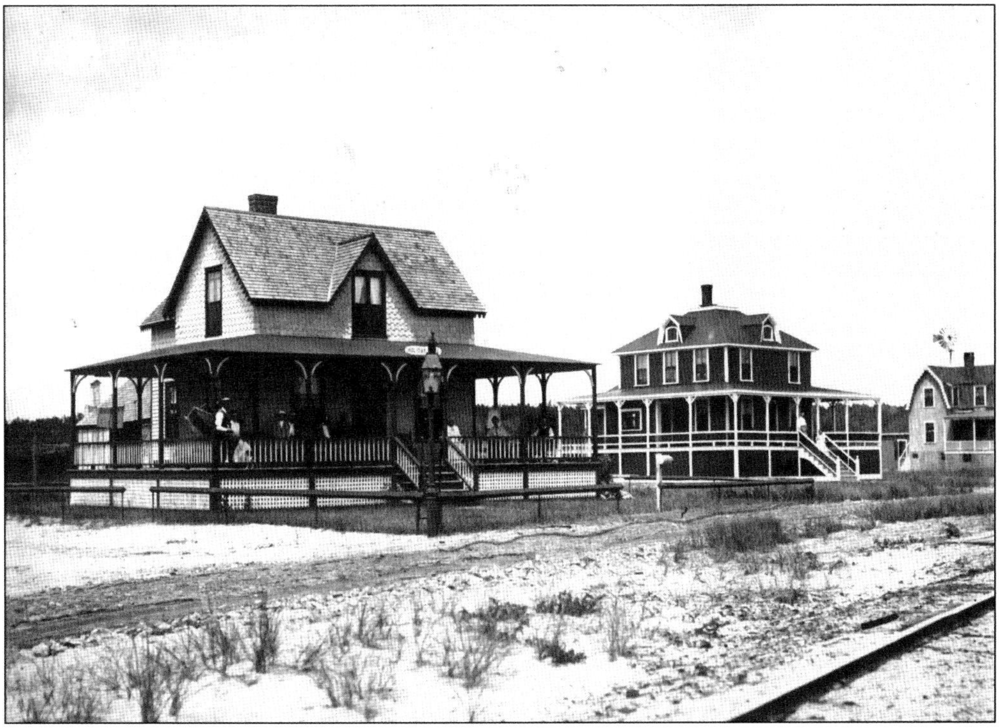

Tracks of the dummy railroad cut across the bottom of this late-19th-century view of Camp Ellis homes. Many wealthy summer visitors built camps, or summer cottages, in and around this spit of land adjacent to Ferry Beach. This photograph shows the cottage known as Holiday Home on the left.

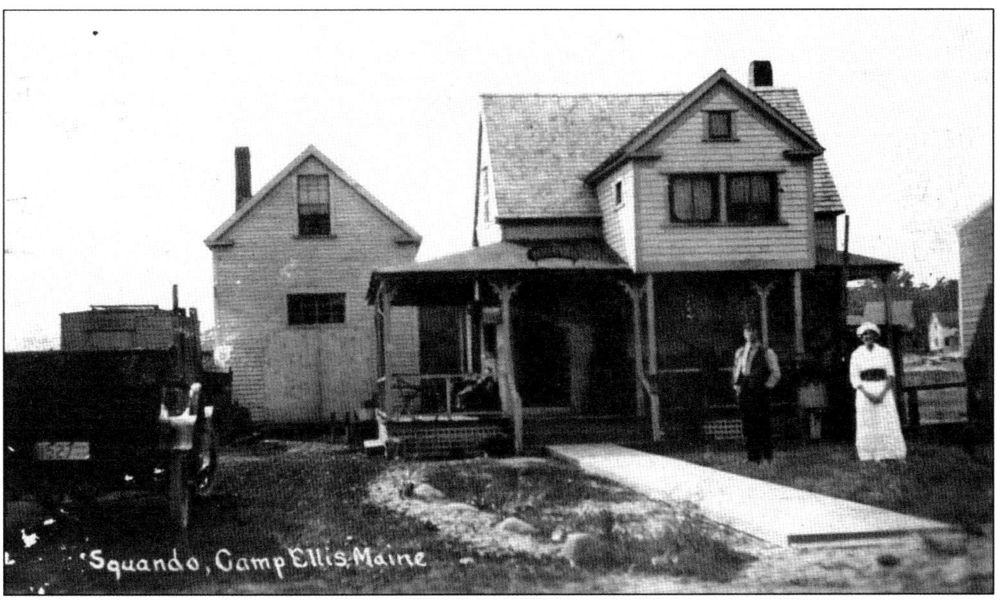

Squando, the Native American chief who famously cursed the Saco River in the 17th century, might be surprised to find his name attached to this attractive seaside cottage from the dawn of the 20th century. Its owners proudly pose in their leisure wear.

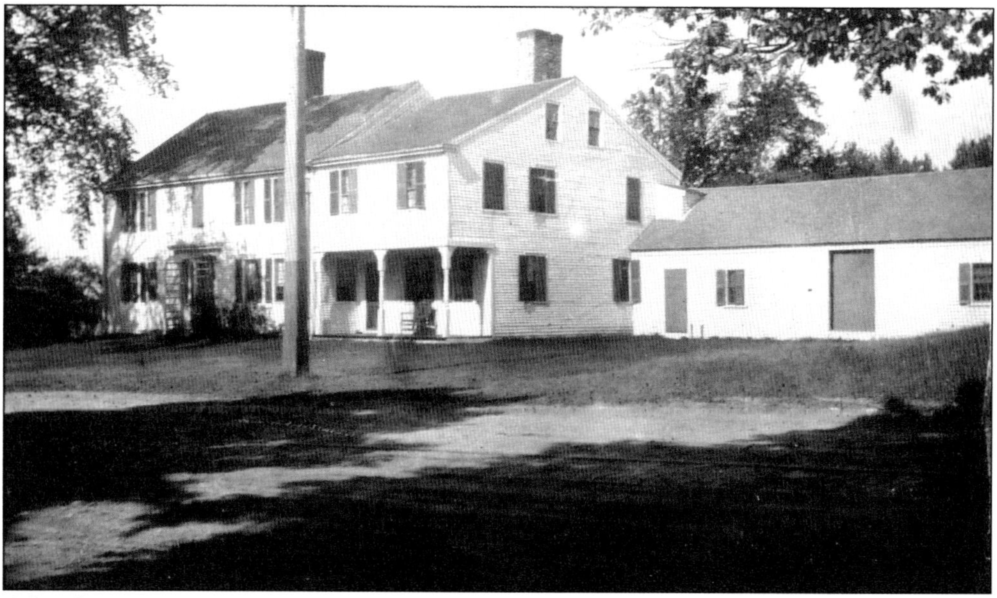

A hand-written notation on the back of this postcard reads, "Scamman Inn, Saco," suggesting a leisure destination for out-of-town tourists. However, the property on North Street was operated by Frank Scamman and his wife between 1902 and about 1907 as the City Farm, a euphemism for "poor farm." The Scamman family ran the facility until 1938; by 1950, it was no longer in use. The defense contractor General Dynamics now occupies the lot, although the building no longer exists.

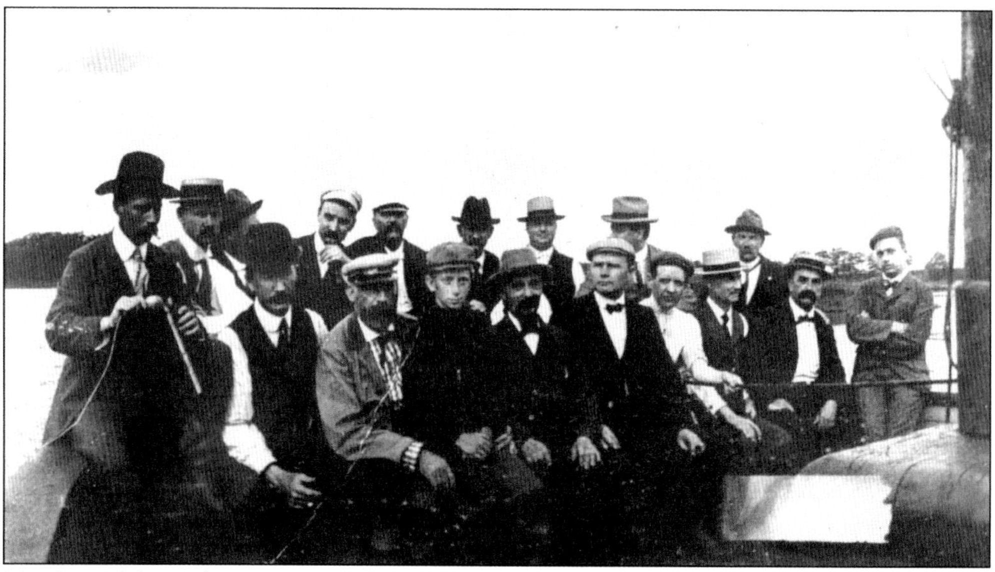

Members of the York County Medical Association gather for an excursion down the Saco River on a steam-powered vessel in 1889. The gentleman to the far left is holding some sort of unusual instrument. (Courtesy McArthur Public Library.)

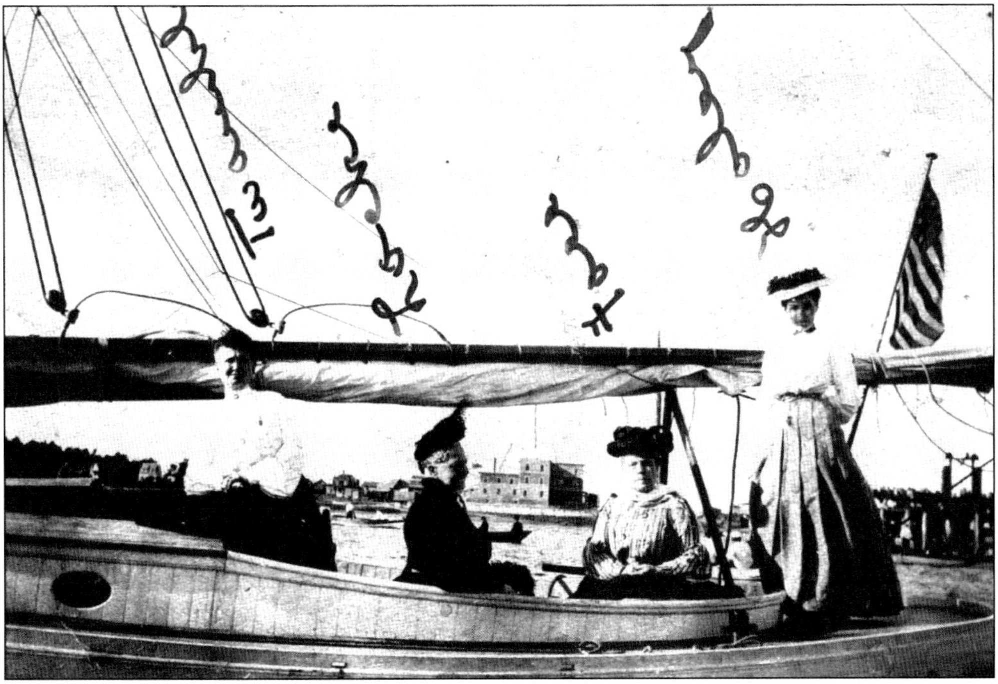

Out for a day's sail around 1900, these prominent ladies have chosen the perfect recreational attire. They are identified by their surnames only. From left to right are ? Twambley, ? Locke (probably Marcia Locke, wife of John S. Locke and mother of Almira Locke McArthur), ? Foss, and ? Haley (probably Adelaide, daughter of John).

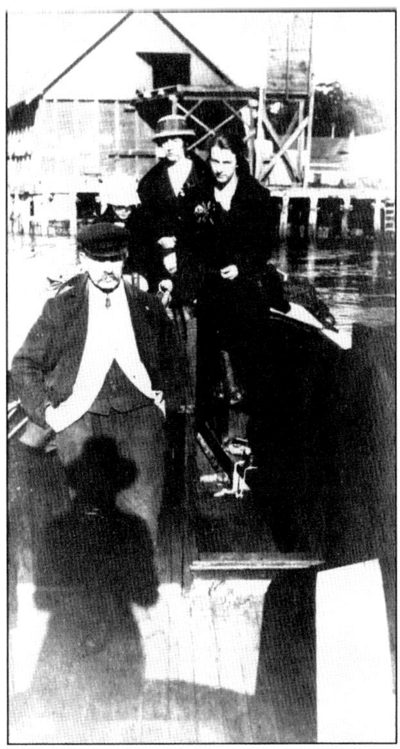

The shadow of the photographer with her box camera partially obscures Frank Leighton on his boat with two lady friends. The coal dock wharf is in the background.

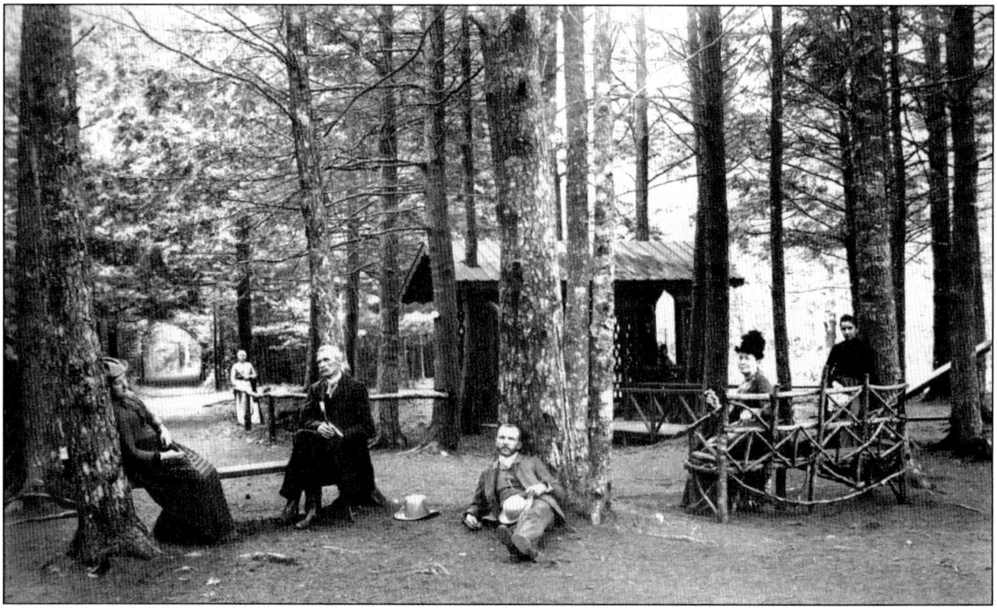

Since the early 1900s, Saco's Ferry Beach has been a popular spot for summer visitors. Its beautiful white sand beaches and unique vegetation made it a frequent destination for tourists and nature lovers, while others were drawn to the growing Unitarian Universalist community there. Since 1901, members of that faith have acquired property there and held annual summertime retreats. Resting after an extensive picnic from left to right are Myra Webster Clark, David Webster, John Emerson, Mrs. Webster, and Marie Webster. Notice the tree growing through the roof of the picnic pavilion.

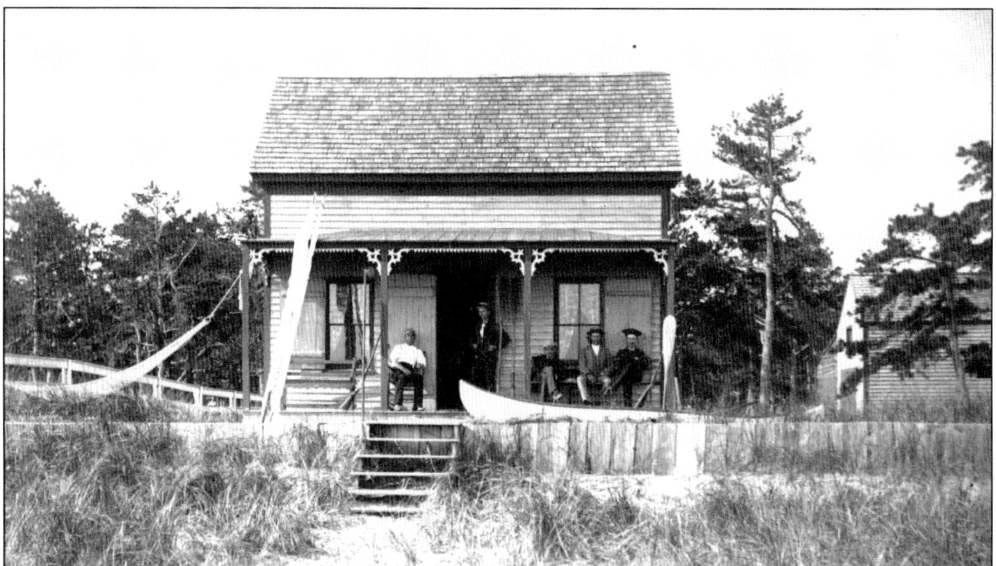

The Unitarian property at Ferry Beach, known as the Pines, included gathering places and summer cottages. Breaking camp at Bradbury cottage on August 25, 1888, from left to right are Dr. Fred Graves, Walter S. Mitchell, S. Lewis Moody, unidentified, and James Vaughan Dennett. Following his customary practice, Dennett sports an unusual cap. Notice the hammock stretched to the left of the building.

Three

PHILANTHROPY

As Saco's economic power grew throughout the 19th century so did the desire to increase the cultural wealth of the area. Institutions of culture and higher learning were founded through the generosity of individuals and the benevolence and foresight of city planners.

The York Institute, now the Saco Museum, was one of the earliest manifestations of this desire for intellectual pursuits and the impulse to preserve history. It was founded in 1866 with a mission "to promote the study of Natural History; encourage Science and Art; also to collect and preserve whatever relates to the Natural and Civic history of York County." The museum's collections to this day reflect those varied goals. The museum's opening was followed by the founding of the Dyer Library, established in 1889 by Olive Dyer in the name of her husband, Oliver. The library shared many of the same ideals as the museum, as well as the mandate to establish a library "which shall ever be free to the citizens of Saco."

Improving the lives of Saco's citizenry was a common refrain throughout the 19th and 20th centuries. Educators, doctors, historians, and other visionaries sought to enhance the physical, mental, and intellectual well-being of the population as a whole. Their efforts supported the creation of venerable institutions—both the human and bricks-and-mortar variety—that endure to this day.

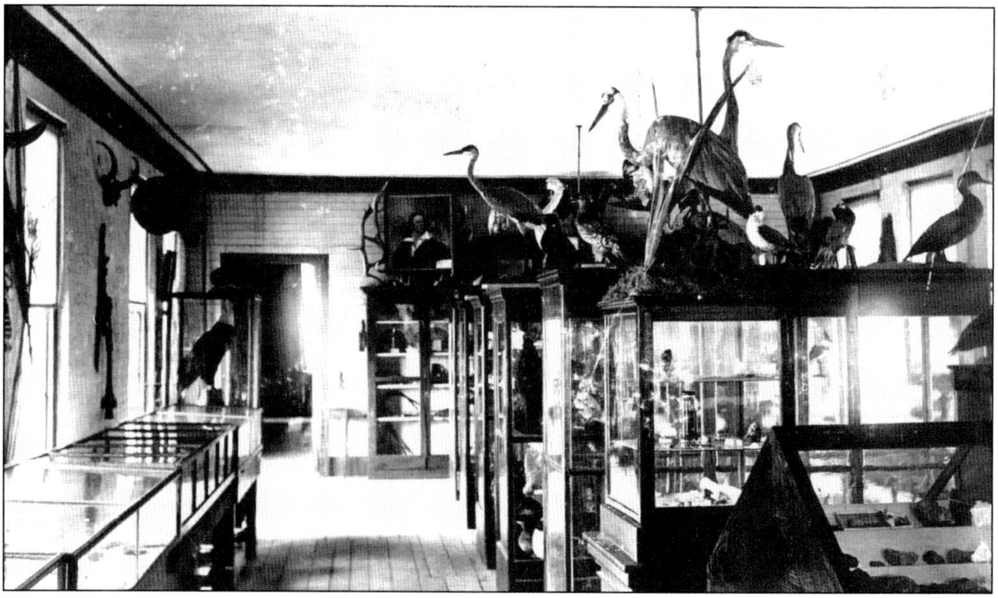

The early collections of the York Institute (now the Saco Museum), founded 1866, featured many natural history objects, including rare birds, eggs, mineral specimens, and seashells. The eagle seen in the background to the left is recognizable to generations of Saco schoolchildren. The York Institute was located in the Sweetser Block near the Saco River from 1890 to 1926, where this photograph was taken. The block also included a large auditorium for public lectures. (Courtesy McArthur Public Library.)

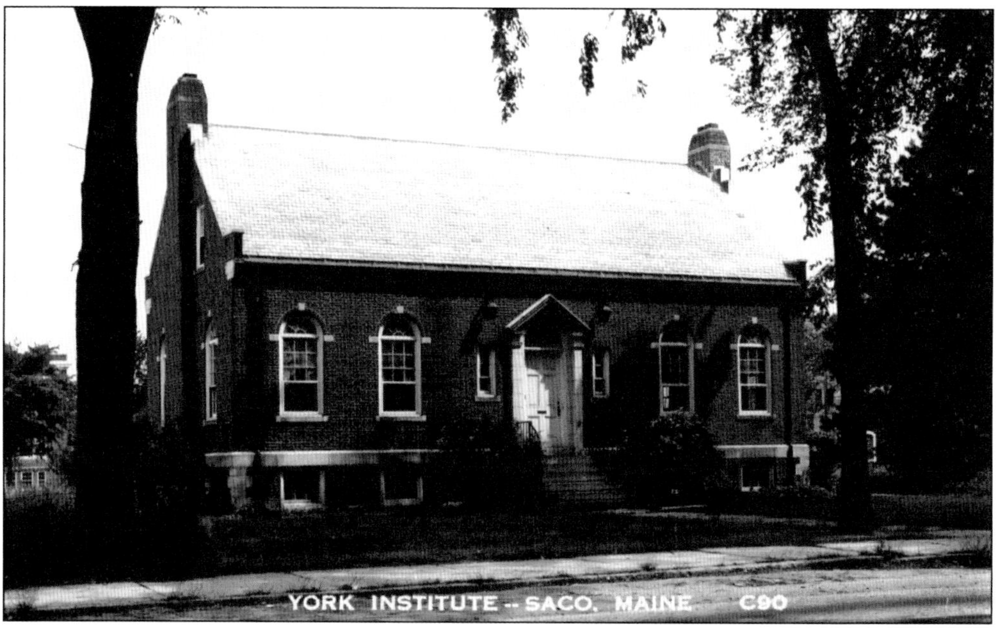

The second home of the York Institute was designed by acclaimed Portland architect John Calvin Stevens and completed in 1926 next to the future home of the Dyer Library. The brick Colonial Revival style of the building emulated the design of local 19th-century homes. The York Institute merged with the Dyer Library in 1976 and changed its name to the Saco Museum in 2000.

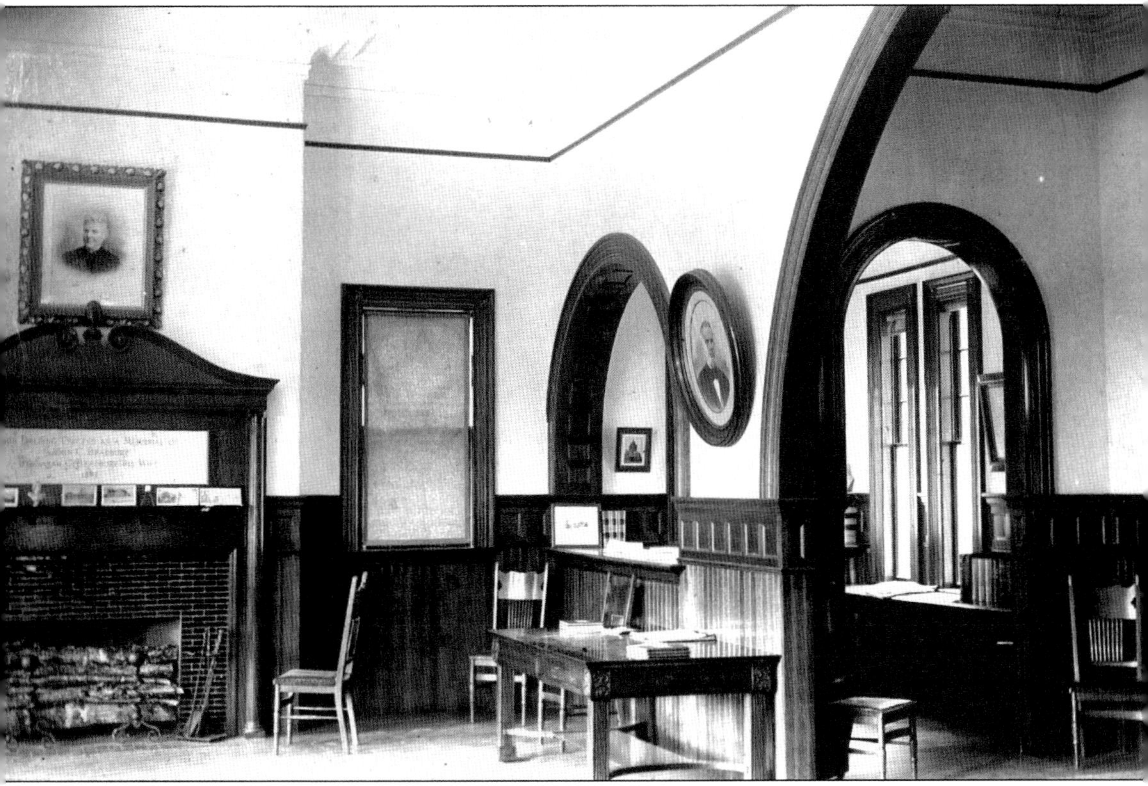

The founder of the Dyer Library, Olive Dyer, stipulated in her will that the money should not go for the purchase of a building, so the library opened for business in the cellar of city hall, where the dirt floor was paved and a small furnace was added. Shortly afterward, the library moved to a new structure next door. Construction of this building was made possible by a gift from Sarah C. Bradbury in memory of her husband, John Bradbury. Construction began in 1893 with Horace G. Wadlin as the architect. The building featured elaborate, well-crafted woodwork. Notice the portrait of Oliver Dyer hanging in the center of this photograph. Olive Dyer stipulated that the photograph of her husband hang in the library for perpetuity. After the Dyer Library relocated to the Deering mansion in 1955, this building became the Saco Police station and currently houses a dance studio.

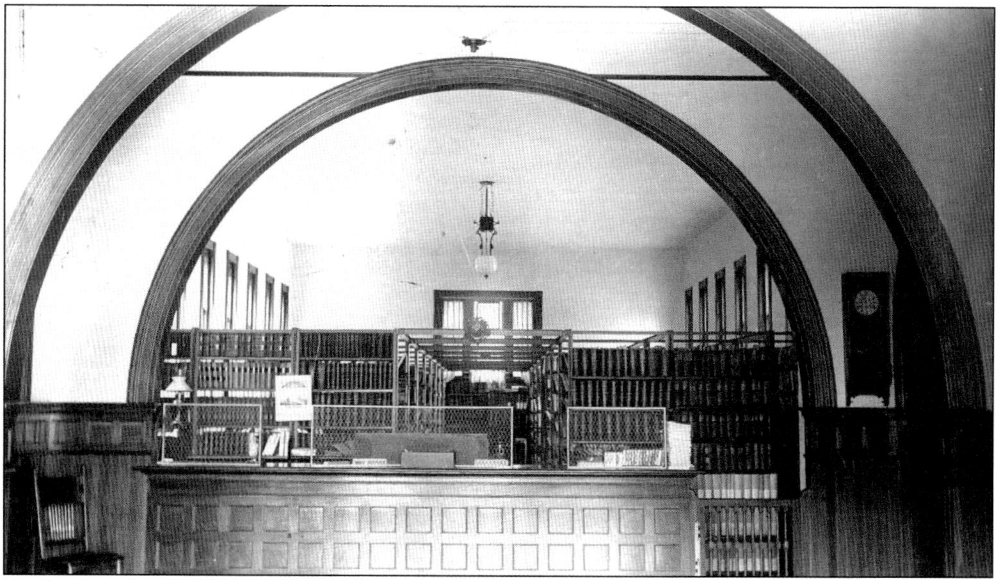

In this view from around 1900, the circulation desk of the Dyer Library stands as a barrier between the public and the books they had to request to check out. Older children and teens frequently had their requests rejected because the librarian judged books to be inappropriate for their age.

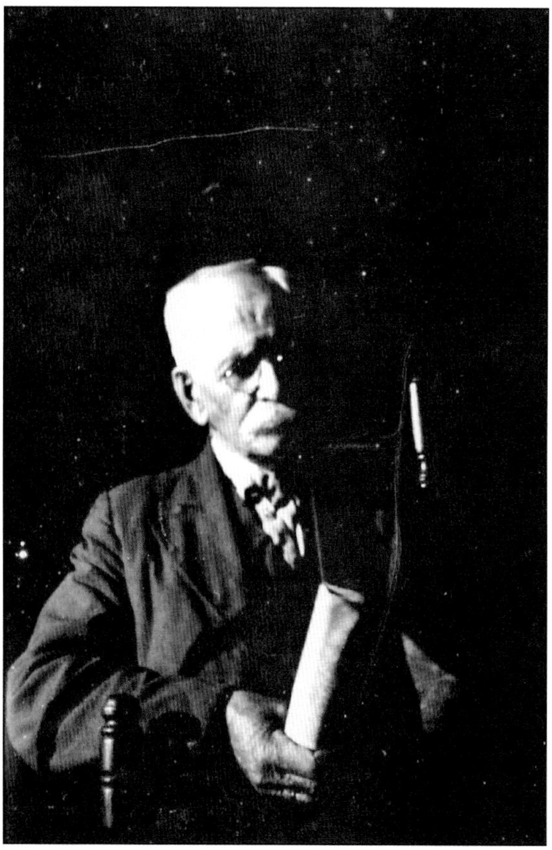

Born on March 3, 1840, John Haley served in the 17th Maine Company I in the Civil War and kept a detailed journal of his experiences. His writings were published as *The Rebel Yell and the Yankee Hurrah* in 1985 by Down East Books. He returned to Saco, worked at various jobs, and finally became the second librarian of the Dyer Library, a position he held until the end of his life. He died on April 17, 1921; this photograph was taken shortly before his death.

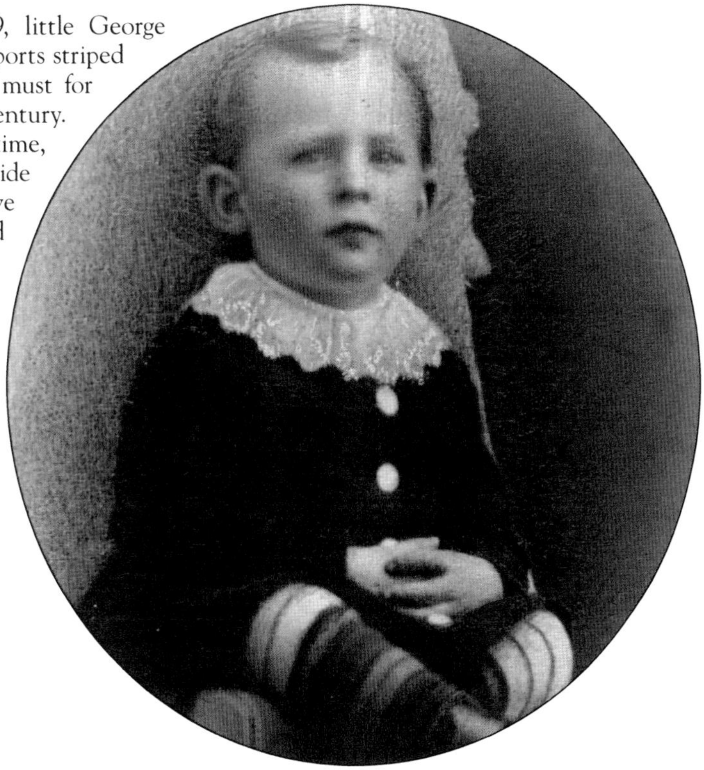

Photographed around 1879, little George Haley, son of John Haley, sports striped socks that were a fashion must for small children in the 19th century. Like most small boys of his time, his hair is parted on the side and he wears an attractive dress. He most likely would have gone into pants at the age of four or five. George Haley went on to become an architect and an artist, with paintings in the collection of the Saco Museum. He lived to the age of 87.

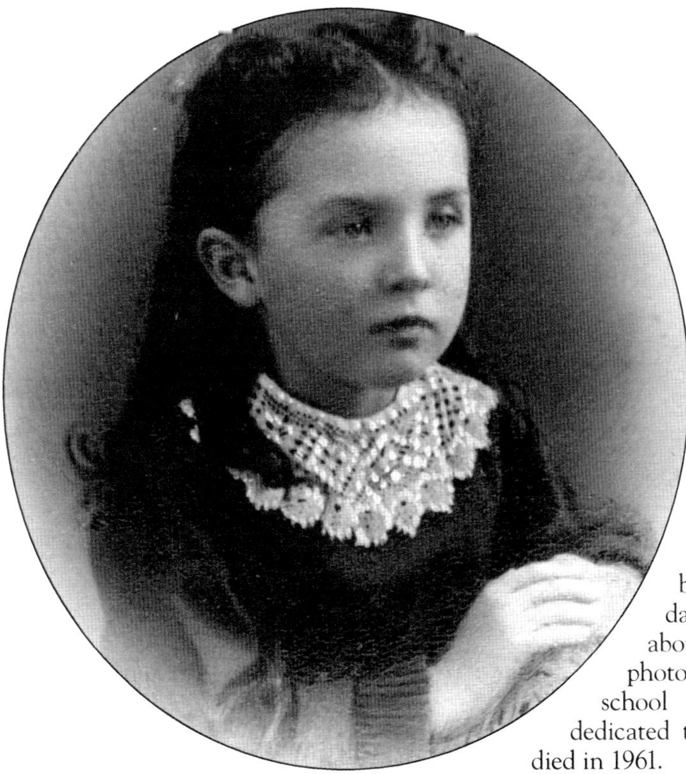

Pictured in a collar that matches her younger brother's, Adelaide Haley, daughter of John Haley, was about five years old when this photograph was taken. She taught school most of her life and was dedicated to documenting history. She died in 1961.

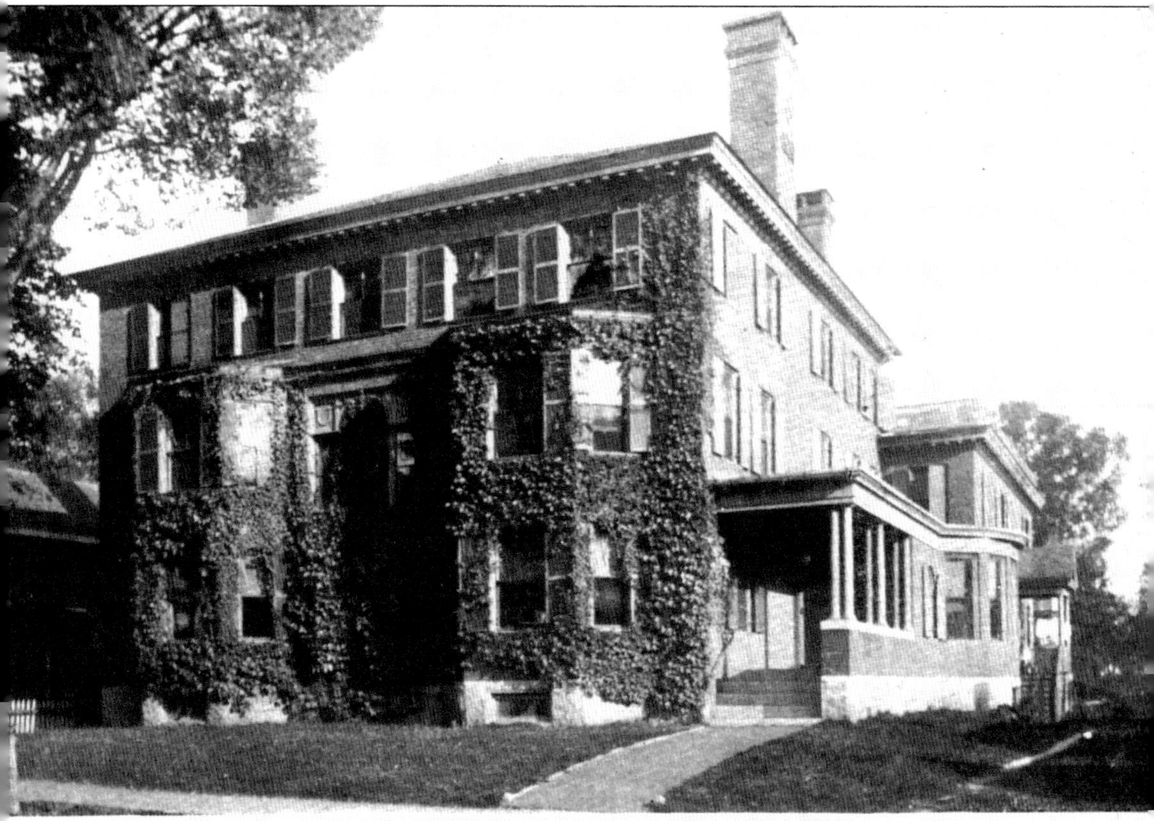

WARDWELL HOME, SACO, MAINE.

The Wardwell Home was founded in 1878 as the "Old Ladies Home of Saco and Biddeford" to address a significant need. Many older women, widowed or never married, had little means to support themselves as they became increasingly infirm. If over the age of 60, they could apply to the home. Upon being "recommended by the committee on admission as proper subjects for the home," the women could pay the (substantial) admission fee of $100, turn over all of their property, and live in a room at the home until death. If the applicant later changed her mind or her "character or conduct is in their [board of directors] judgment detrimental to the welfare or comfort of the Home," she could leave with her property—less the cost of board—returned to her. Philanthropist John S. Locke was an early president of the home, which continues to serve Saco today.

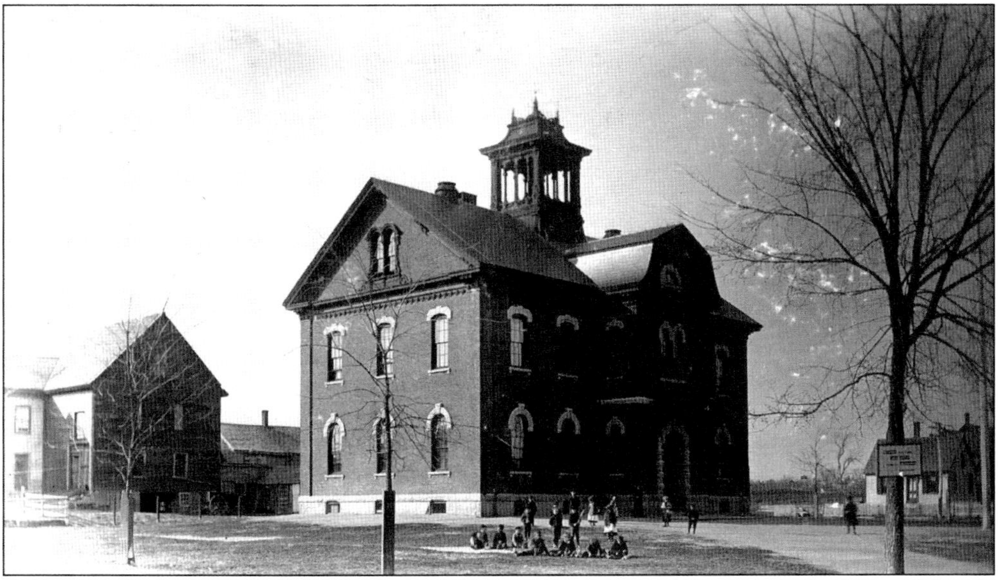

Photographed in the 1880s, the Spring Street schoolhouse later became the Sweetser School, named for Cornelius Sweetser, whose significant philanthropy continues to affect many of the citizens of Saco and Biddeford. The boys gathered in front appear ready to start up a game of baseball, still a relatively new game at this time. The little girls' white pinafores are visible beneath their winter coats. Behind the school, a wagon stands ready next to the barn.

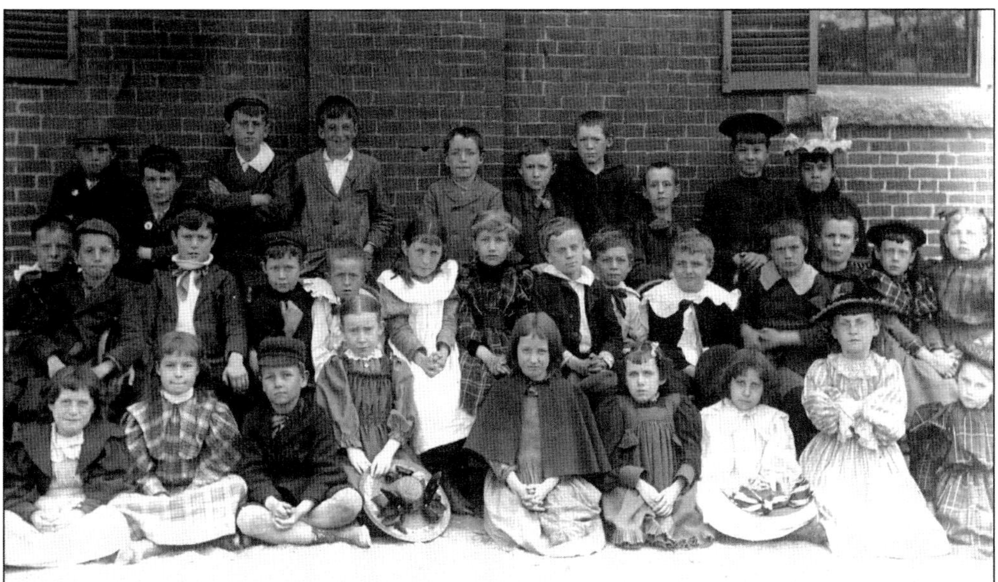

The fourth-grade class of the Sweetser School gathers beside the building for a photograph around 1895. Their teacher, Nella L. Allen, lived on Spring Street in Saco and taught Saco children for many years. She died in 1915.

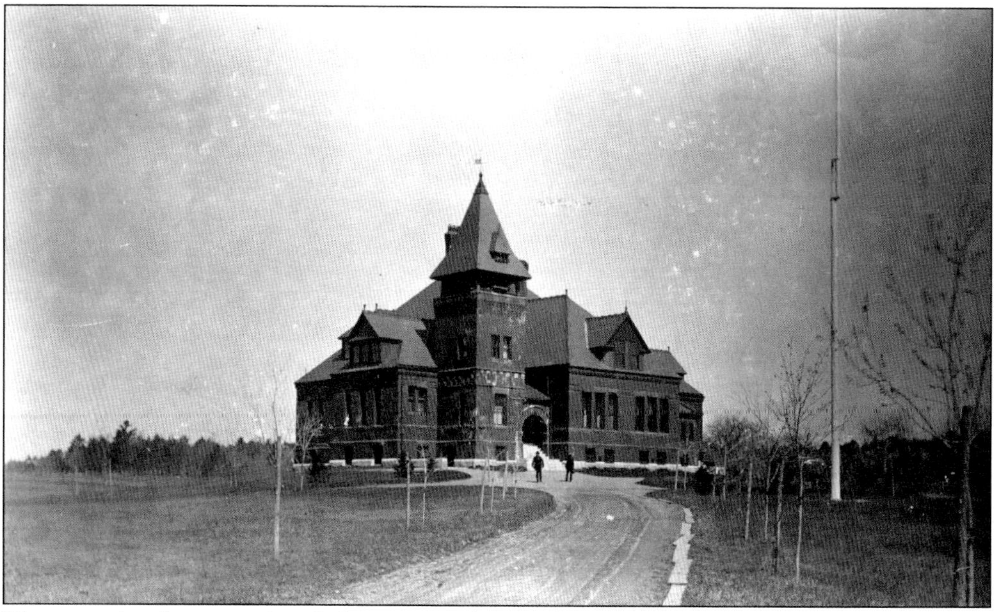

Thornton Academy was founded in 1811 and opened in January 1813. The original Thornton Academy burned to the ground in 1848, at which point the new Saco High School took over secondary education in the city. Eventually Thornton Academy was rebuilt and Saco High School was closed. The tall flagpole to the right shows up in many other early photographs, although most do not show it entirely since it was so tall.

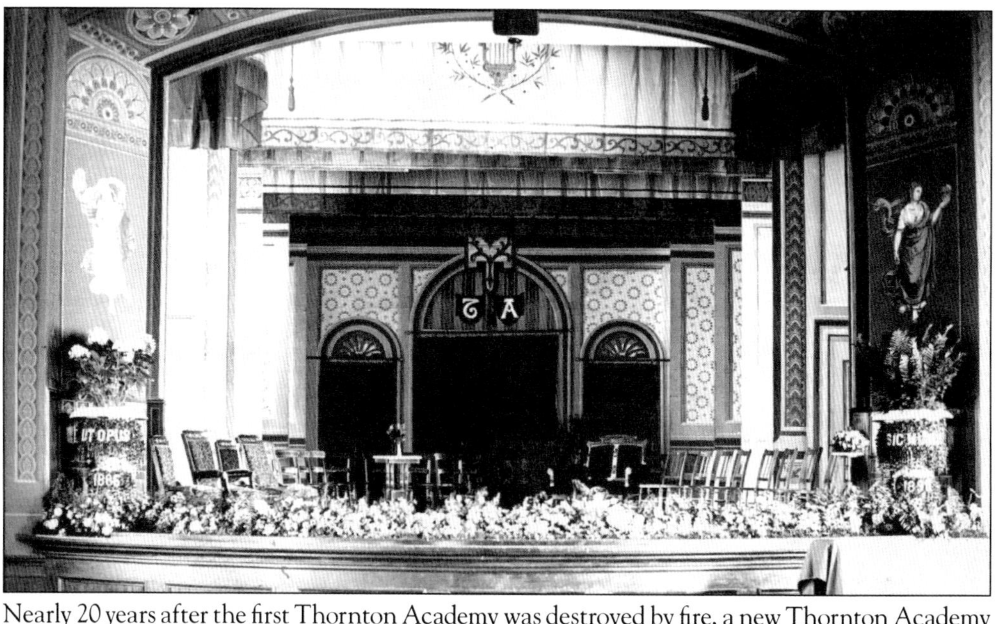

Nearly 20 years after the first Thornton Academy was destroyed by fire, a new Thornton Academy was established as a corporation in 1886, and on June 20, 1890, the first class graduated. This photograph shows the Saco City Hall stage set up for that ceremony. The kindergarten founded just the year before by the Women's Educational and Industrial Union (see page 88) held classes in a room directly underneath this stage.

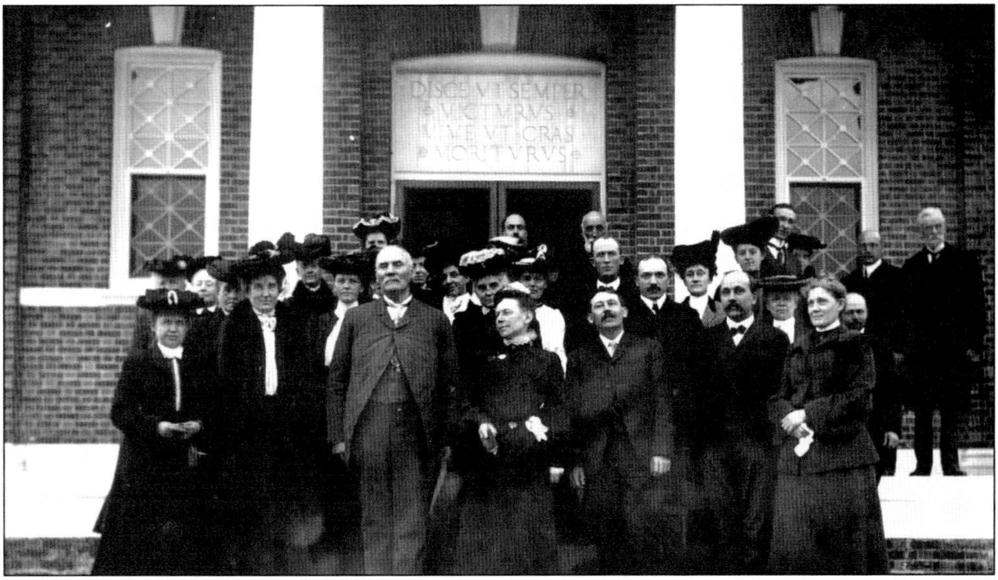

George A. Emery (1839–1933), far right, poses here in front of the Charles G. Thornton Memorial Library, completed in 1902 on the Thornton Academy campus. Emery's donation made the George Addison Emery Gymnasium possible in 1913. Prior to that time, indoor gymnasium classes were held at Hamilton Hall on Storer Street, a considerable distance from campus. Emery, whose dedication to the school earned him the nickname "Mr. Thornton," was also a founding member of the York Institute, now the Saco Museum. (Courtesy McArthur Public Library.)

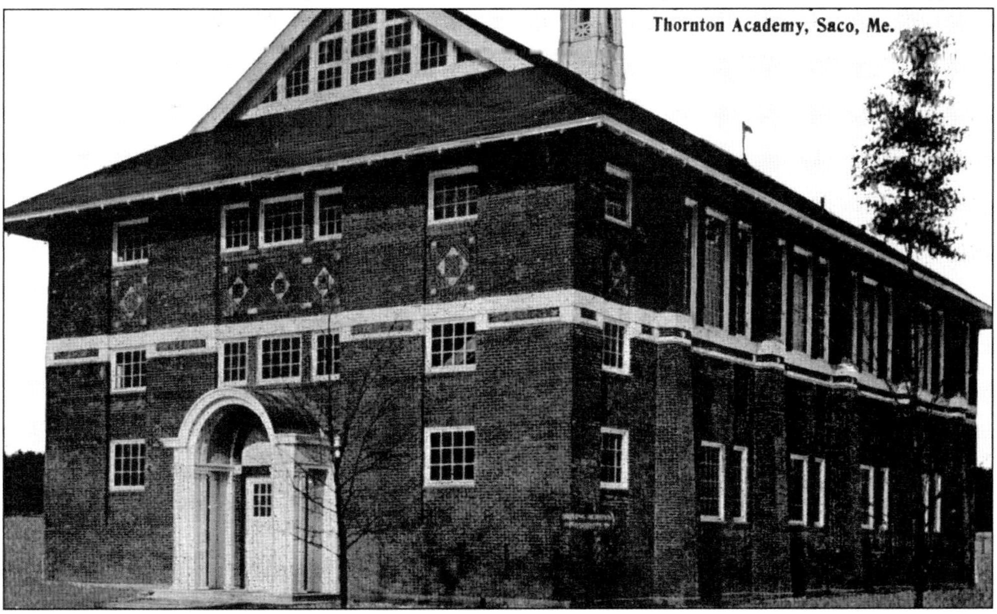

The George Addison Emery Gymnasium was dedicated at Thornton Academy on February 13, 1913. It was the fourth building erected on campus and constructed of "mill fire-proof or, more to the point, slow burning" materials. The exterior was brick with marble trim, and interior partitions were also brick. The lower floor housed a 24-by-51-foot gymnasium, and a larger one was on the main floor. The height of luxury, the building included shower rooms. Although the building still stands, a new gymnasium replaced it for athletic use in 1963.

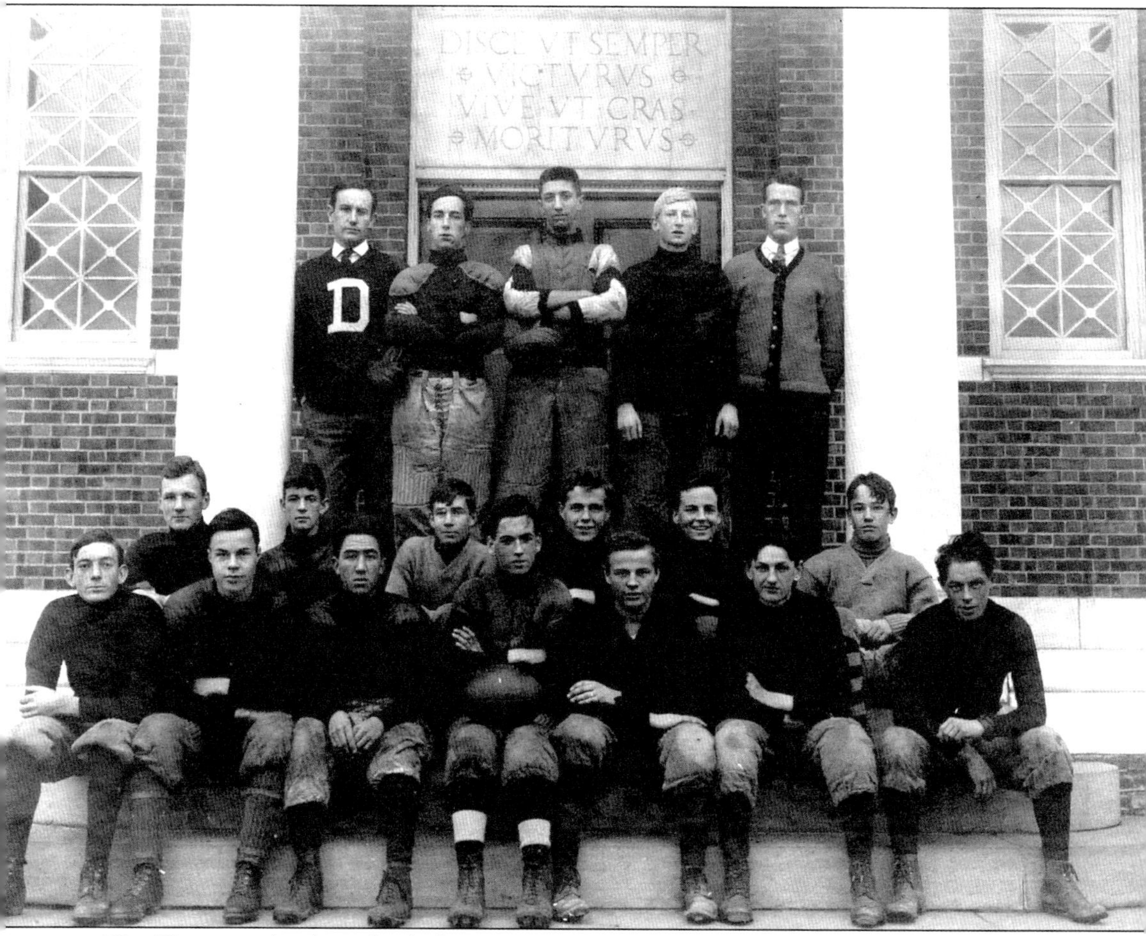

The Thornton Academy football team was founded in 1893, and by the 1920s, its rivalry with neighboring Biddeford High School was well established. The annual meeting between the two teams became known as the "Battle of the Bridge." Wearing the minimal padding of football uniforms of the period, the 1923 Thornton Academy football team gathers for a photograph on the front steps of the Charles G. Thornton Library. Only a few of the names are remembered. From left to right are (first row) F. Mattley, ? Winslow, unidentified, Bob Burns, S. Harper, unidentified, and Doc S. Walker; (second row) F. Wiggin, George Norwood, unidentified, unidentified, Allan Burns, and Howard Morrill; (third row) unidentified, Nathaniel Mitchell, Phil Towle, Ray Emery, and unidentified. The academy team was average in the 1920s but became a powerhouse in the 1930s and 1940s under coaches Robert Bowie and George Martin.

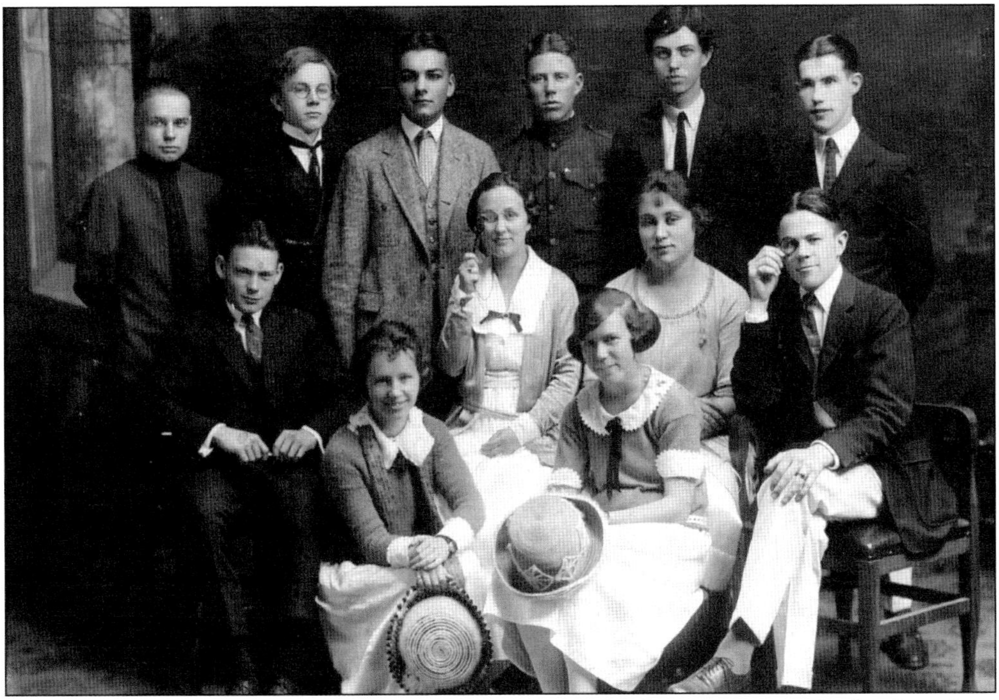

In 1922, the Thornton Academy junior class presented *The Wrong Mr. Wright*. Seen here with monocles in evidence, from left to right, are (first row) Josephine Chadborne and Althea Macoumber; (second row) Paul S. Hill, Althea Lombard, Jeanette Ross, and Nelson Mitchell; (third row) Leon Libby, Alfred Mitchell, Maurice Roux, Lloyd Armstrong, Harry Sawyer, and Hugh Carson.

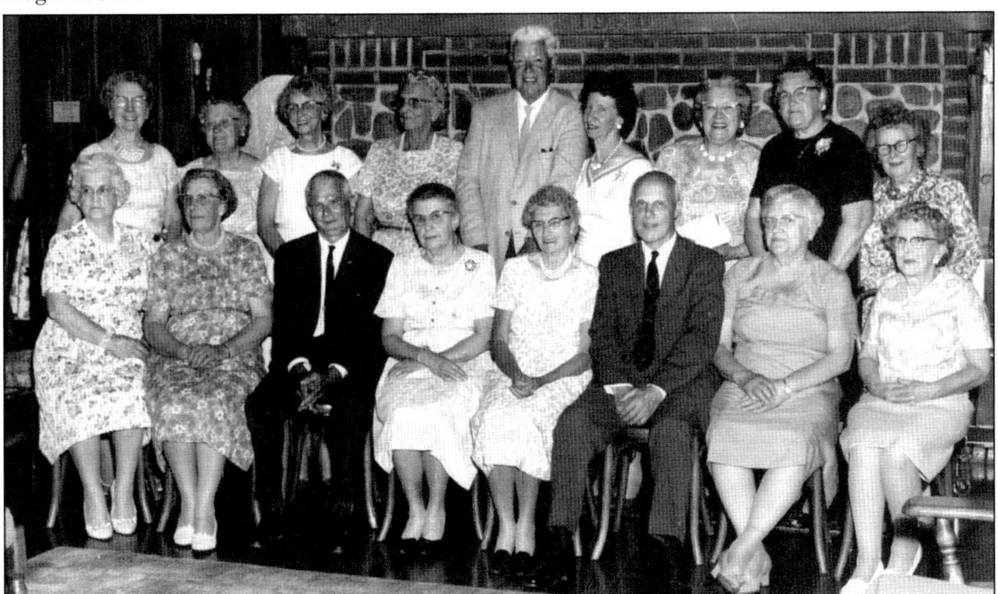

In the summer of 1964, the Thornton Academy class of 1914 gathered for their 50th reunion. Four members of the girls' 1914 state championship basketball team were present. Their coach, Elizabeth Wilson Robinson, also attended the reunion.

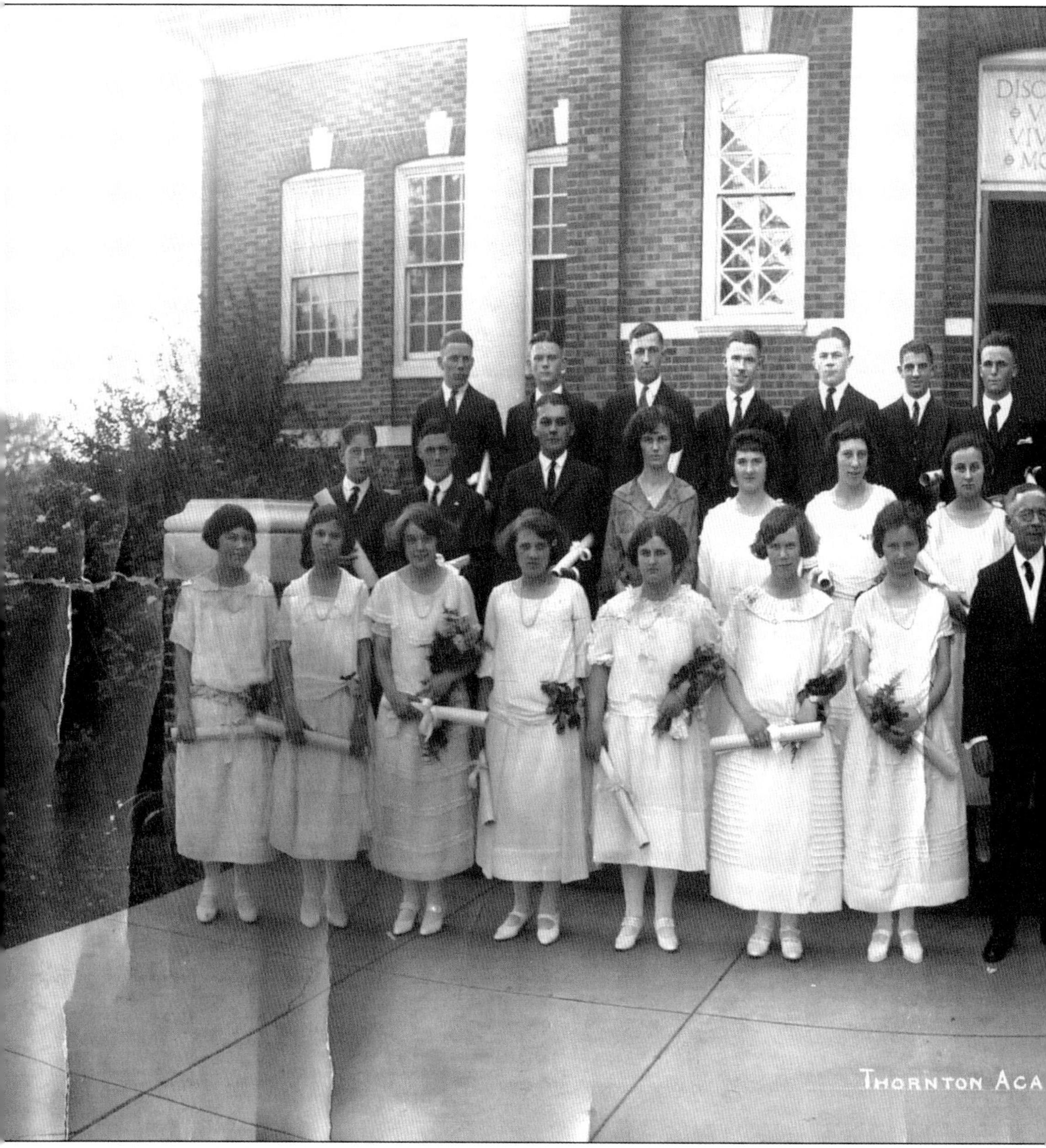

With the girls looking lovely in their finery and the boys having neatly slicked down hair, the Thornton Academy class of 1923 gathers for a final photograph. On the far left in the first row stands Clair Matthews. In 1930, she married classmate Paul S. Hill, who served in World War II

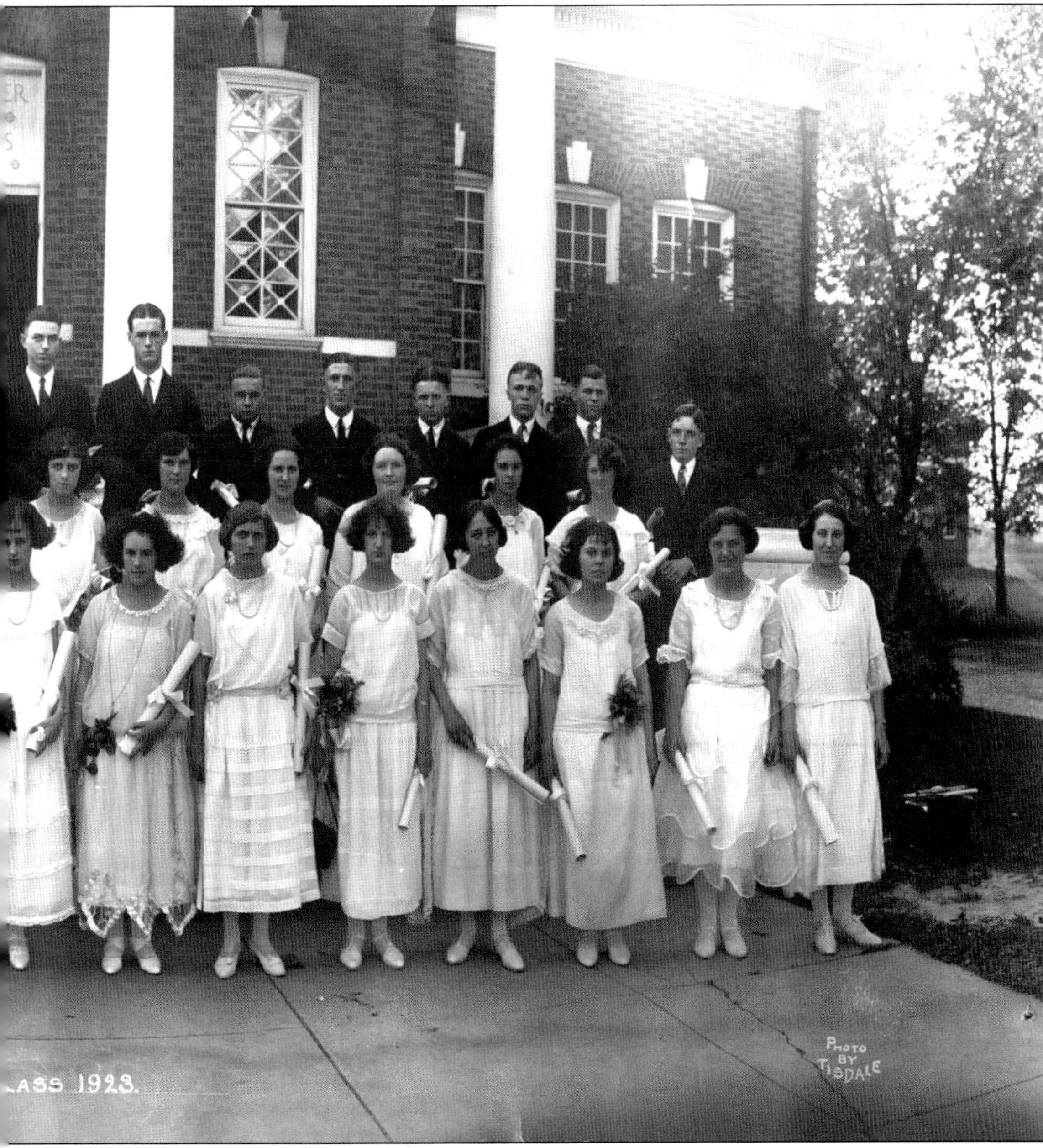

as a physician to Gen. George S. Patton and continued to practice after the war in Saco (see page 115). Hill stands third from the left in the second row.

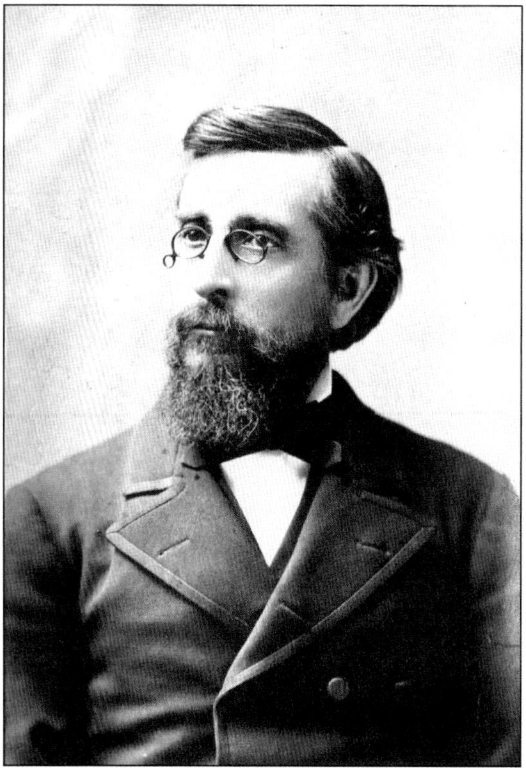

Marshall Pierce (1823–1900) was born in Standish and spent most of his adult life in Saco. He operated a successful grain business in Portland. By 1880, when this photograph was taken, he had relocated to California. Later in life, he began to assemble a large collection of newspapers from earlier in the 19th century. Many of these newspapers were donated to the York Institute. The Dyer Library still holds a substantial portion of his original gift.

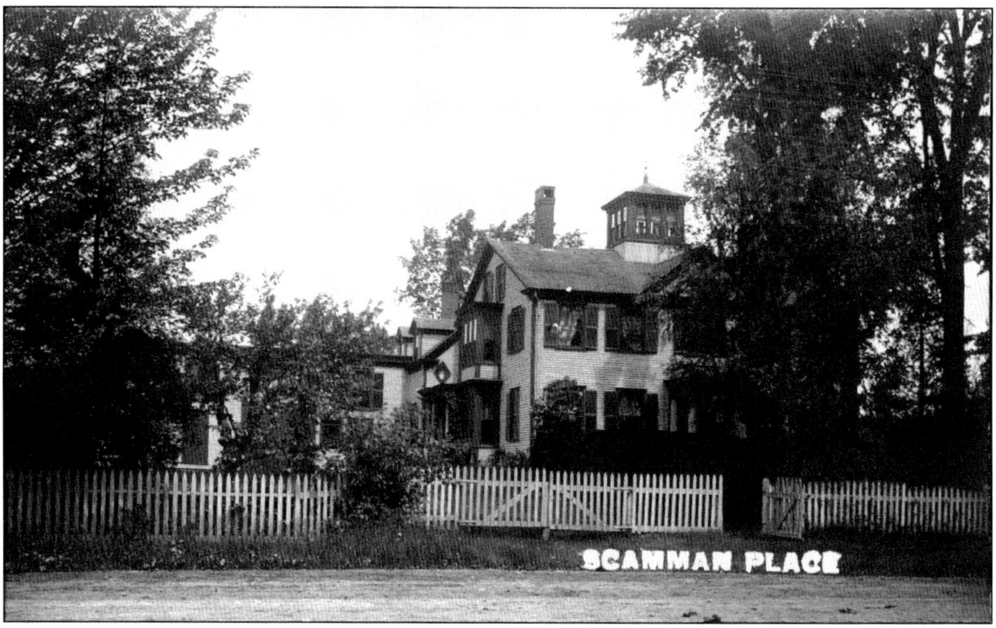

Noted botanist Edith Scamman was born in Saco in 1882 and was based here for much of her life. Through courses she took at Radcliffe later in life, she became an expert in ferns and contributed extensive specimens and scholarship to the Gray Herbarium at Harvard University. In 1967, she bequeathed her Saco home to Thornton Academy. It was later razed to provide room for athletic fields, and the site is now the home of the international dormitory.

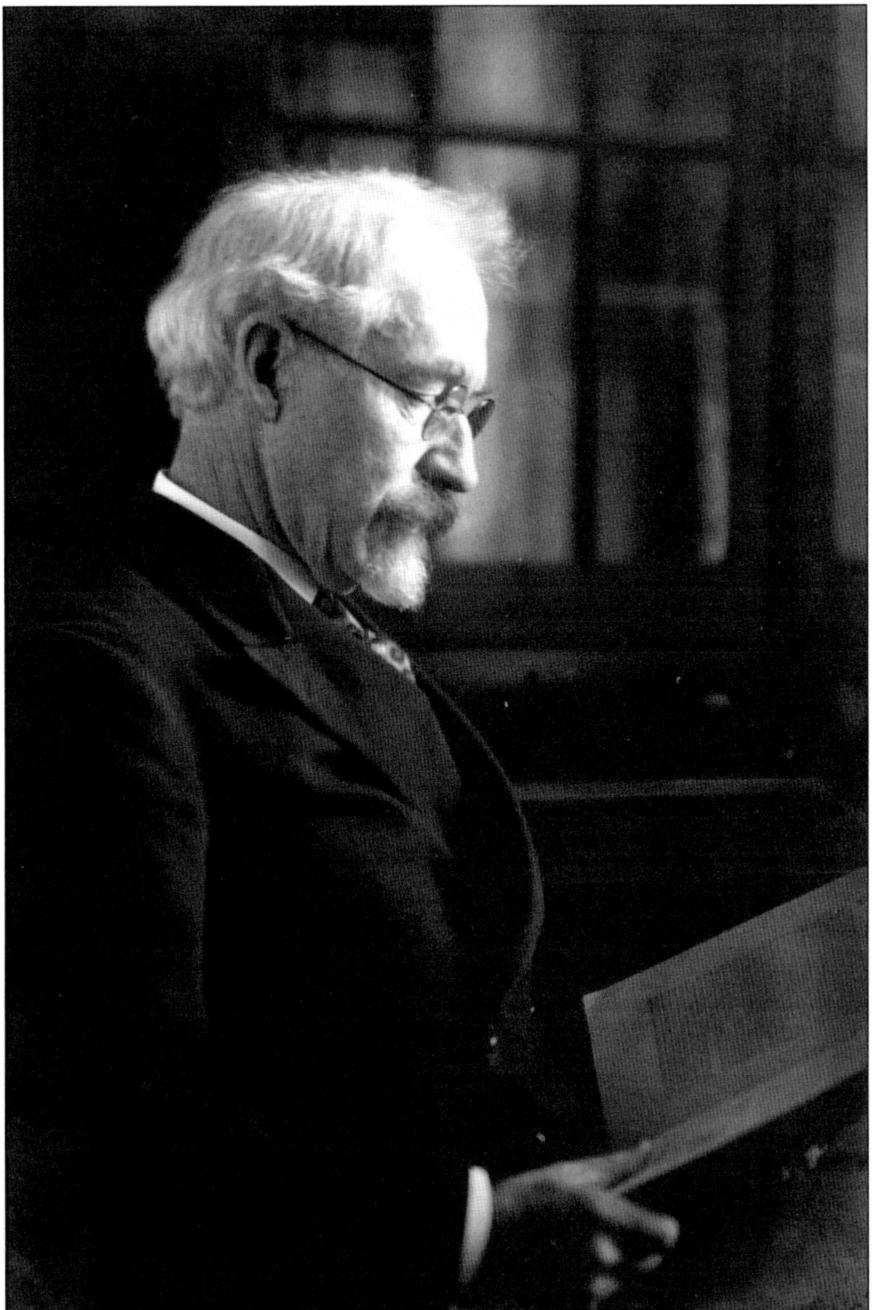

Saco native James Vaughan Dennett (1867–1959) attended the Massachusetts Institute of Technology and became a pioneer in construction in Boston, creating several landmark buildings there. After retiring in Saco, Dennett became president of the York Institute (now the Saco Museum), which his father, Dr. Roscoe Dennett, helped to found. James Vaughan Dennett's daughter Dorothy bequeathed a large collection of furniture, decorative arts, papers, and photographs to York Institute in her father's memory; a gallery in the museum is named in his honor.

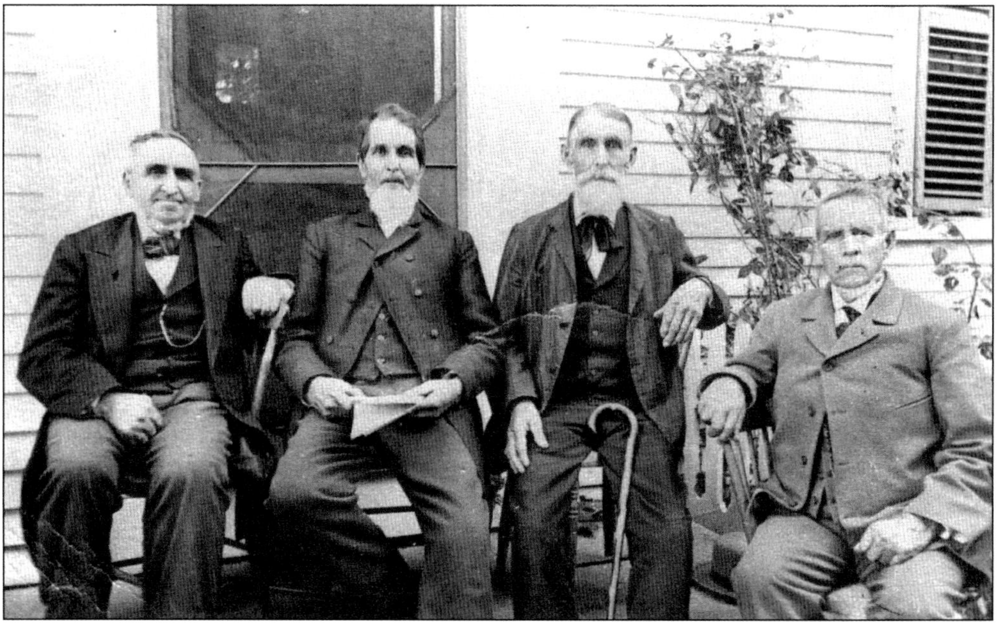

Farmer, tax collector, and surveyor William Deering and his wife, Eunice, had six sons. Four of them are pictured here. From left to right are William Harper, Jonathan Rumery, James Madison, and Joseph Godfrey. Joseph Godfrey, known as J. G. Deering, ran Deering Lumber Company and also built the brick mansion at 371 Main Street that his grandchildren Joseph and Katherine donated to be the third and present home of the Dyer Library. James Madison Deering helped to found Laurel Hill Cemetery.

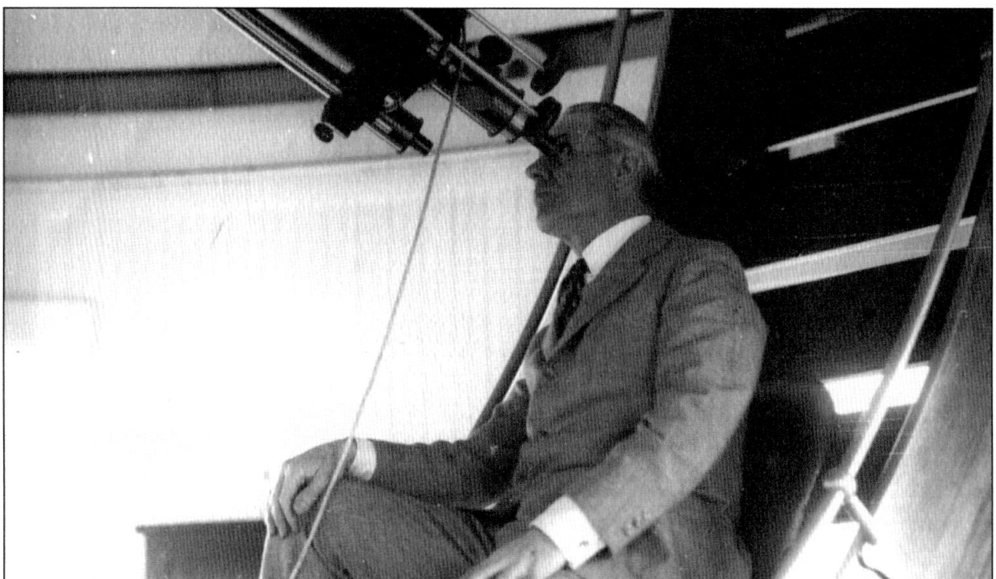

Frank Cutter Deering (1866–1939) was the son of Joseph Godfrey Deering. Along with being an avid amateur astronomer, he was also a trustee of Thornton Academy, treasurer of Laurel Hill Cemetery Corporation, owner of the Deering Lumber Company, vice president of York National Bank, and an avid collector of "captivity tales"—stories of colonists captured by Native Americans who returned to tell their stories.

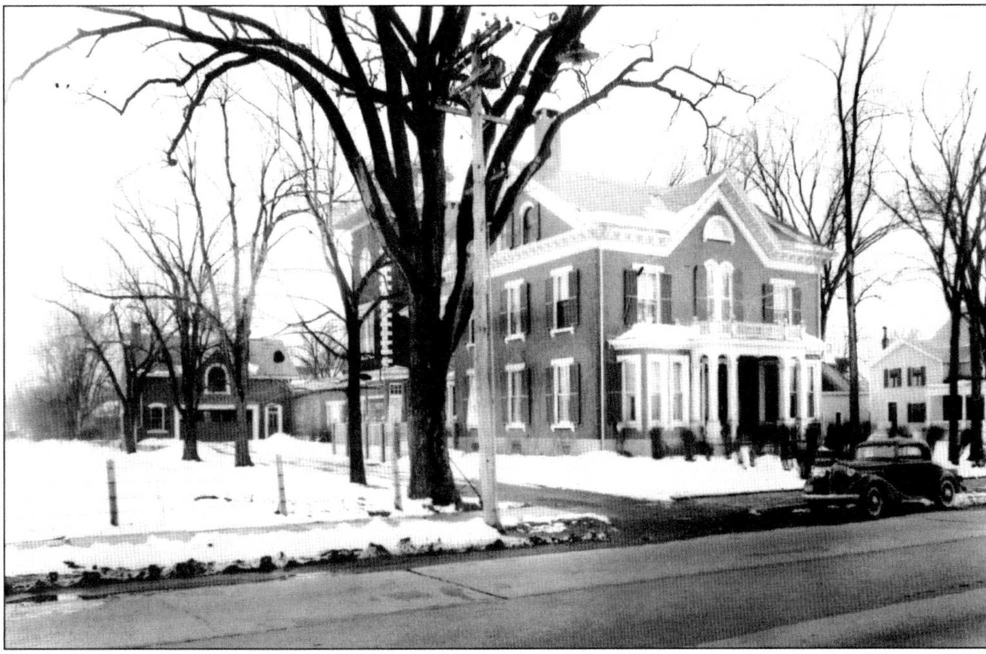

Photographed around 1940, this is the Deering family mansion on 371 Main Street, which later became the home of the Dyer Library. Before the conversion to a library, the observatory behind the main house was moved to Thornton Academy, where it stood for many years. When the supporting structure became unstable, the dome was placed on the ground near the football field, where it remains. By the time this photograph was taken, the large rear wing that included a parlor and linked it to the carriage house had already been constructed.

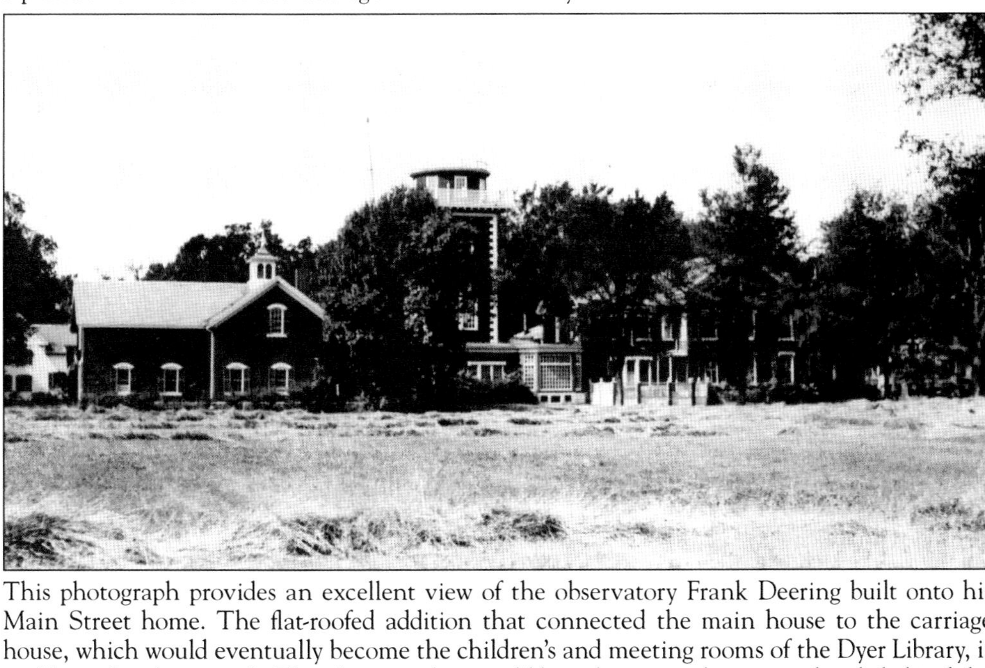

This photograph provides an excellent view of the observatory Frank Deering built onto his Main Street home. The flat-roofed addition that connected the main house to the carriage house, which would eventually become the children's and meeting rooms of the Dyer Library, is visible in the photograph. The photographer would have been standing immediately behind the Saco Museum (then the York Institute) around 1930.

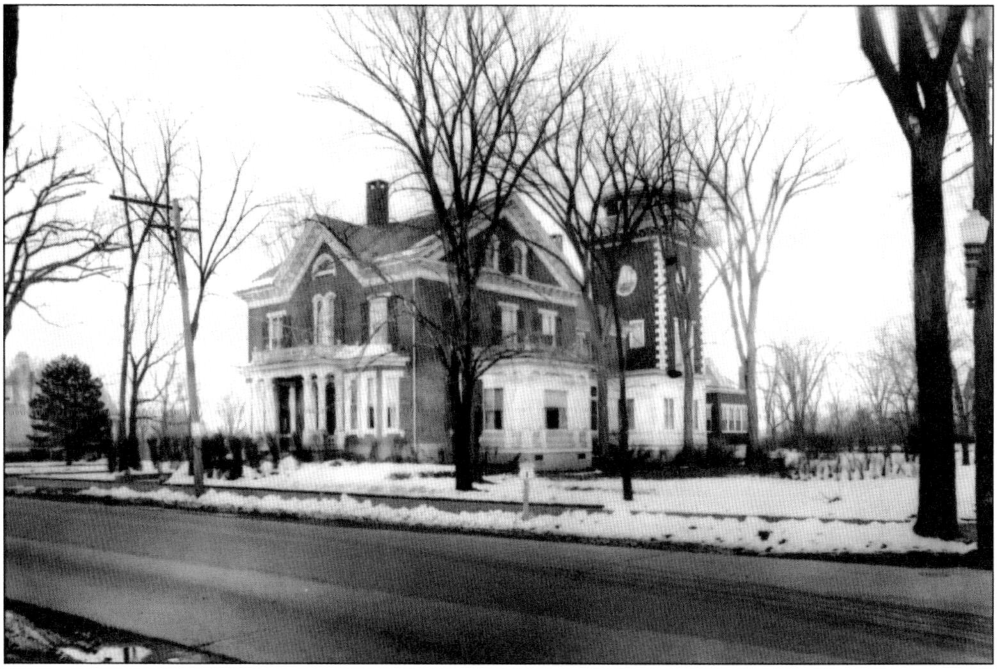

In this view of the Deering mansion from 1937, the York Institute (now the Saco Museum) is just visible to the far left.

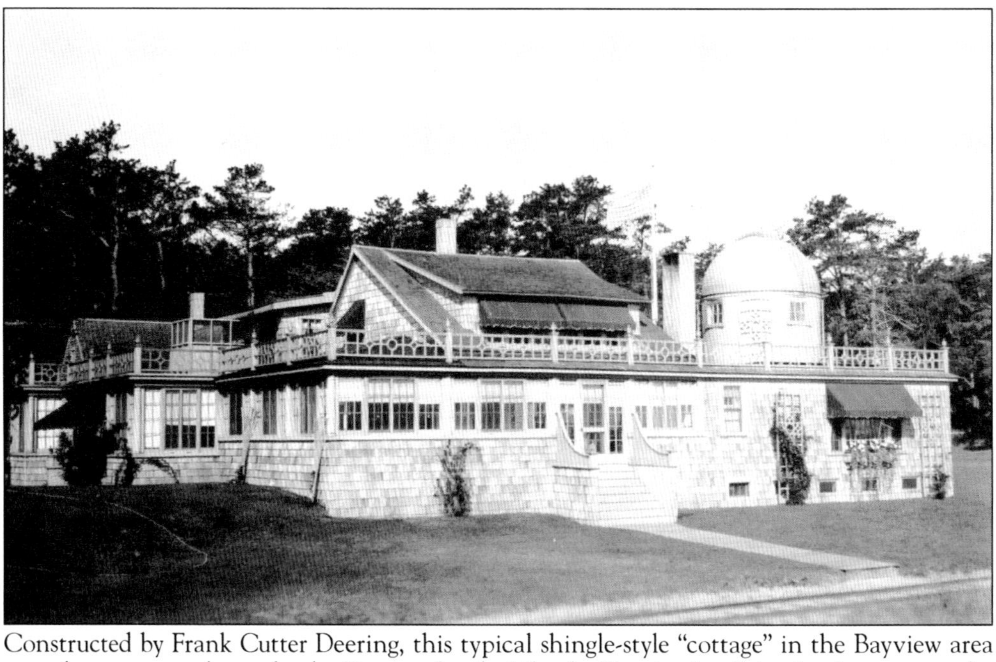

Constructed by Frank Cutter Deering, this typical shingle-style "cottage" in the Bayview area served as a summer home for the Deering family. Like the Deering family's other home, now the Dyer Library, it featured an observatory.

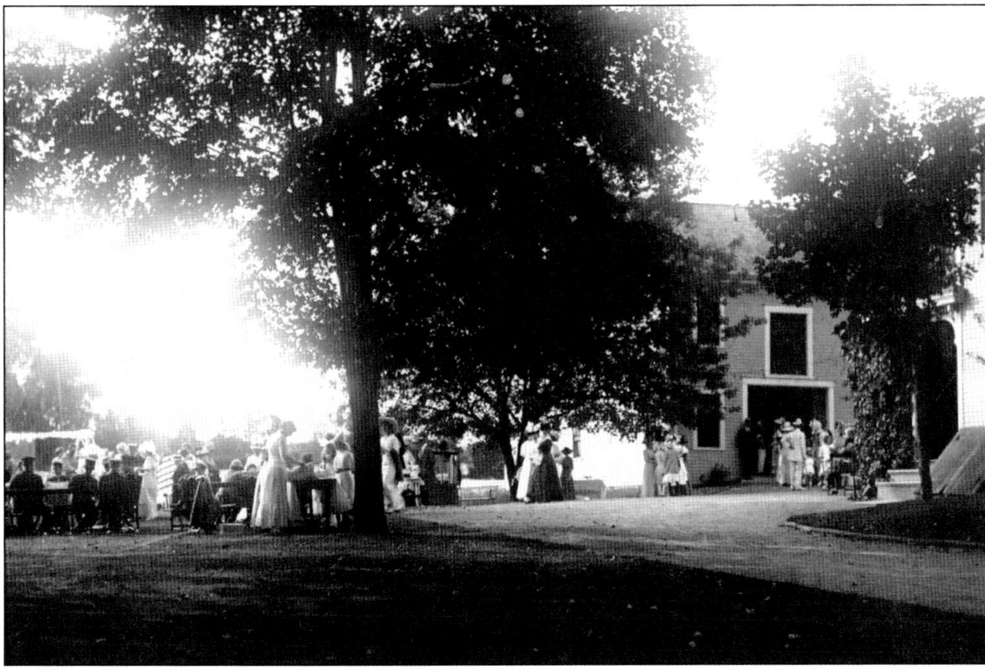

Ladies gather on a Saco lawn around 1910 for a party. A small band provides entertainment. Events like these were not just social occasions; they also could serve as fund-raisers for a variety of causes. (Courtesy McArthur Public Library.)

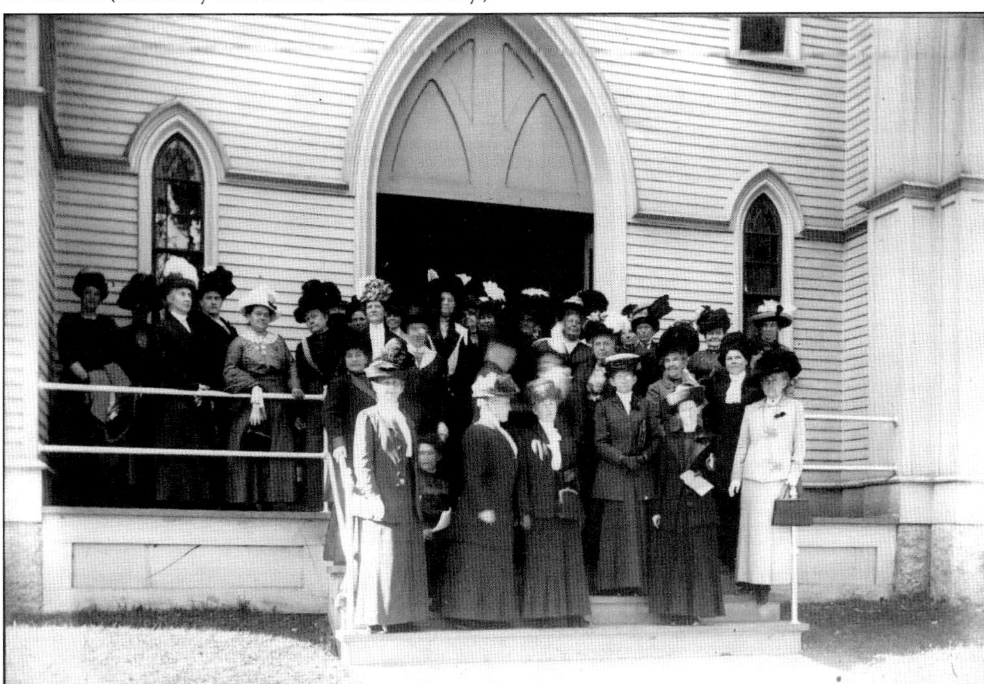

Sporting their finest bonnets, these ladies convened in 1911 for the Maine State Federation of Women's Clubs. They represented women's groups all over the state, with most groups actively performing philanthropic works. (Courtesy McArthur Public Library.)

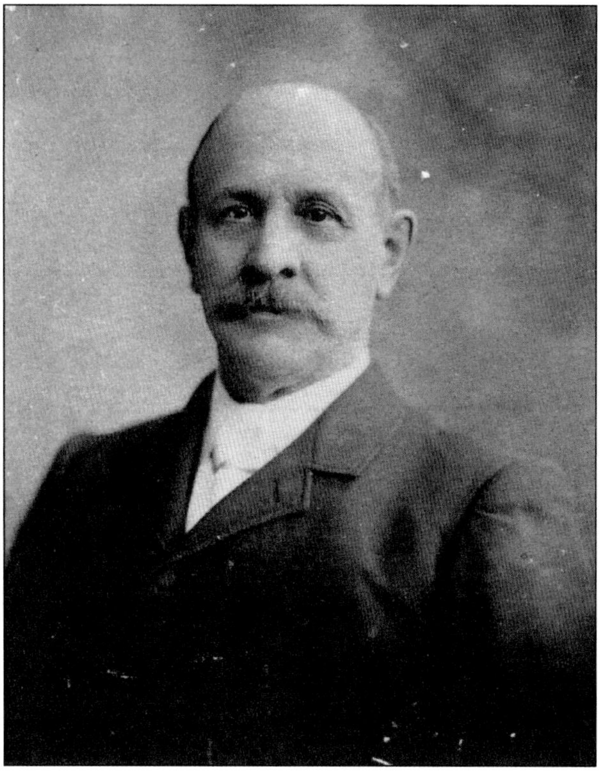

John S. Locke (1836–1906) served as the superintendent of Saco schools from about 1894 to around the time of his death. The Middle Street School was later renamed the Locke School in his honor. It was probably during his tenure as superintendent that he sat for this photograph. An esteemed author and publisher, he also played an important role in the start of the York Institute.

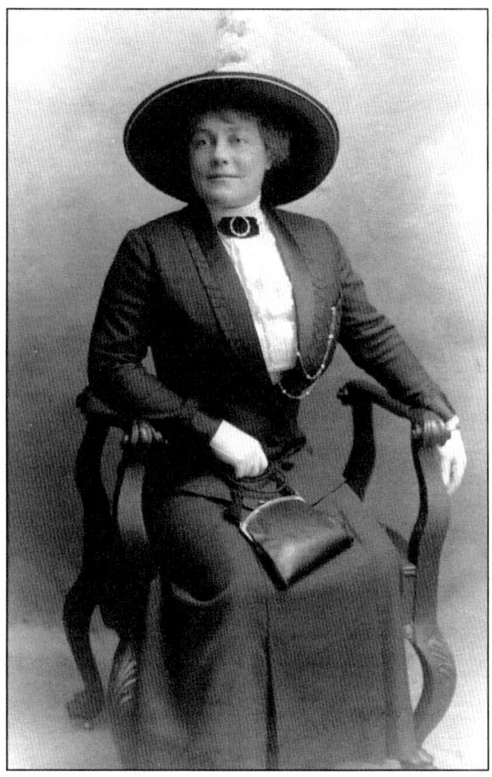

Almira Locke McArthur, daughter of John S. Locke and wife of George McArthur, went on to become a major philanthropist in the Saco area. In 1950, she bequeathed most of the contents of her home to the York Institute. After posing for the photographer between 1900 and 1910, she wrote on the back of this postcard, "How do you like the shape? (It's really a fake) I am not nearly as small as I look."

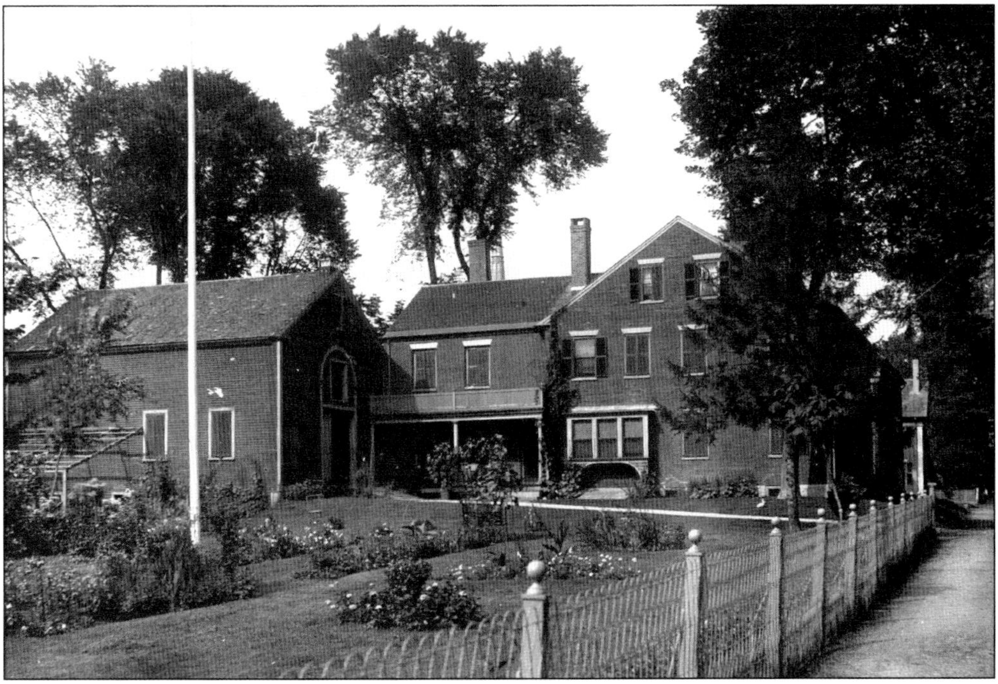

This brick house was built for lumber merchant Joseph Leland around 1820. He also built Thornton Hall (which later became the home of philanthropist Sarah Fairfield Hamilton) around 1801. The building seen here eventually became the home of John S. Locke, Saco's first superintendent of schools, for whom Locke School was named. Almira Locke McArthur grew up there and later married George McArthur. The house still stands at 90 Middle Street.

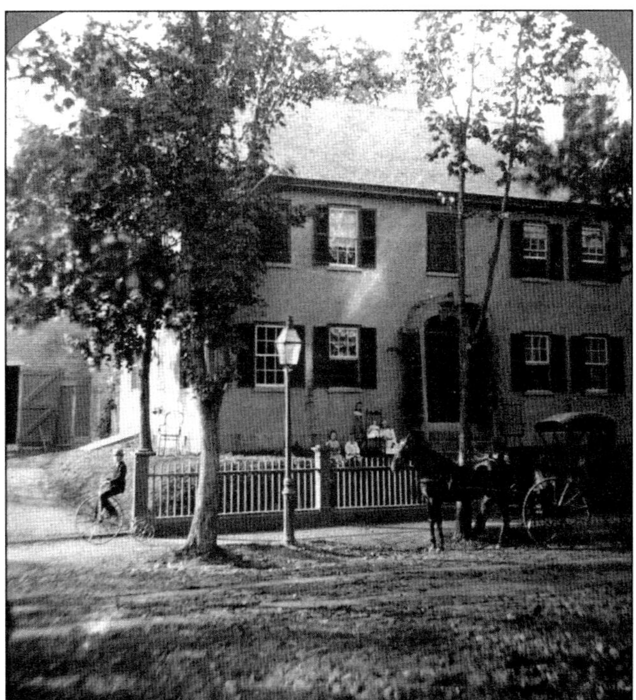

This is an earlier view of the Locke-McArthur house taken around 1880. Notice the man pedaling by on his tricycle and the group of children gathered on the front step. Almira Locke McArthur is probably one of the three little girls; an only child, she was about nine years old when this photograph was taken.

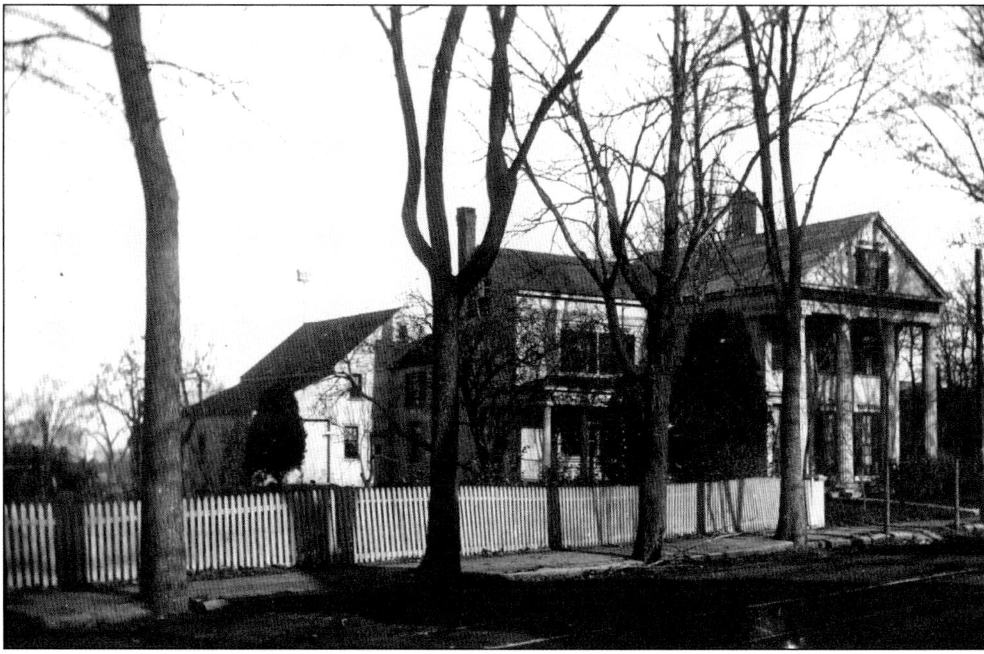

This is the Ferry Road childhood home of Sarah Fairfield Hamilton, daughter of the Honorable John Fairfield, who eventually became governor of Maine. Shortly after her 1853 marriage to Benjamin Franklin Hamilton, she became a force for social change, encouraging her husband to hire single, middle-class women as clerks in his store. This resulted in a scandal and a boycott of the Hamilton store that was reported in newspapers throughout New England.

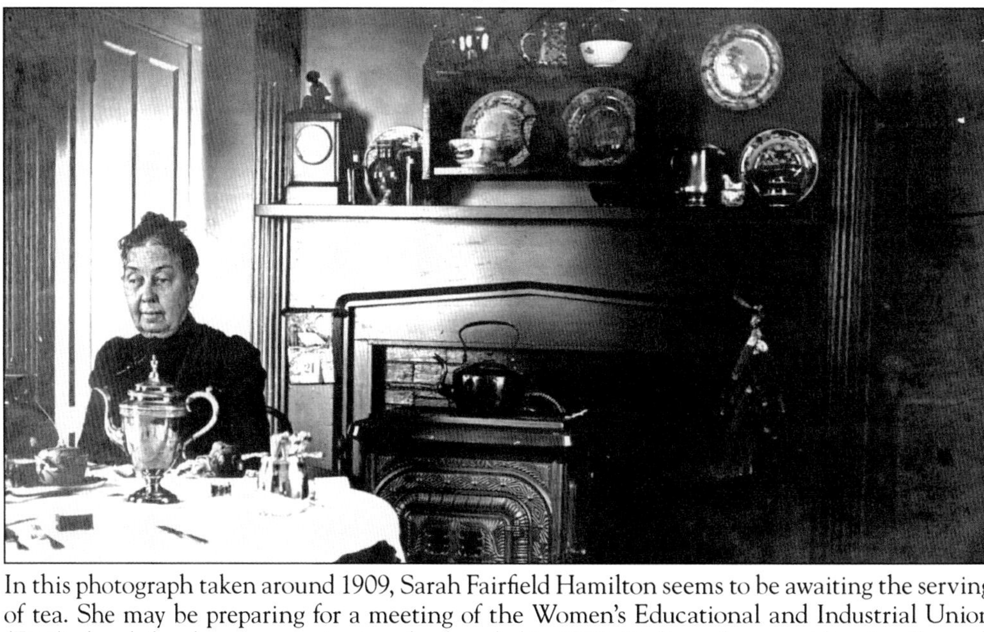

In this photograph taken around 1909, Sarah Fairfield Hamilton seems to be awaiting the serving of tea. She may be preparing for a meeting of the Women's Educational and Industrial Union (E&I), the philanthropic organization she founded in 1888. Dedicated to providing intellectual, vocational, and physical education opportunities to all genders and classes of local residents, the E&I, among other things, established Saco's first kindergarten, which met in a ground-floor room underneath the stage at city hall.

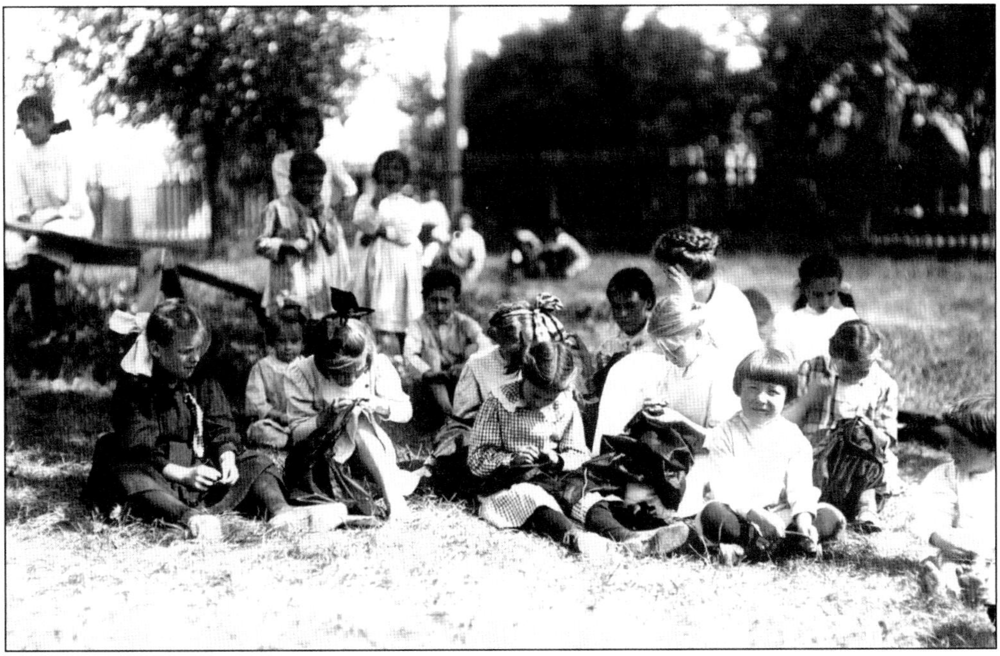

The E&I conducted and financed this summer playground, located near Pepperell Park and Bonython School. Since one of the goals of the E&I was for women to have skills that would aid them in becoming self-sufficient, a sewing class for little girls must have seemed especially appropriate. Notice that the few boys present are *not* sewing. (Courtesy McArthur Public Library.)

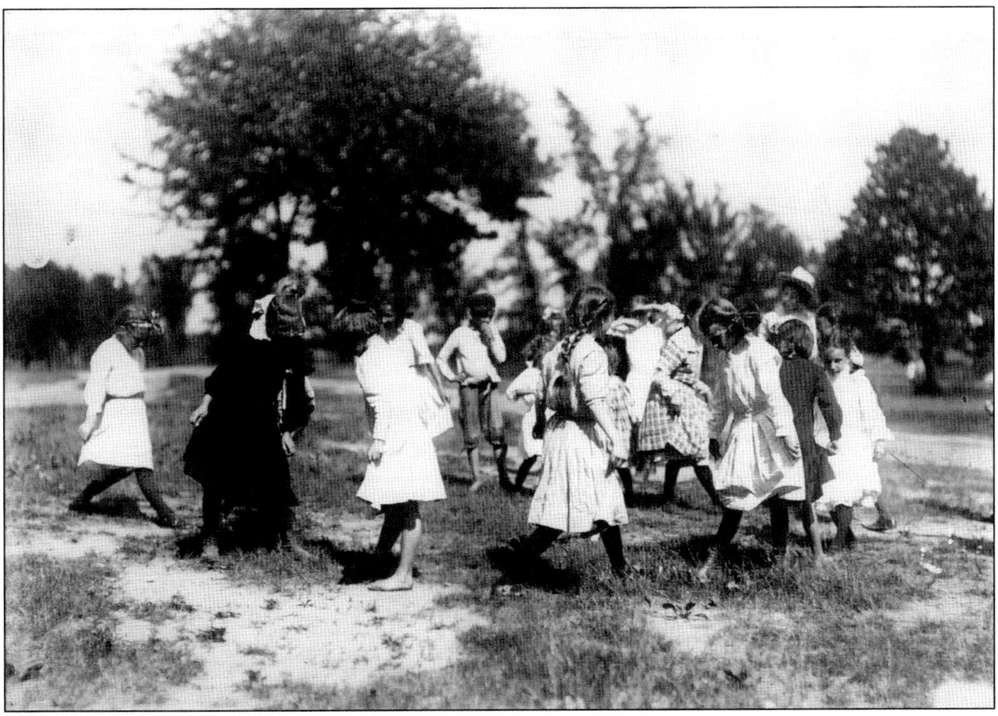

A little boy in the background seems bemused by the many little girls curtseying to each other in a very organized playground game in this 1913 photograph. (Courtesy McArthur Public Library.)

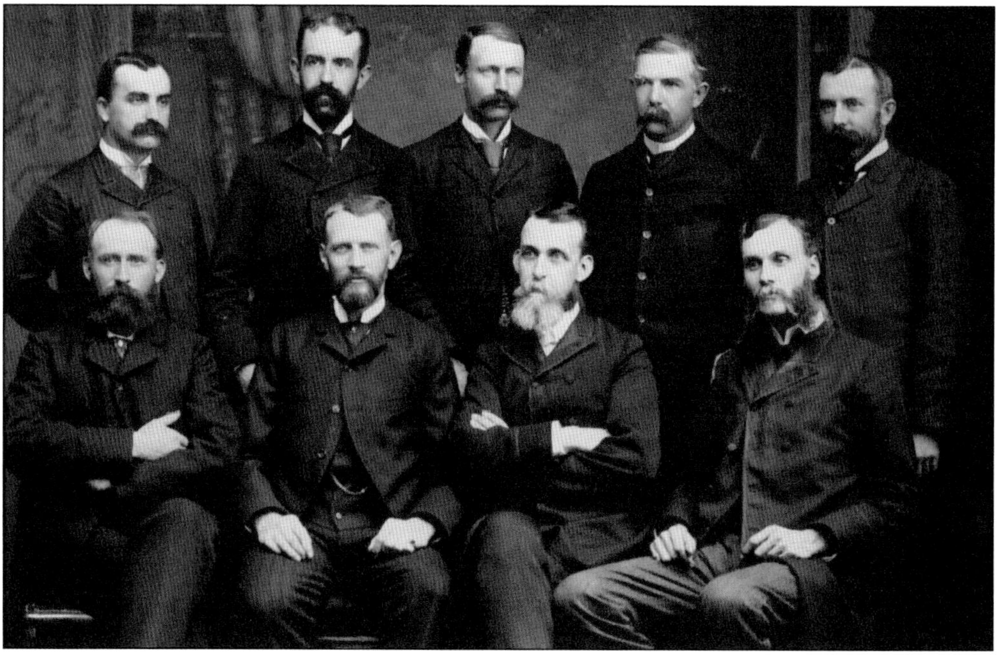

Community members shared the E&I's concern for public health. In the early 1900s, this group of Saco and Biddeford physicians posed for a formal group portrait. They are identified as Dr. Davis (Biddeford), Dr. Harwood (Saco), Dr. Cochrane (Saco), Dr. Goodale (Saco), Dr. Maxey (Saco), Dr. Dennett (Saco), Dr. Cobb (Biddeford), Dr. Bassford (Biddeford), and Dr. Pillsbury (Saco). Their first names are not given. A note accompanying the photograph says that it was "presented to the City of Saco by Walter E. Scamman, 1924."

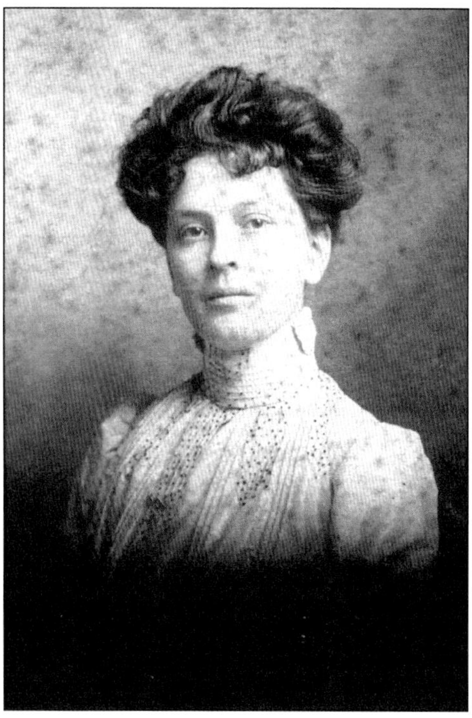

After completing an internship at the College of Physicians and Surgeons in Boston, Dr. Laura Stickney opened a practice in Saco in 1906 and became a beloved family doctor. She became the first female city physician, appointed in 1913. Stickney was also an advocate for women's rights: she was a charter member of the Saco Equal Suffrage Club and subsequently ran for mayor, losing by only a small margin. (Courtesy Marian Stickney.)

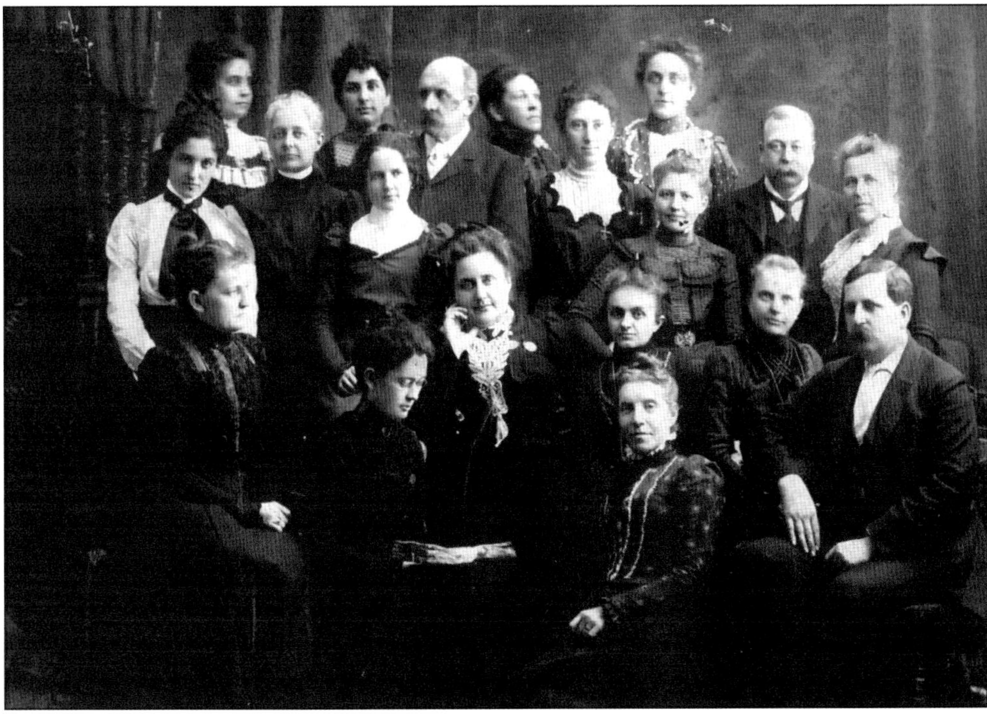

This photograph shows a number of Saco teachers around 1891. Identified are Alice Fogg, Henrietta Gay, Alvin Merrill, Ada Hill, Elizabeth Mahoney, Myra Hooper, Myra Conforth, Florence Mack, Annie Cobb-Smith, Isabel Baker, Lillian Tarbox, John Locke, Harriet McKeen, Theo T. Young, Mary Mitchell, Nella Allen, and Eva Thompson.

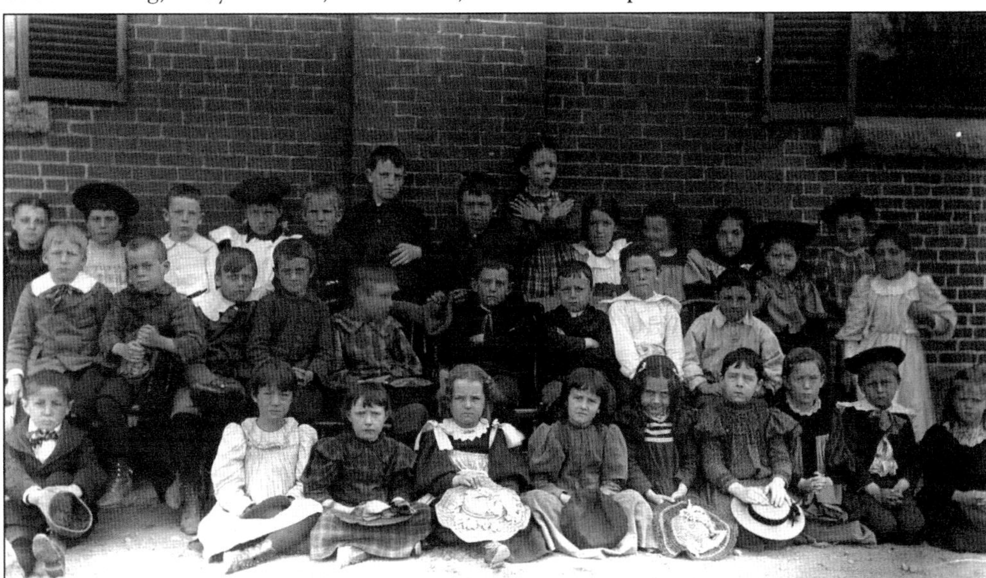

The fourth-grade class of Eva Thompson posed for this photograph about 1894. By 1913, Thompson had become the principal of Moody School on Spring Street, which was located across the street from the Sweetser School. Note the little girl in the center of the back row with her unusual pose.

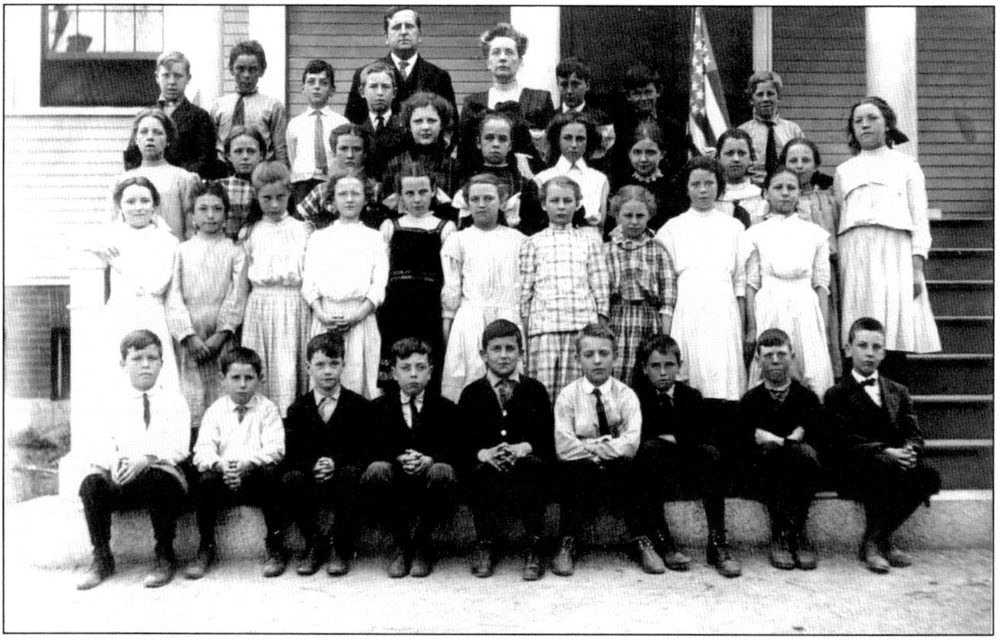

The fifth-grade class of the Bonython School is pictured here in May 1911. Standing in the center back are Elvira J. Lord, classroom teacher, and Alvin R. Merrill, the writing and drawing teacher employed by the public schools. The Bonython School was located on School Street opposite the Unitarian church in Saco. A wood-framed building with two levels and six classrooms, the school closed down in 1960 or 1961 and later burned.

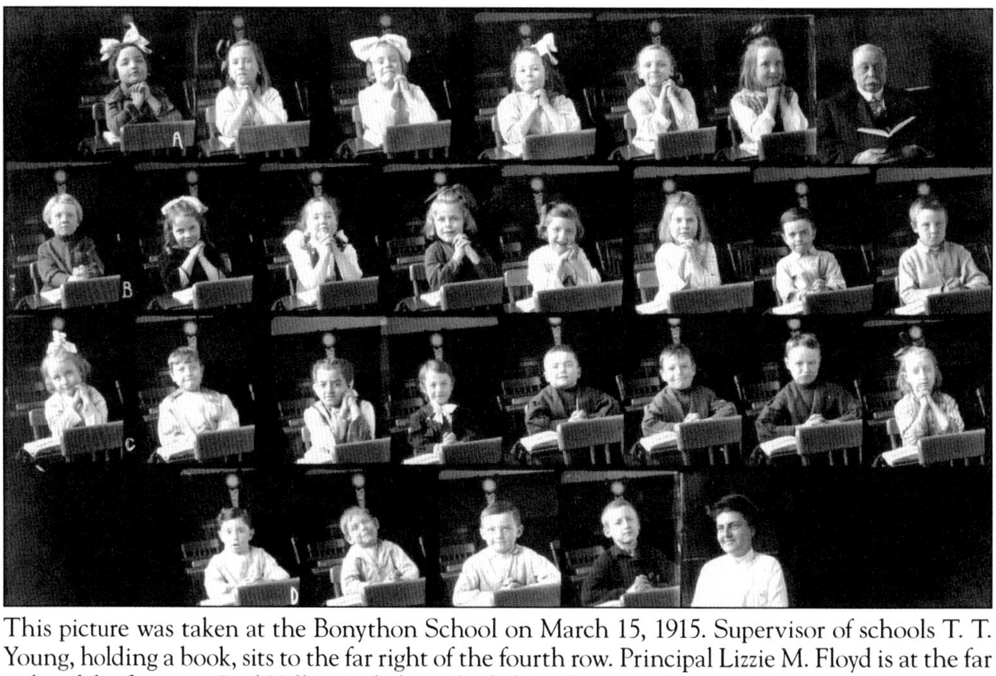

This picture was taken at the Bonython School on March 15, 1915. Supervisor of schools T. T. Young, holding a book, sits to the far right of the fourth row. Principal Lizzie M. Floyd is at the far right of the first row. Paul Hill is sixth from the left in the second row. He became a physician to Gen. George S. Patton in World War II (see page 115). Notice the difference between the boys' and the girls' poses: the boys look determined and the girls look sweet.

Lizzie M. Floyd began teaching at the Bonython School around 1913. She continued to teach up until about 1940 and in later years worked at C. K. Burns School, where she served as principal. She lived at the Wardwell Home until she died in 1957.

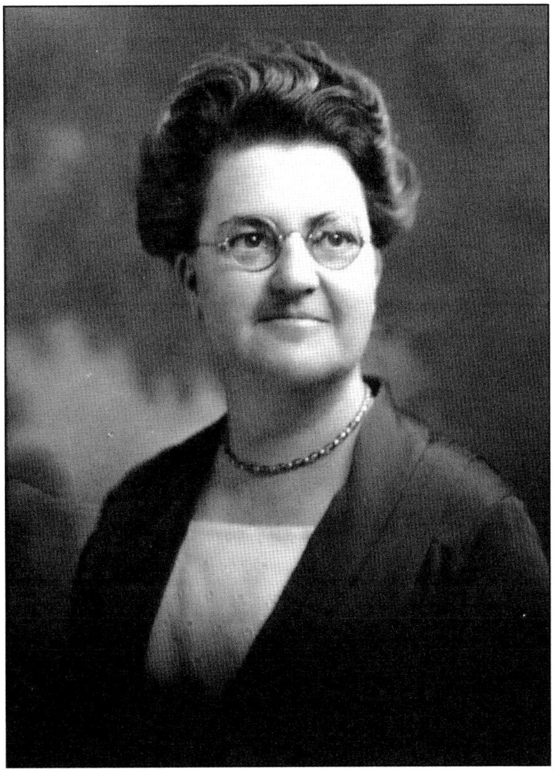

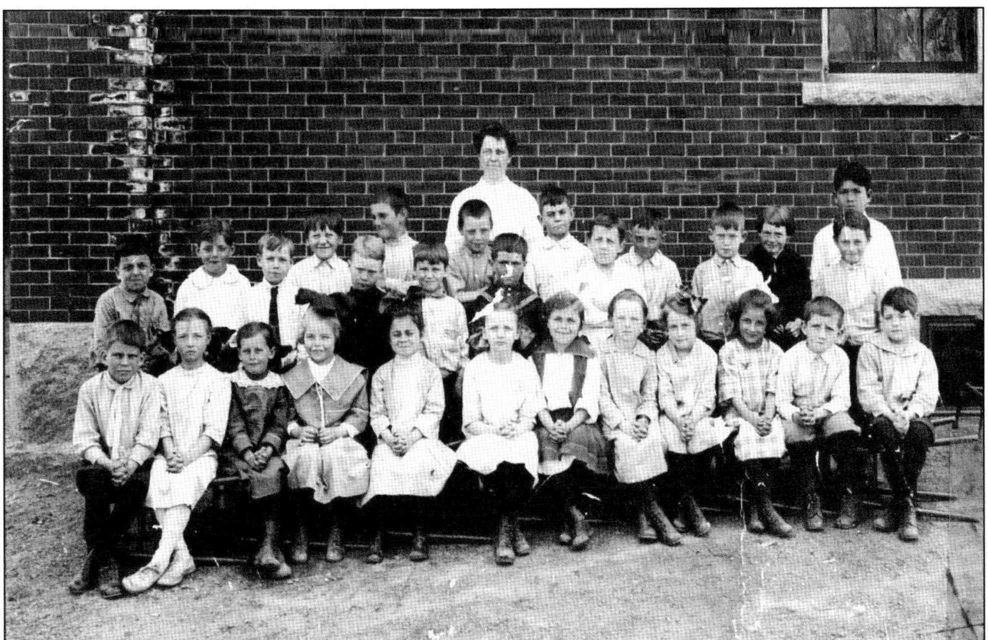

Lutie Harmon poses here with her first-grade class at Jordan School in Pepperell Park in 1916. Clearly the children in the first row have been told to clasp their hands and cross their ankles; only some of them remembered. Harmon taught in both Maine and Massachusetts and worked as a substitute when she retired from regular classroom work.

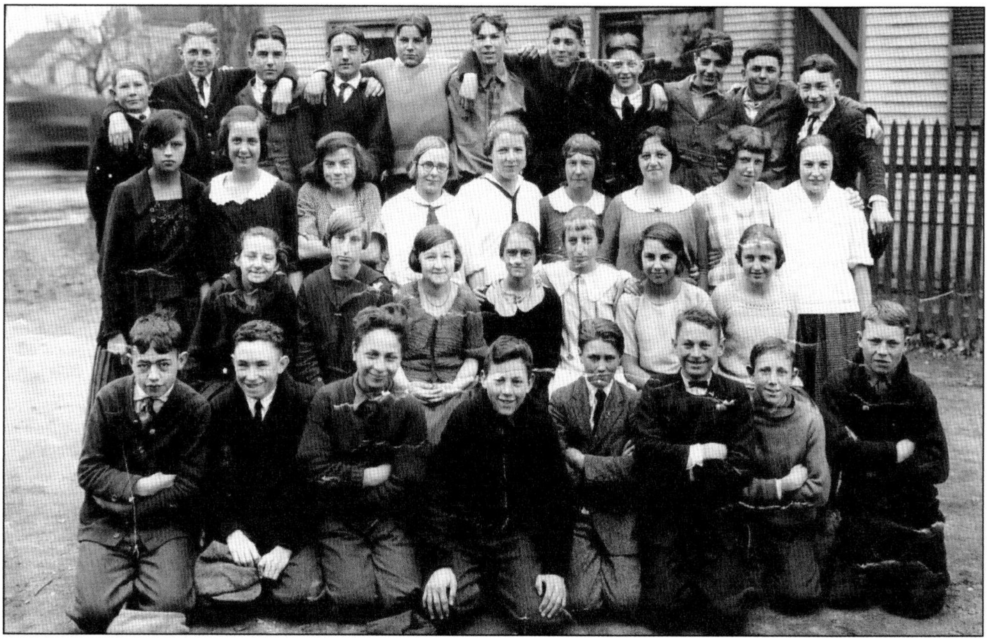

The ninth-grade class of the Locke School is pictured here in 1923. From left to right are (first row) James Scott, Samuel Rankin, Morris Shapiro, Carlton P. Sanborn, Douglas I. Pate, Milton A. Thompson, John G. Smith, and Alexander Stackpole; (second row) Jennie M. McKeen, Sarah Noble, Jeanette Scott, Olive E. Smith, Grace Noble, Miriam Macomber, and Josephine M. Towne; (third row) Dorothy Richards, Ruth E. Tuttle, Evelyn Sleeper, Jessie Viets, Martha L. Smith, Estther A. Rankeillor, Doris C. McKenney, Dorothy Ridlon, and Margaret McCaughlin; (fourth row) Charles S. Towle, Lawrence J. Smtih, Earl Rumery, John Strickland, Millard G. Patterson, Alton L. Thurston, Everett Whitten, Lawrence K. Wakefield, Arthur Oldread, Laurence Roussin, and Everett O'Neill.

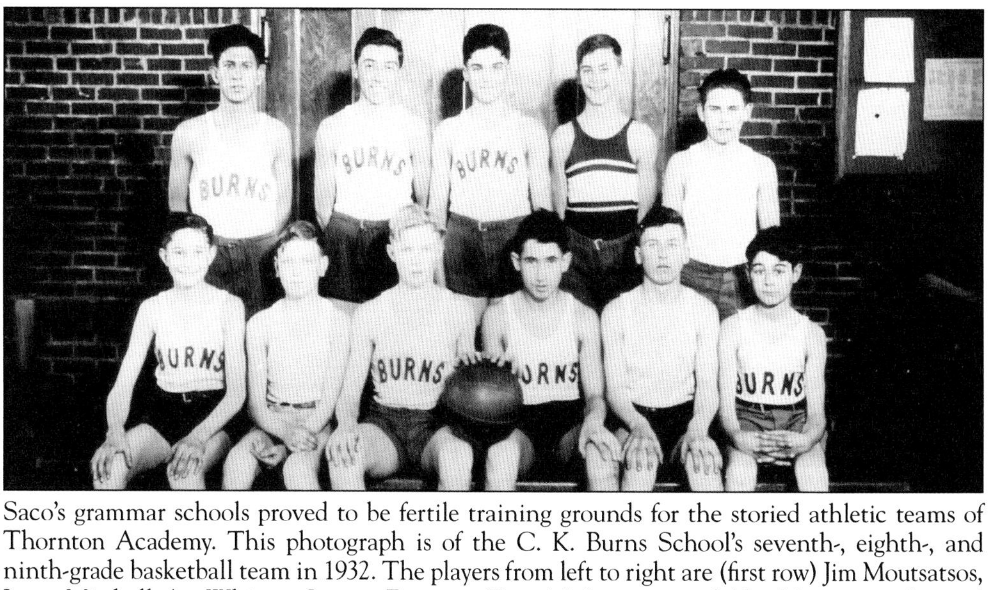

Saco's grammar schools proved to be fertile training grounds for the storied athletic teams of Thornton Academy. This photograph is of the C. K. Burns School's seventh-, eighth-, and ninth-grade basketball team in 1932. The players from left to right are (first row) Jim Moutsatsos, Leroy Mitchell, Art Whitney, Leavitt Emmons, Terry McSweeney, and Alex Moutsatsos; (second row) Emanuel Hàràmis, Charles Mistos, Nick Sarelas, Art McDougall, and Wendell Willett.

Hampden Fairfield (born 1835), son of Gov. John Fairfield, posed for this photograph on May 30, 1889. He was an attorney in the law firm of Hampden Fairfield and Luther R. Moore. He lived for many years at 56 Beach Street and was president of York National Bank. He served as the president on many local nonprofit boards and played important roles in Laurel Hill Cemetery, the Dyer Library, and Thornton Academy.

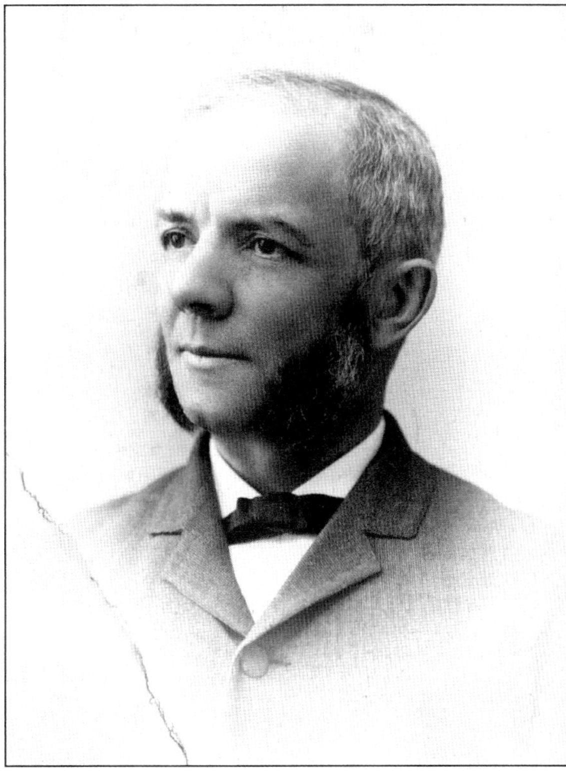

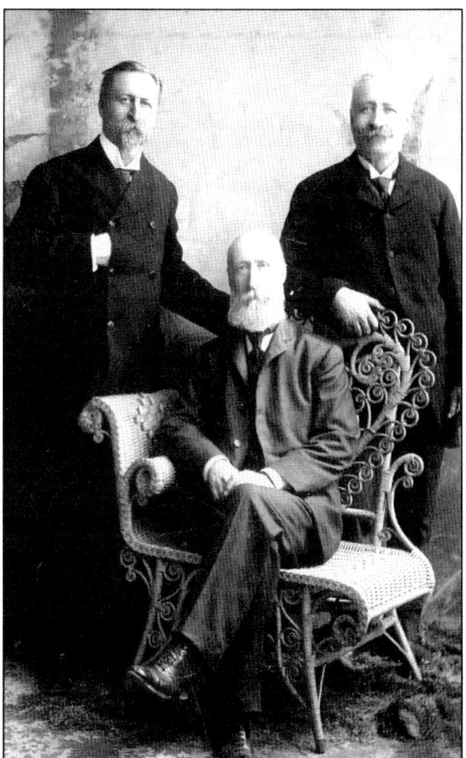

Although Charles Way Shannon (right, pictured with his brothers Richard Cutts Shannon, left, and Jame Shannon, seated) served as organist and musical director at several churches throughout Maine, he held a post at Saco's First Parish Church almost continuously for nearly 50 years. Shannon also helped to found and direct the Bangor Conservatory of Music and ran his own successful school in music rooms on Saco's Main Street. He also ran a music store with the school, selling and renting pianos and organs as well as sheet music.

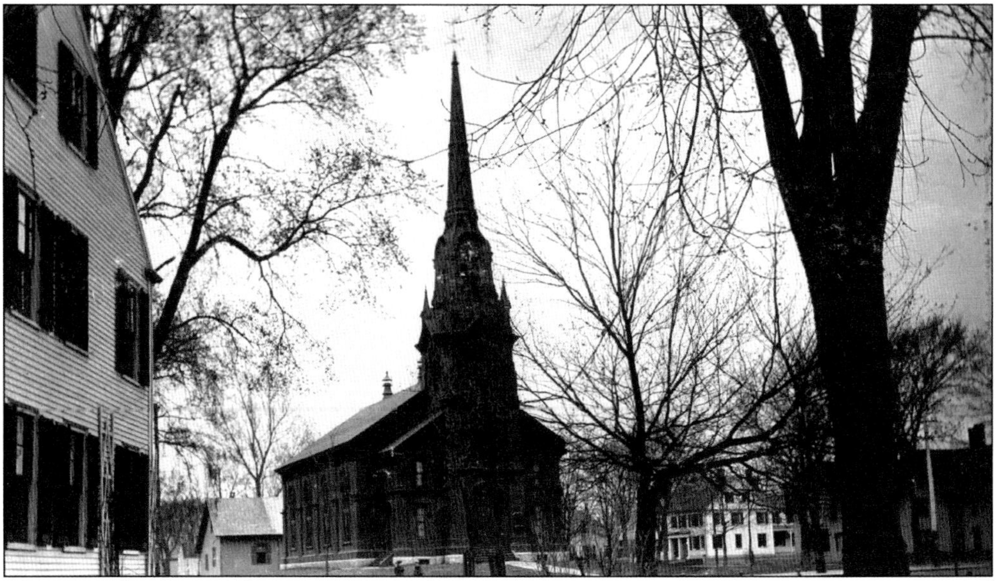

The second First Parish Congregational Church was constructed in 1863 after the original building was lost to fire in 1860 (see page 120). Salvaged metal from the original bell—cast by famed Boston silversmith Paul Revere—was used to make the new bell for this building. When the church burned again in 2000, metal from the bell was again reused for the bell of the present building (see page 121).

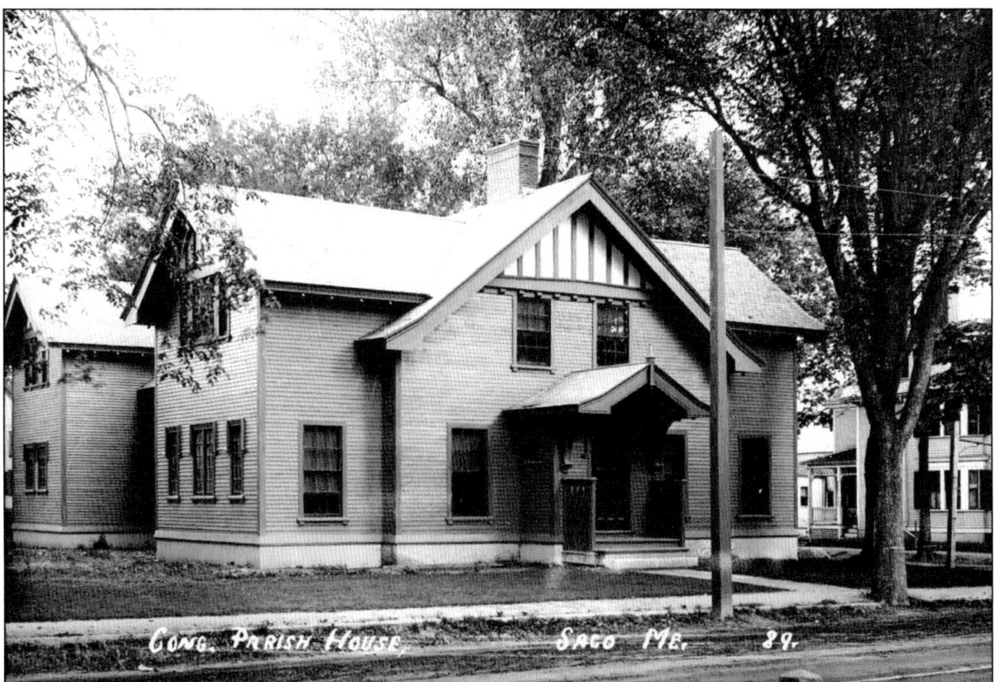

The parish house for the First Parish Congregational Church stood at 39 North Street until it was destroyed by the 2000 fire. Built in 1859, it featured a two-story frame construction with a cross-gable roof. This photograph shows additional alterations completed in 1910. (Courtesy Penobscot Marine Museum.)

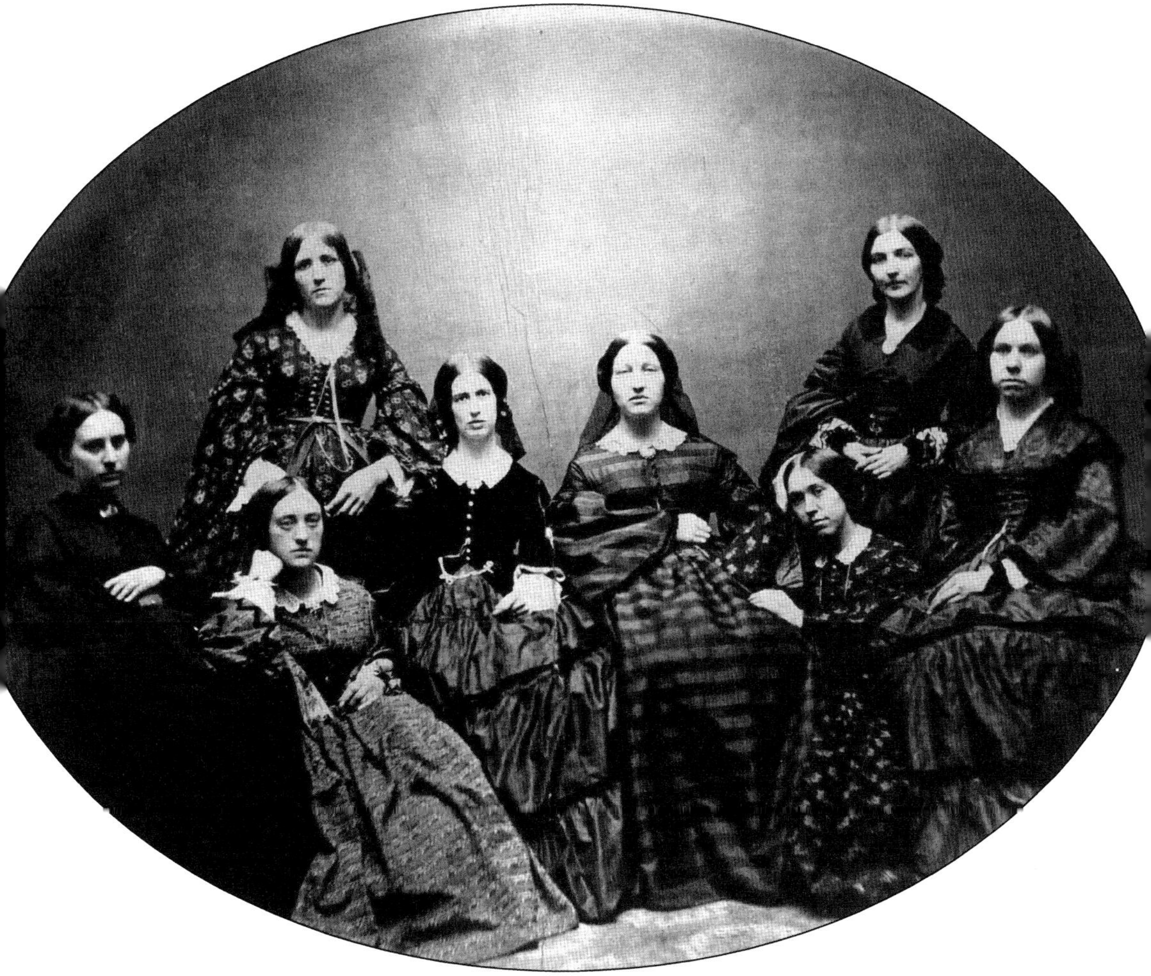

Gathered here in their Sunday finery are the eight members of Stephen L. Goodale's Sunday school class of the First Parish Congregational Church in 1859. Bell-shaped sleeves, large-print fabrics, and white Jenny Lind collars were the fashion orders of the day. If these women had been standing, it would be possible to appreciate their enormous hoop skirts. Stephen Goodale, in addition to being a Sunday school teacher, also served as the first secretary of agriculture for the state of Maine. From left to right, are (first row) Miss Cheney, Miranda P. Sawyer, Aseneth Monroe, Mary Sands, Frances M. Lathe, and Lizzie Deering; (second row) Lucinda R. Allen and Sarah A. Mansfield.

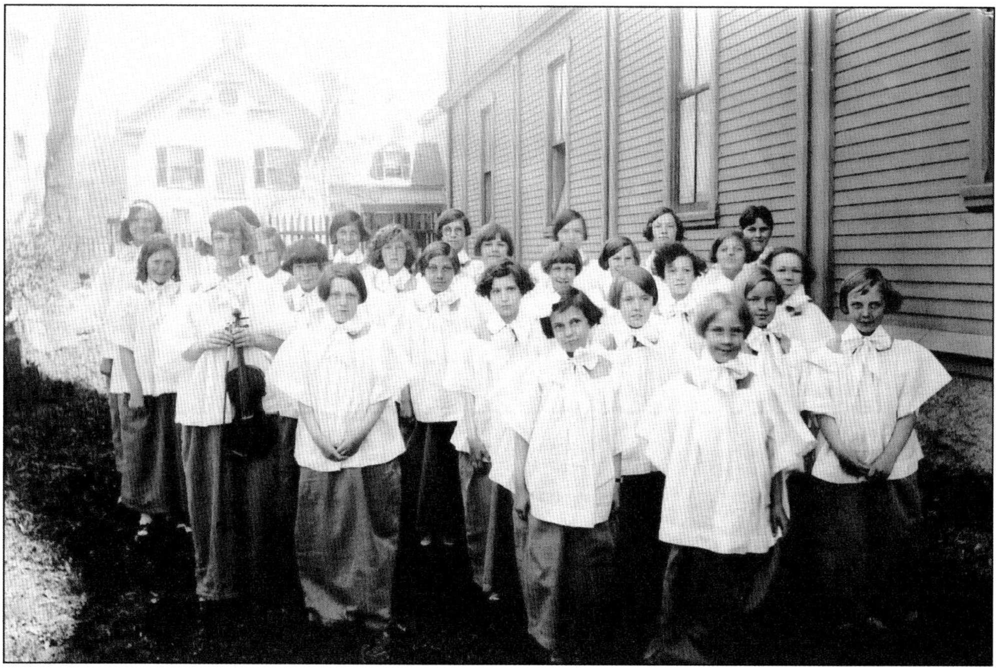

The junior choir of the School Street Methodist Church is assembled around 1930. Ruth Olive Roberts was the director, church organist, and a local music teacher. She was a fixture on the Saco music scene until 1984. Identified here are Sylvia Sinclair, Marjorie Clark, Marian Holt, Margaret Bean, Barbara Lamb, Peggy West, Evelyn Parslow, Barbara Small, Althea Fogg, Gertrude Merrill, Barbara Parslow, Catherine Crowley, Ernestine Knight, Dorothy Bowie, Phyllis Boothby Vining, Esther Smith, Dorothy Pike, Dorothy Bean, Dorothy Meserve, Frances Smith, Pauline Elia, Pauline Fairfield, and Marion Lamb.

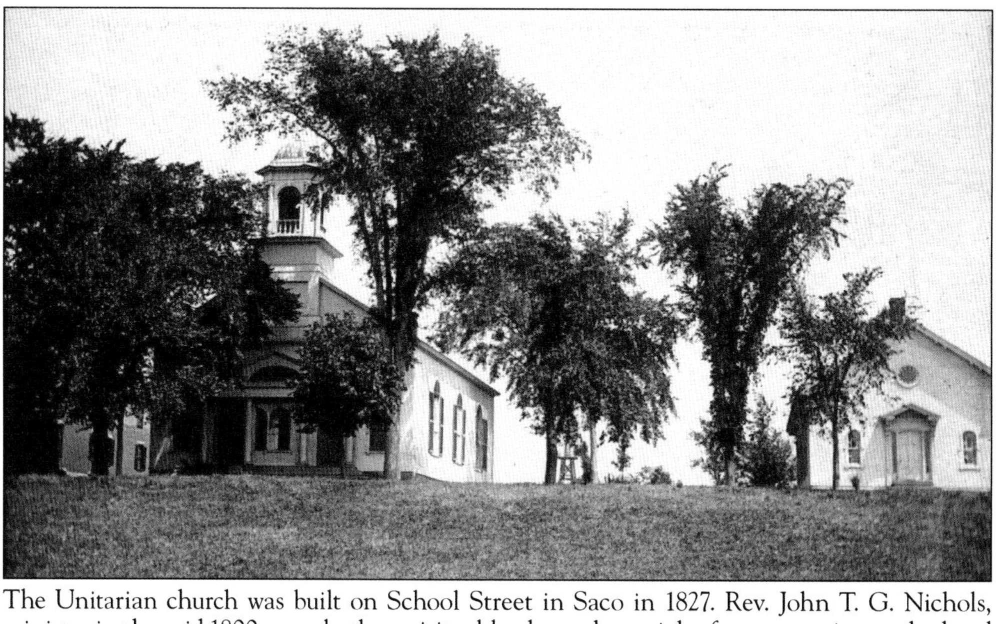

The Unitarian church was built on School Street in Saco in 1827. Rev. John T. G. Nichols, minister in the mid-1800s, was both a spiritual leader and a social reformer, serving as the head of Saco's school committee.

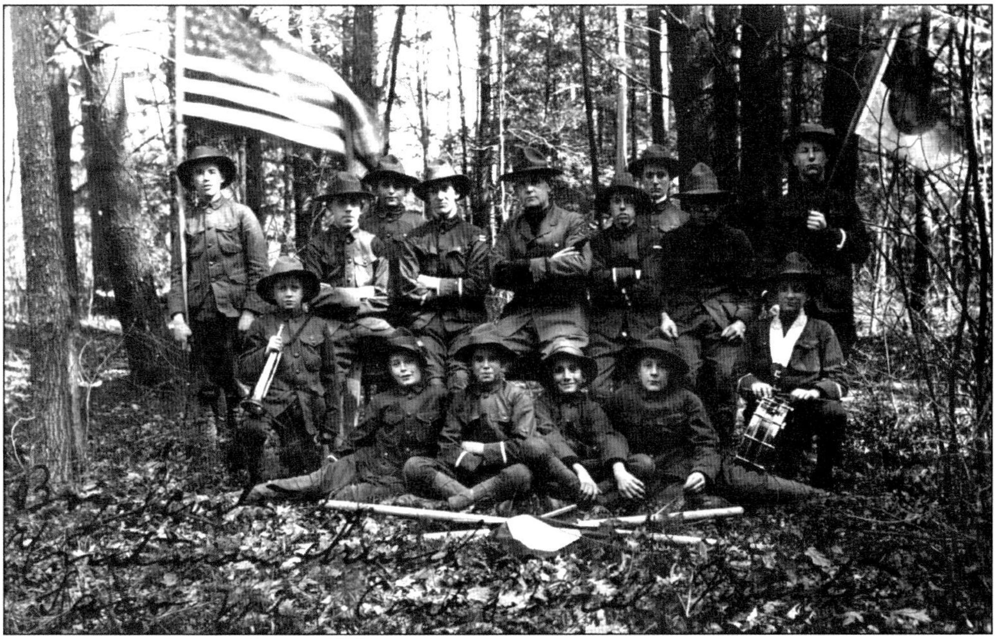

Boy Scout Troop No. 1 was photographed in Saco in March 1913. Considering that the Boy Scouts of America signed their charter on March 8, 1910, and suffered notable growing pains as they dealt with other contemporaneous scouting organizations, this troop must have been on the cutting edge of scouting. It is interesting to note that they had both a bugler and drummer to help with their scouting activities.

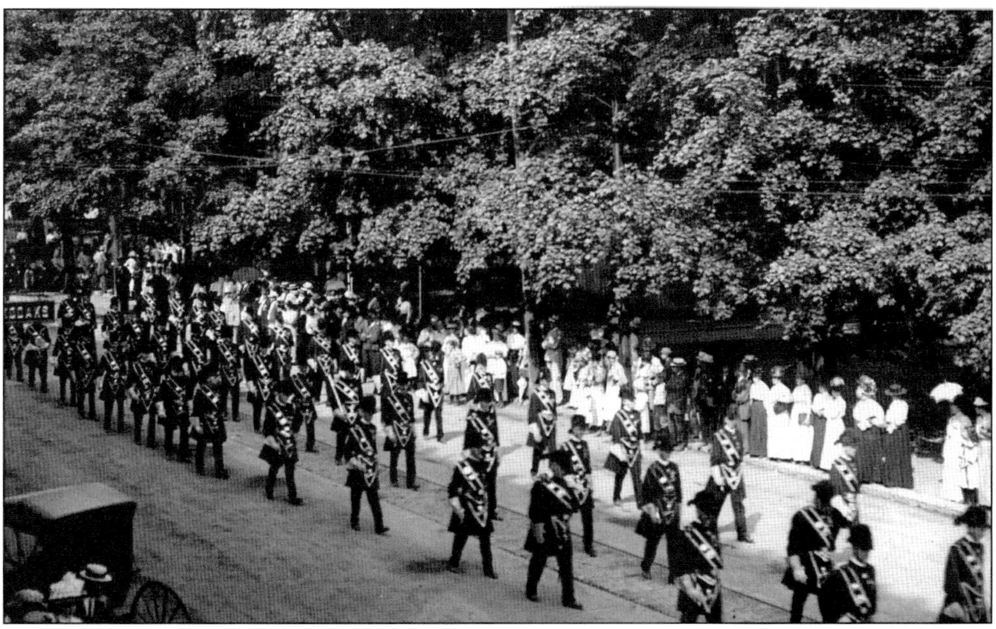

The Knights of Columbus was founded as a Catholic fraternal benefit society in 1882, with founding principles of charity, unity, and fraternity. They paraded through Saco on June 24, 1912, in front of a large group of bystanders. This parade preceded the founding of Holy Cross Trinity Church by four years.

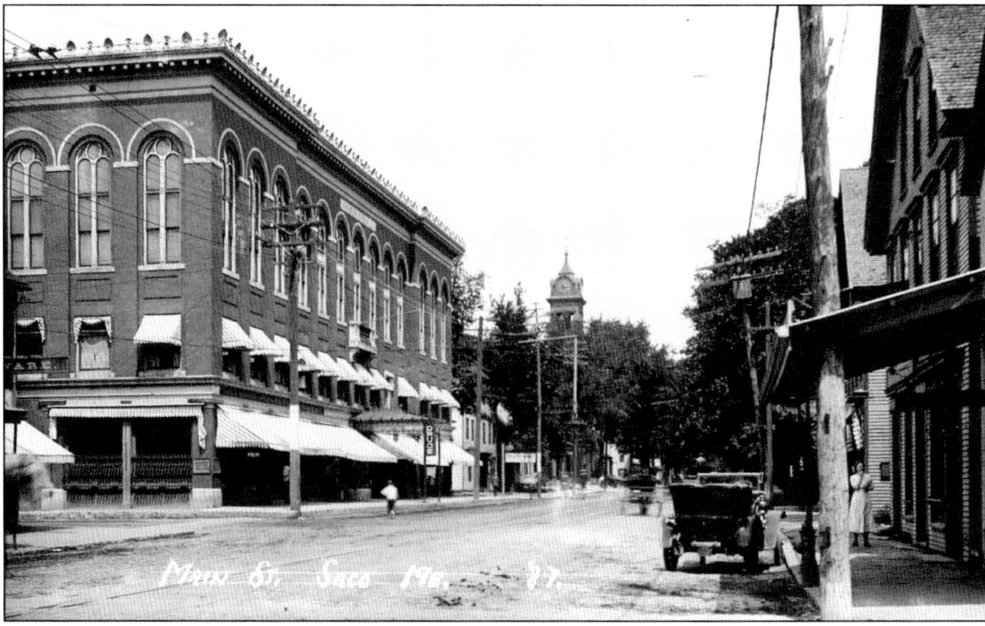

This view of Main Street from the south shows the impressive facade of the Masonic Block at 252 Main Street, built in 1907. The block features multistory windows with arched tops and trefoil tracery as well as decorative metal roof cresting. It was designed by Penn Varney of Lynn, Massachusetts. It is notable for retaining two of its original occupants: Saco and Biddeford Savings Institution and the Masonic lodge. (Courtesy Penobscot Marine Museum.)

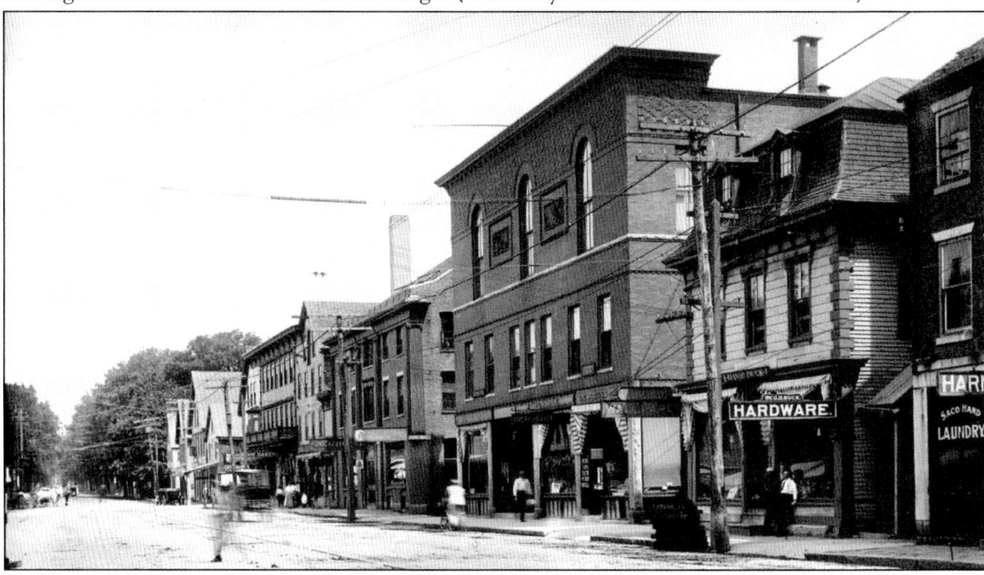

The William Pike Block at 199 Main Street was originally two stories tall with a mansard roof like the wooden block next door. In 1896, the Saco Chapter of the Independent Order of Odd Fellows—a charitable organization dedicated to "improving the character of mankind"—hired Portland architect John Calvin Stevens to remodel the block as its lodge hall. The patterned brickwork and terra-cotta panels were added by Stevens. In 2001, the Saco lodge of the Odd Fellows disbanded, and much of their ceremonial regalia was given to the Saco Museum. (Courtesy Penobscot Marine Museum.)

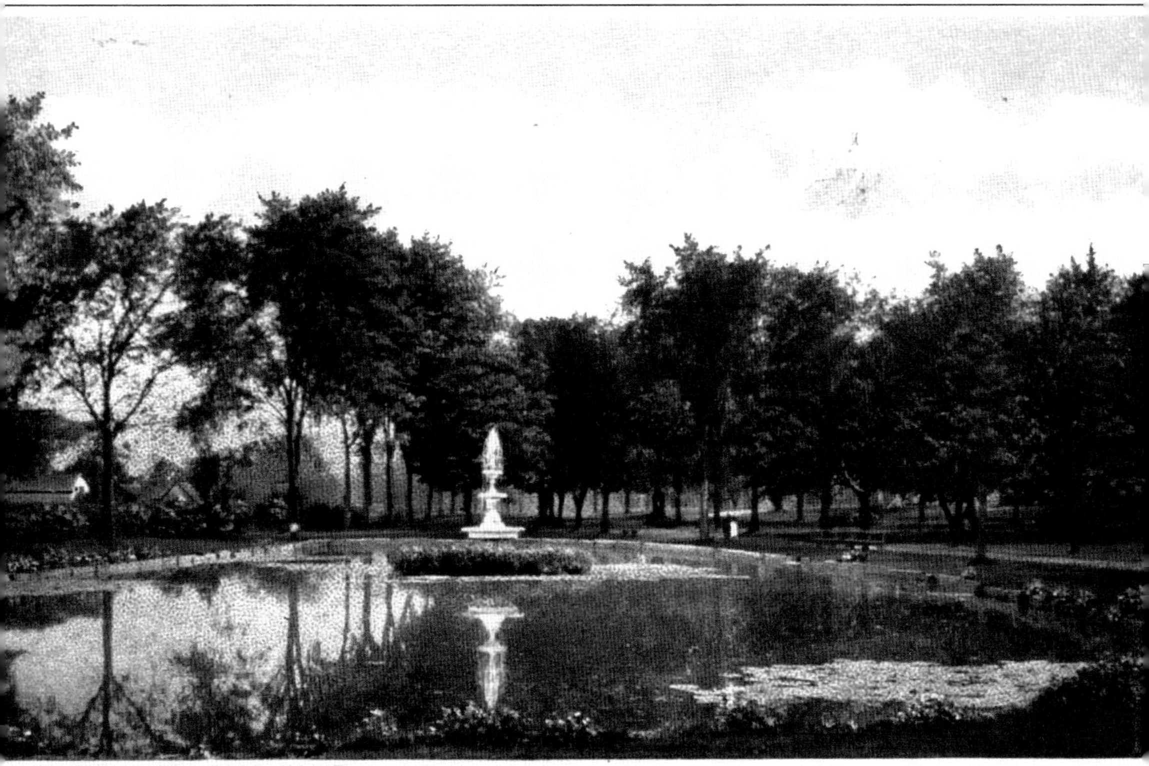

PEPPERELL PARK, SACO, MAINE.

In 1881, Cornelius Sweetser bequeathed $10,000 to the City of Saco to make Pepperell Park "a place of exceeding beauty." The park was originally conceived by colonial landholder Sir William Pepperrell (the second *r* in his last name was eventually dropped) on October 9, 1752, as a burial place adjacent to Saco's first meetinghouse. Yeoman Robert Gray of Biddeford added two more acres to Pepperrell's original four. Gray's donation was made just in time because his wife, Jane, died the following day and became the first person buried there. Burials were discontinued by the time Laurel Hill Cemetery was created in 1843, and time had taken its toll. Jane Gray's stone is one of only a handful that exist today, and it no longer stands in the cemetery. In the 19th century, as picnicking in the cemetery became popular, it evolved into an attractive, well-landscaped park. A sparkling fountain, picnic areas, a trotting park, a bandstand, gravel pathways, lush lawns, and tall shade trees were among the features of this centrally located attraction. The ornamental pond seen here was also popular with ice-skaters for many years.

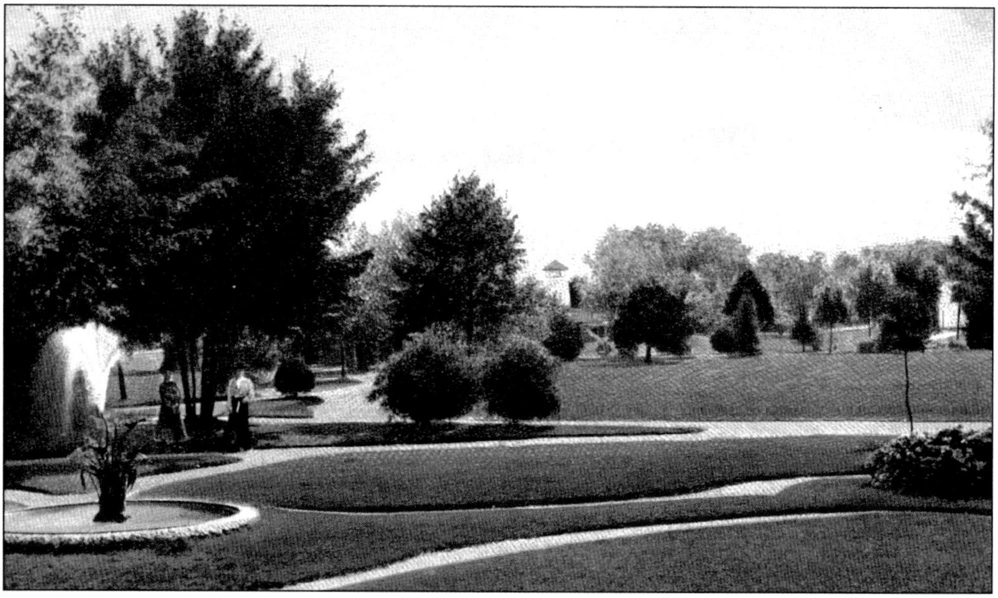

A newspaper article from June 15, 1889, states that Pepperell Park featured nearly 1,000 trees of at least 36 different varieties. In this postcard from about that time, ladies are seen enjoying their shade. The new water tower stands in the center background. It was constructed in 1889 from plans drawn up by architect H. G. Wadlin, who also designed the first Dyer Library and the main building of the second Thornton Academy.

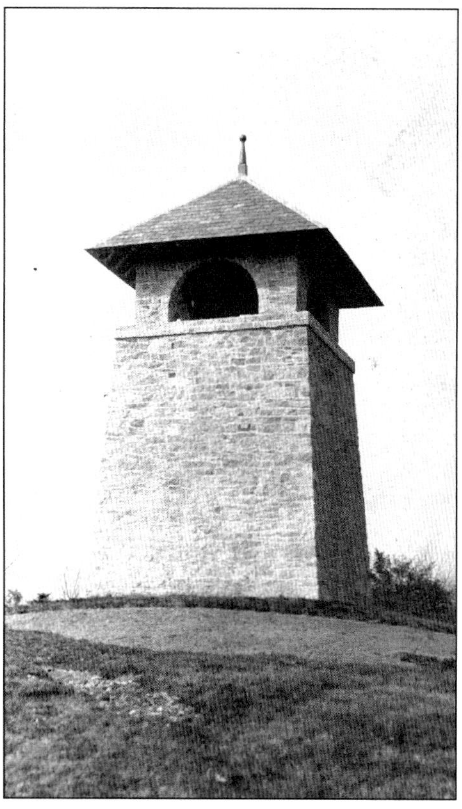

Photographed around 1895, the Pepperell Park tower stood above a 200-foot-deep artesian well. An adjacent windmill pumped the water to the surface, supplying the fountains and pond. The hammered granite tower, which park commissioners described as "a handsome ornament to the park," is 15 feet at the base, stands 18 feet tall, and has a capacity of 7,680 gallons of water. Although the Gov. John Fairfield School replaced most of the park's features, the tower remains.

Four

PATRIOTISM

Since the American Revolution, the men and women of Saco have represented their country in every major conflict. Some served in battle farther south or overseas, some were stationed here to keep watch over Maine's vulnerable coast, and many did what they could to support war efforts from the homefront. Even in peacetime, patriotism ran high, with various drum corps providing the sound track to parades, celebrations, and holidays.

Patriotism was manifested in another way, as Saco was a local example of America's famed melting pot. Drawn by the promise of steady jobs in the factories, many immigrant groups made their way to Saco in the 19th and 20th centuries. As the French Canadian, Greek, and Jewish communities, among others, became woven into the fabric of this American town, they nevertheless held on to their unique traditions. The result is a patois of cultures that is fundamental to Saco's (and America's) history and character.

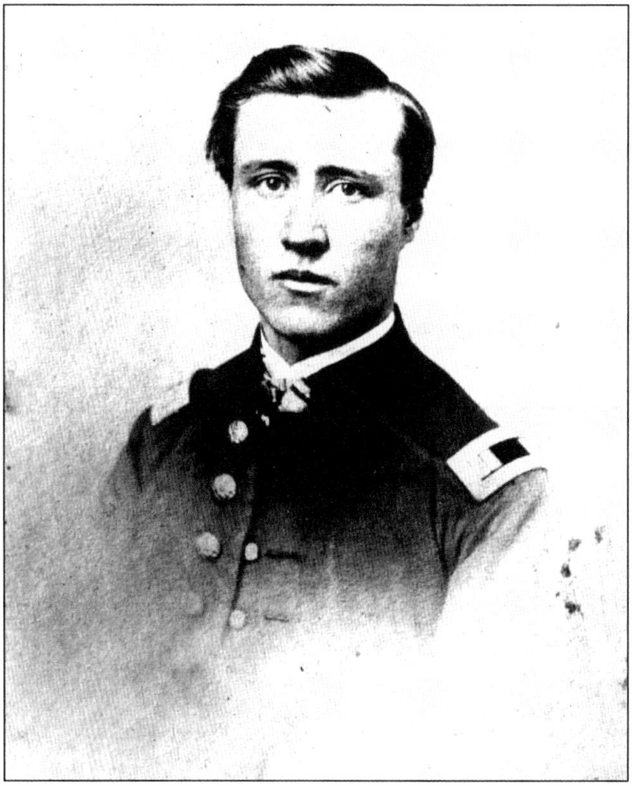

Saco resident James H. Shannon poses in the Civil War uniform of the 1st U.S. Cavalry of Tennessee. He later transferred to the regimental band of the Fifth Main Infantry, Company H. Born in 1841, Shannon married Susan Greenwood and then died in 1916. He remained active in Grand Army of the Republic reunions throughout his life and is buried at Laurel Hill Cemetery.

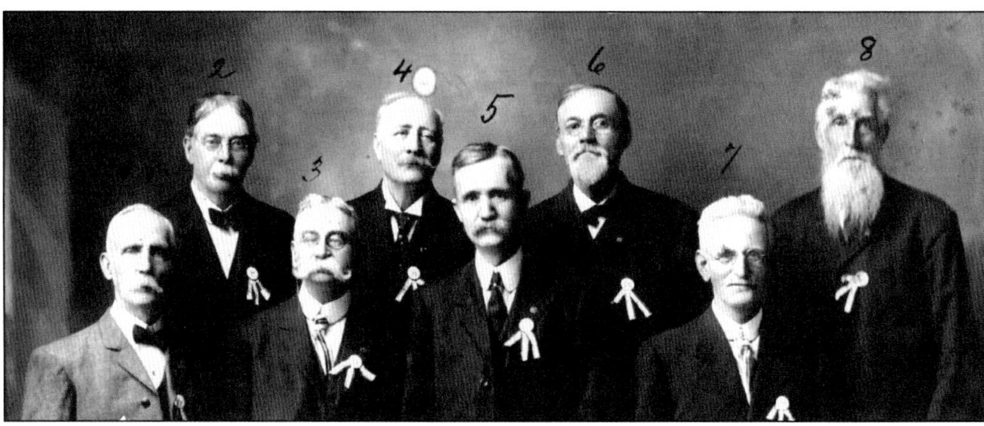

Years after the preceding photograph was taken, James H. Shannon appears again with surviving members of Company H, 5th Maine Regiment Infantry Volunteers, who are gathered for a reunion in Portland in 1911. Shown are (1) Orin F. Pettingill, (2) Sgt. J. G. Sanborn, (3) Capt. George E. Brown, (4) Shannon, (5) Sgt. Joseph E. Taylor, (6) Sergeant Hannaford, (7) Daniel H. Towle, and (8) Corporal Chase. Listed as absent are Col. R. C. Shannon, Adjt. George W. Bicknell, and Sergeant Jordan.

Joseph T. Wentworth (1835–1917) poses proudly with his Grand Army of the Republic medal pinned to his lapel. He served for a year as a corporal in Company G, 11th Regiment Infantry Maine Volunteers. After the war, he worked as a store clerk and operator in the mills. E. E. Sawtelle operated a photograph studio in Biddeford from about 1880 until the late 1890s.

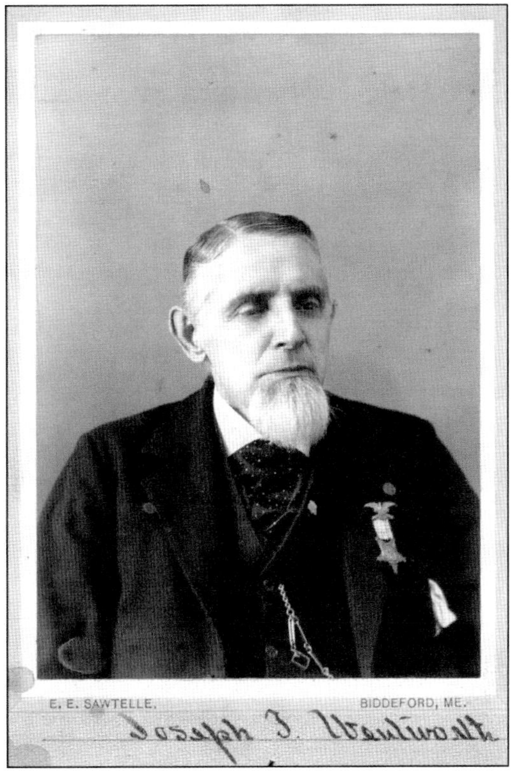

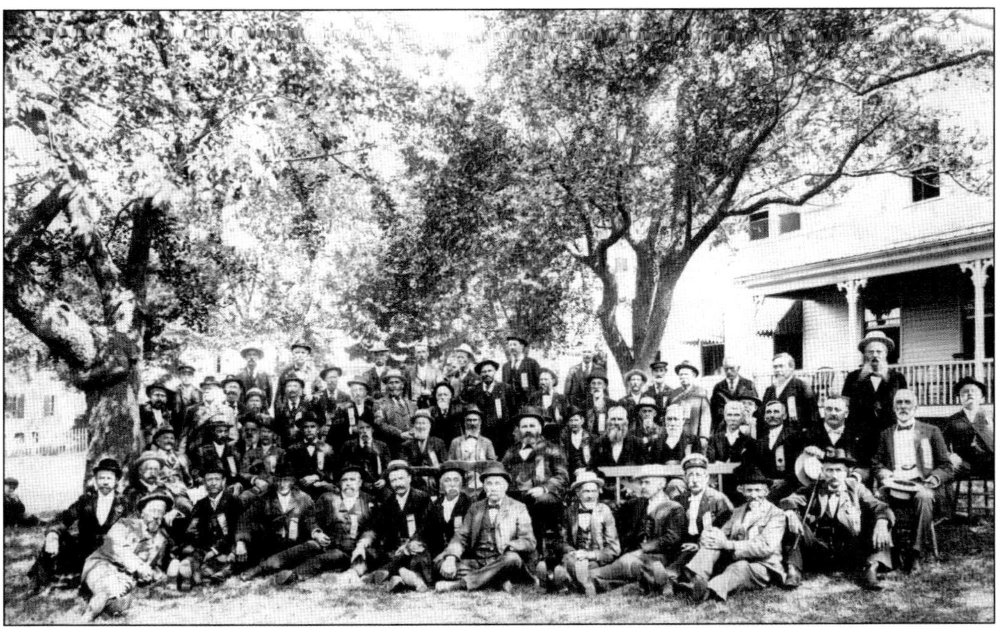

The 1898 reunion of the 17th Maine Infantry Regiment is pictured in this photograph titled, "36 Years Later: 1862–1898." The photograph is from the papers of Dyer librarian John Haley, who is thought to be the gentleman in the center of the farthermost row with a white hat, looking directly at the camera. Haley devoted much of his life to promoting Civil War memorial activity and has been described as a "one-man agency" to help veterans.

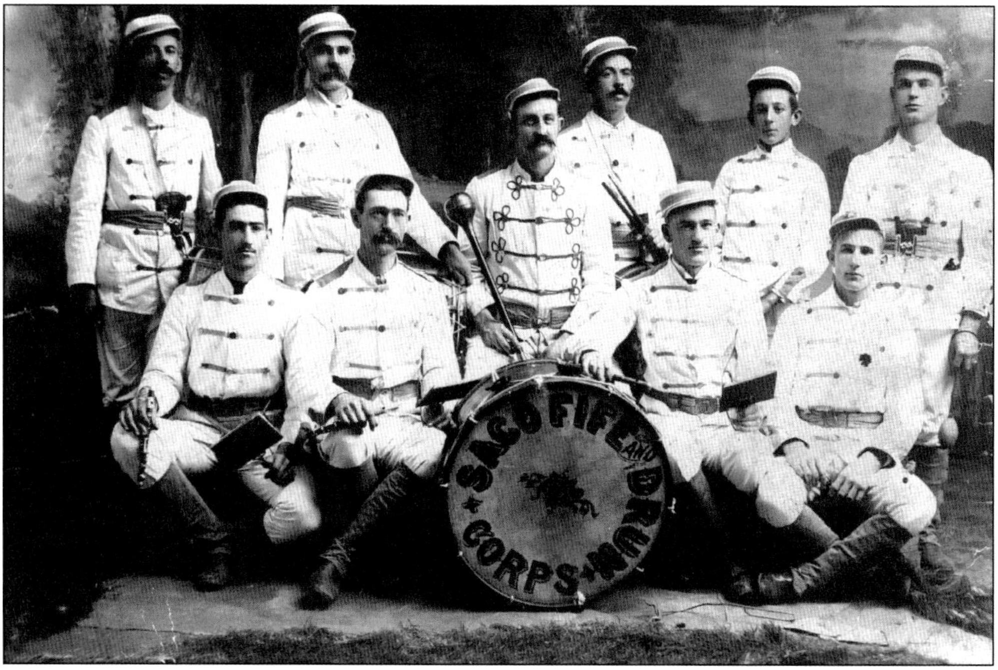

The Saco Fife and Drum Corps poses for a photograph in 1886. An offshoot of military drum corps, city drum corps were often sponsored by local veterans' groups or churches. The Saco Fife and Drum Corps was on hand for parades and celebrations. A wide range of ages are represented here. A few of the fifers have their sheet music on underarm music stands. One of the music stands can be more clearly seen on the ground to the right of the drum.

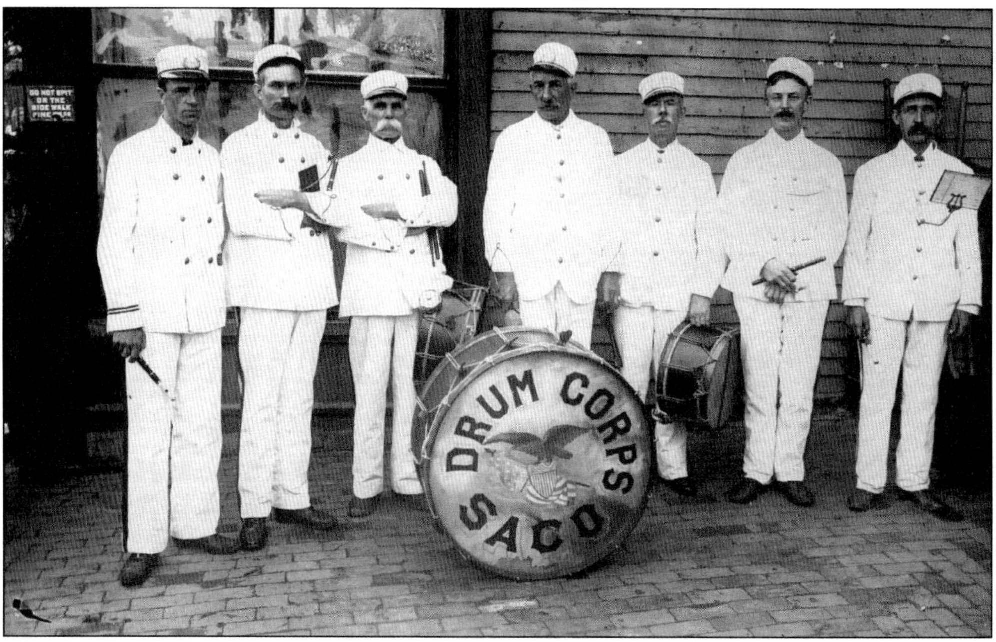

The Saco Drum Corps, probably a later manifestation of the group pictured above, assembled on Labor Day in 1908. The military and patriotic origins of the drum corps are evident here in the elaborate and pronounced design of an eagle, shield, and American flag on the bass drum.

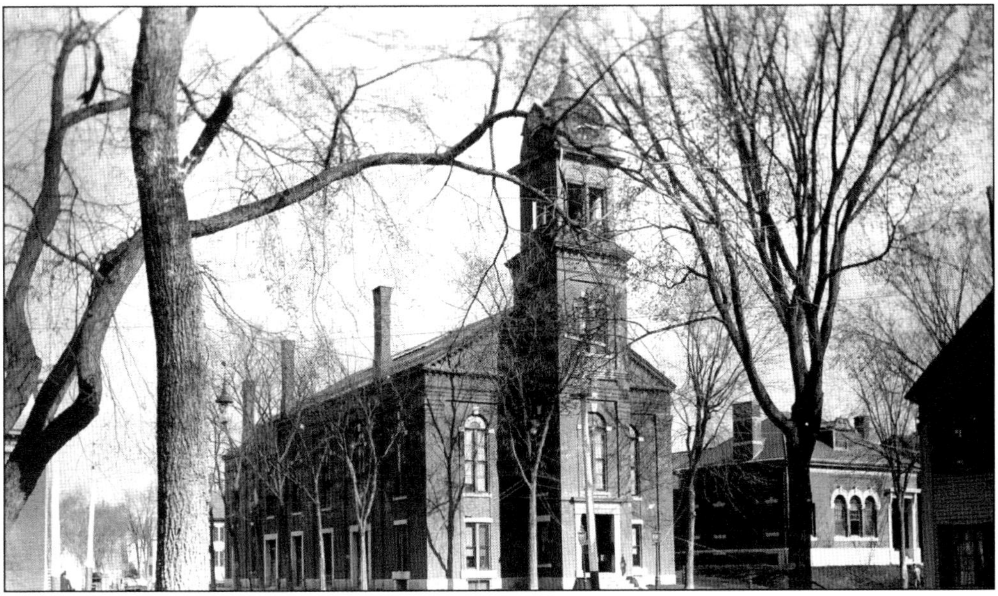

Originally constructed as the town hall in 1856, the building at 300 Main Street was rededicated as city hall following Saco's incorporation in 1867. The clock tower pictured here was completed in 1881. Next door is the original Dyer Library, built in 1893. In 1955, the library moved to its current location in the Main Street house built by Joseph Deering. Budding elm trees form a cathedral-like arch over Main Street in this photograph from 1896.

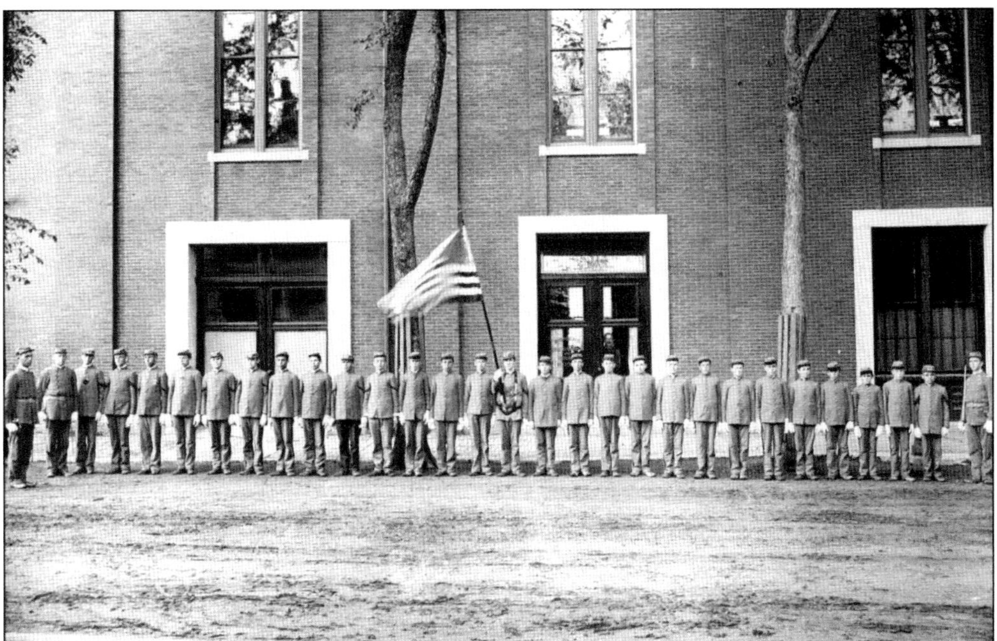

Thirty members of the Thornton Academy Cadet Corps are pictured at Saco City Hall. The cadet corps was a school drill team that existed from 1889 to 1893.

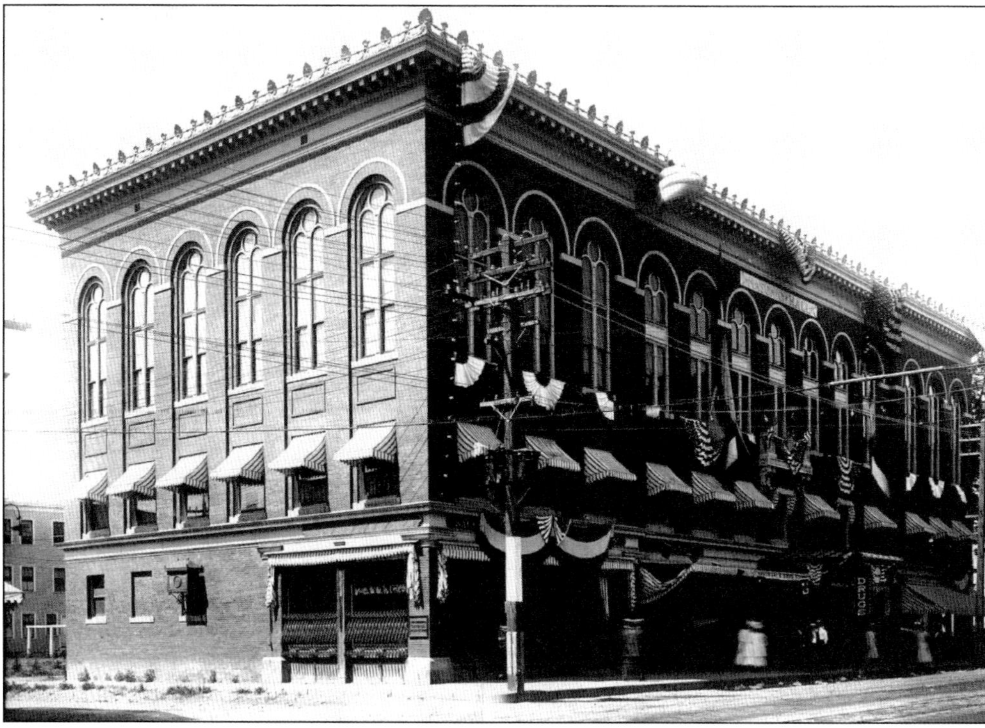

Patriotically decked out, the Masonic hall, built in 1907, had recently become home to Saco and Biddeford Savings Institution, which was previously located on Factory Island. Bradbury Drugs opened in the Masonic building at about the same time and closed about 1930.

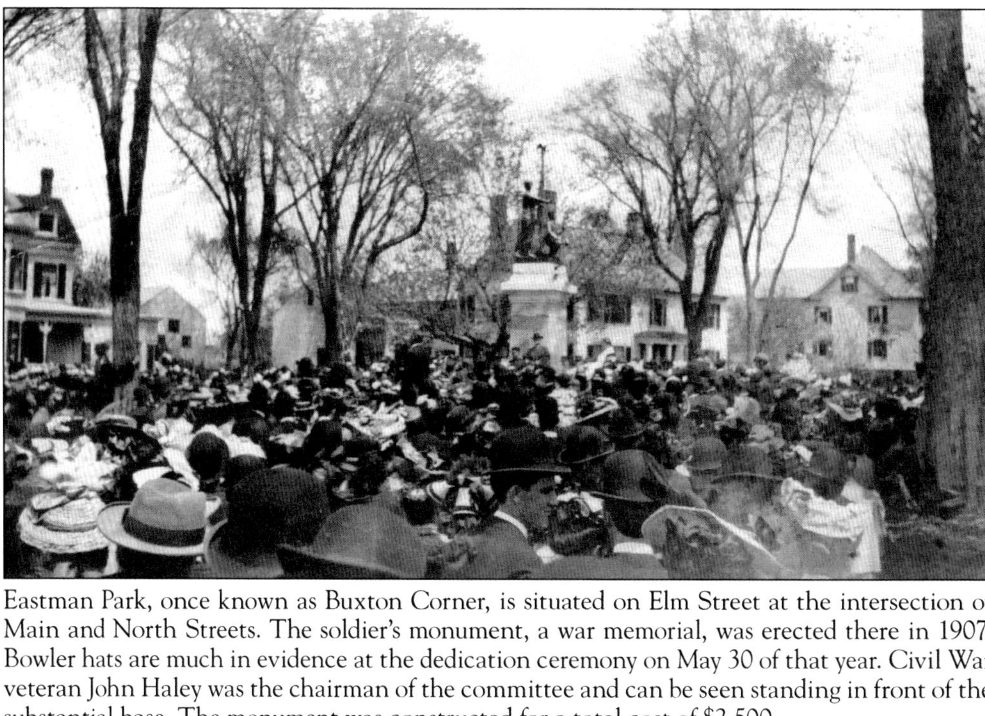

Eastman Park, once known as Buxton Corner, is situated on Elm Street at the intersection of Main and North Streets. The soldier's monument, a war memorial, was erected there in 1907. Bowler hats are much in evidence at the dedication ceremony on May 30 of that year. Civil War veteran John Haley was the chairman of the committee and can be seen standing in front of the substantial base. The monument was constructed for a total cost of $2,500.

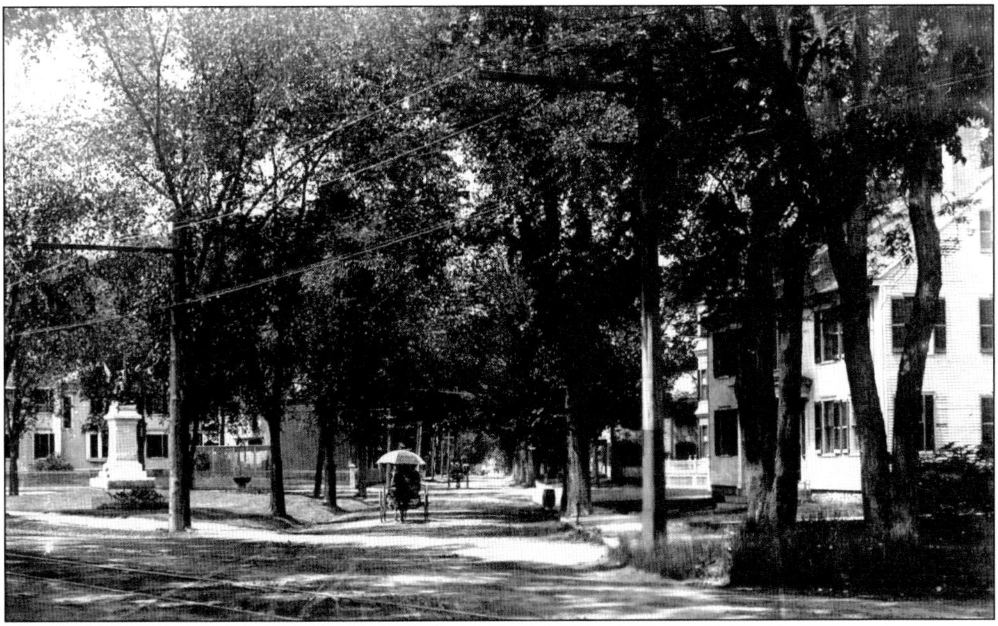

This photograph by Charles Moody shows Eastman Park around 1910. The umbrella over the horse-drawn wagon reads, "Low & Co. Clothiers." Eastman House (Prescott House) at 146 Elm Street (right side) is an example of a late Federal-style home with a Greek Revival porch and doorway.

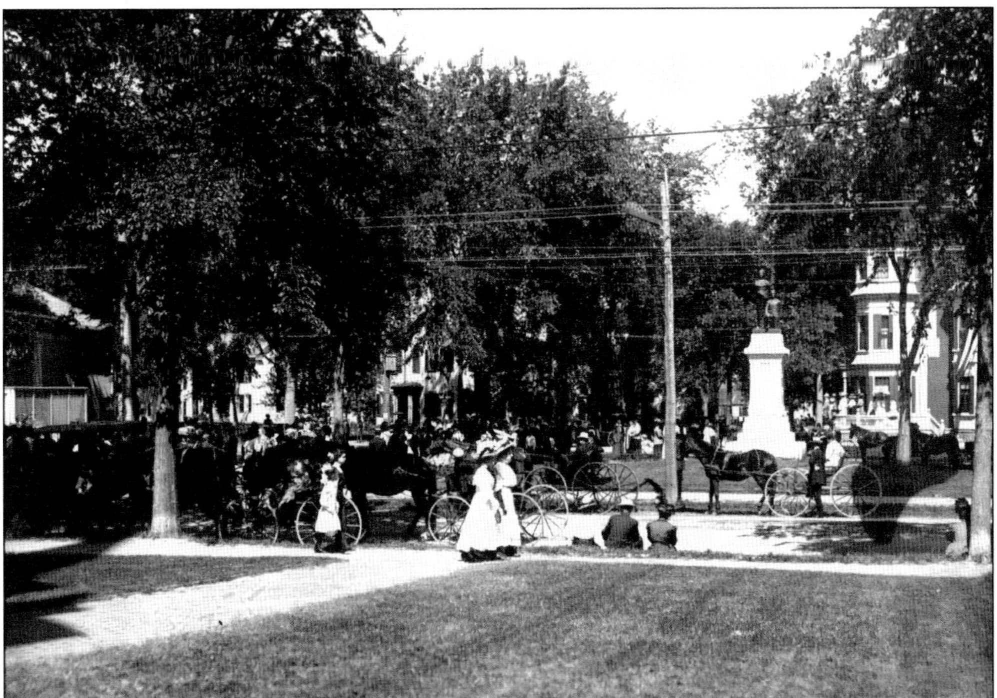

These ladies await the parade in Eastman Park in this 1912 photograph, taken from in front of the First Parish Congregational Church at the corner of Beach and Main Streets. (Courtesy McArthur Public Library.)

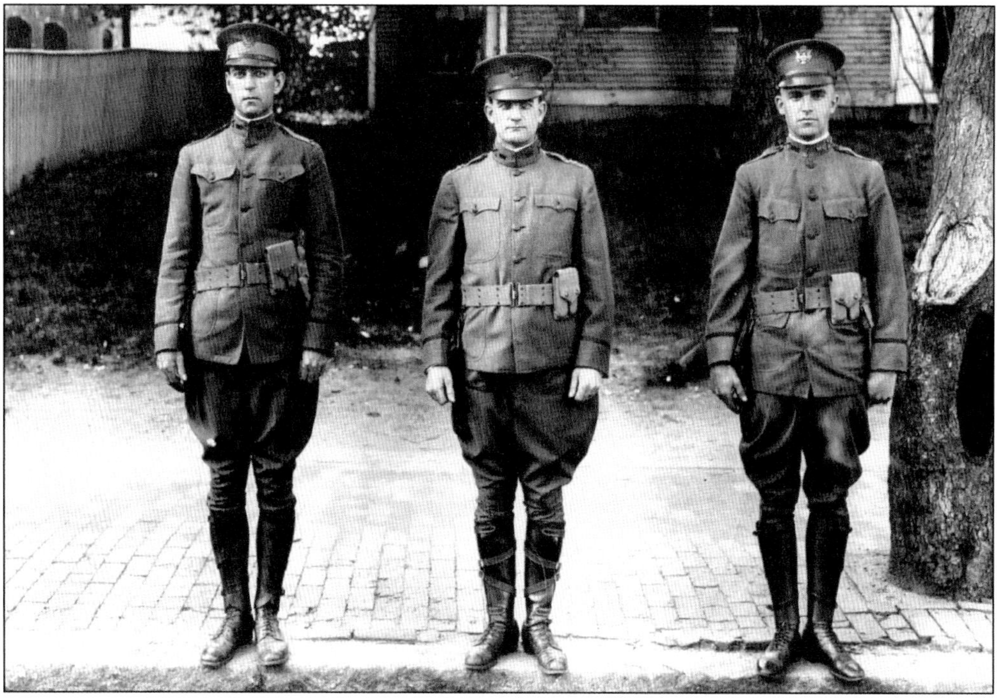

Three men in World War I uniforms stand on Main Street in Saco. The man in the middle is Clarence E. Holt, co-owner of Knight-Holt Company of Motor Car Electricians on Portland Road in Saco.

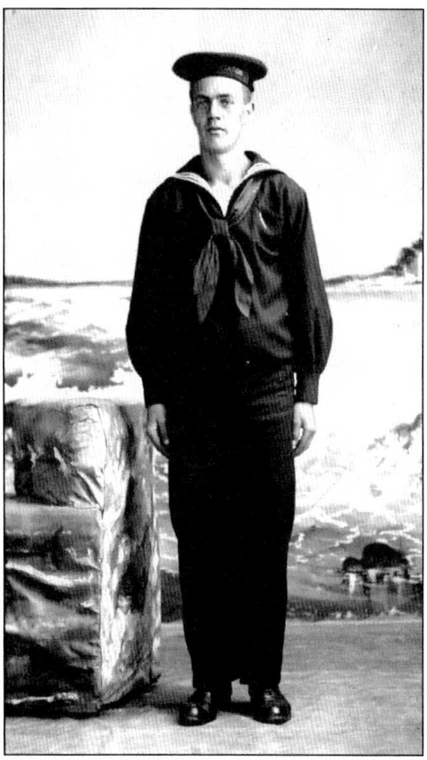

Frank Leighton (pictured around 1917) was about 18 years old when he sent this carefully posed postcard home to his parents when they lived on Deering Avenue. The photograph was clearly taken in a photographer's studio; note the painted backdrop. Leighton survived the war and returned to Saco, where he worked as a clerk. He died in 1949.

Elroy Booth of Saco was one of the many young local men to serve in World War I. Later a carpenter, Booth died in 1969.

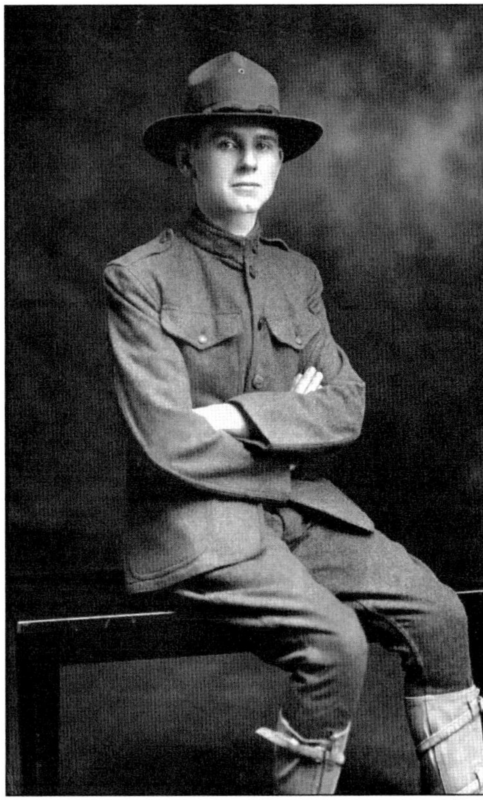

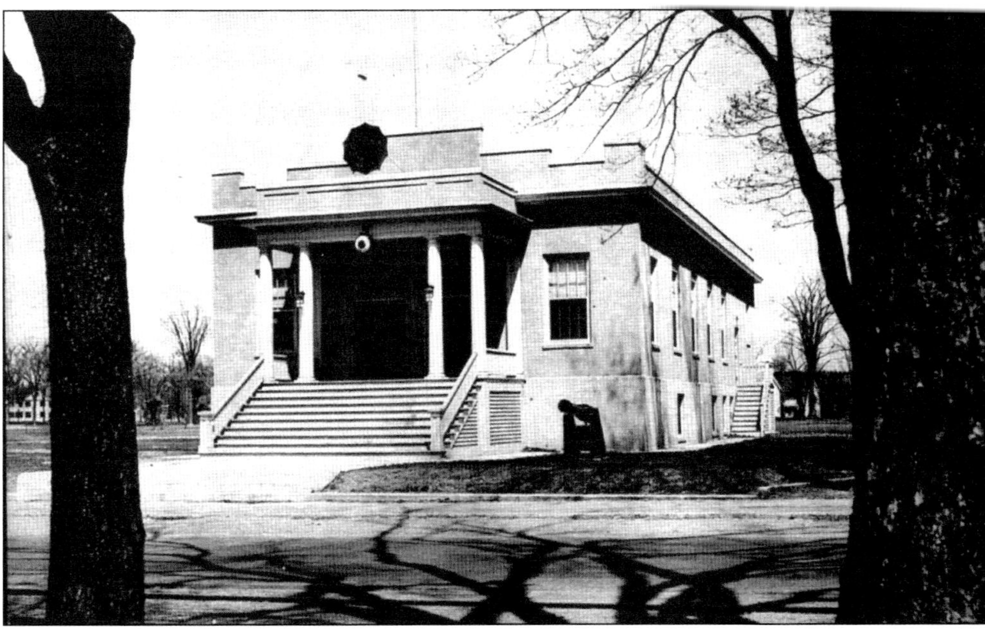

The R. C. Owen American Legion post, built in 1935 on Beach Street, was named for Richard C. Owen, who was killed in action on September 26, 1918, in France during World War I. He was 22 years old. The American Legion was chartered by Congress in 1919 as a patriotic veteran's organization. The post's drum and bugle corps was a prominent feature in area parades.

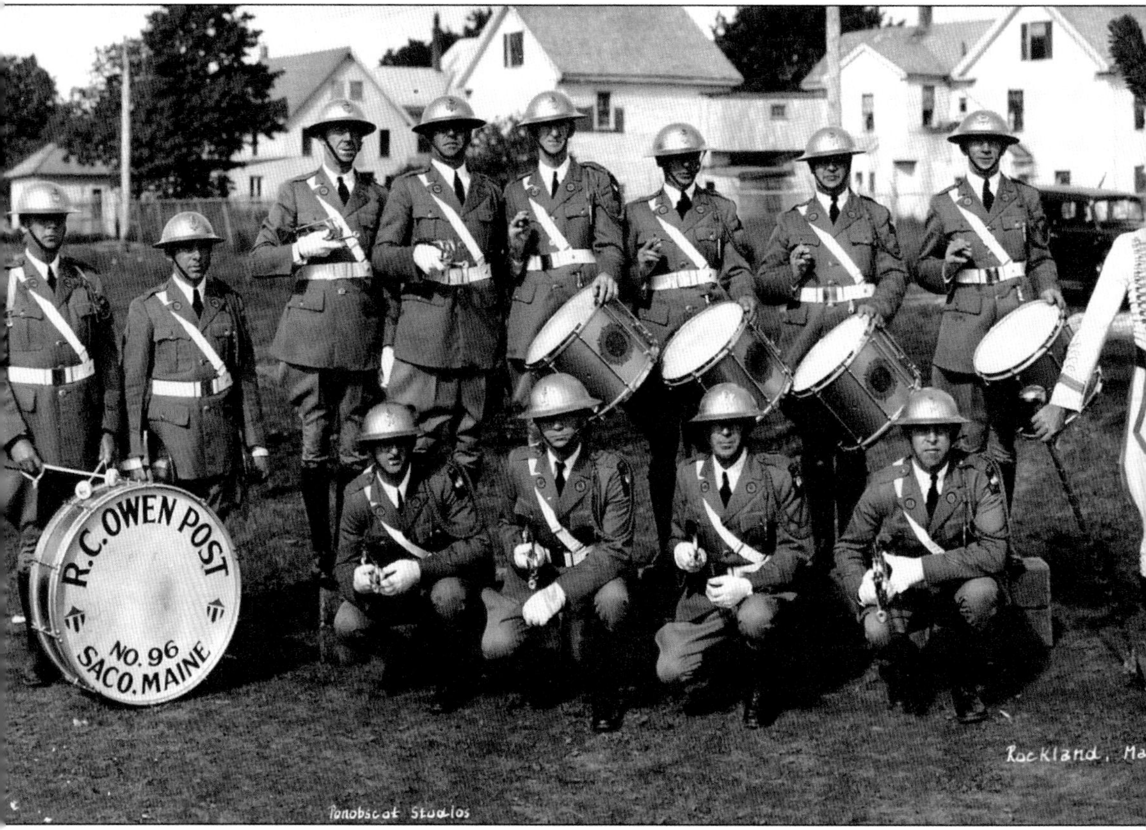

The drum corps of the R. C. Owen American Legion post, now known as the Owen-Davis post, poses in Rockland on June 18, 1935. This band superseded the earlier Saco Fife and Drum Corps

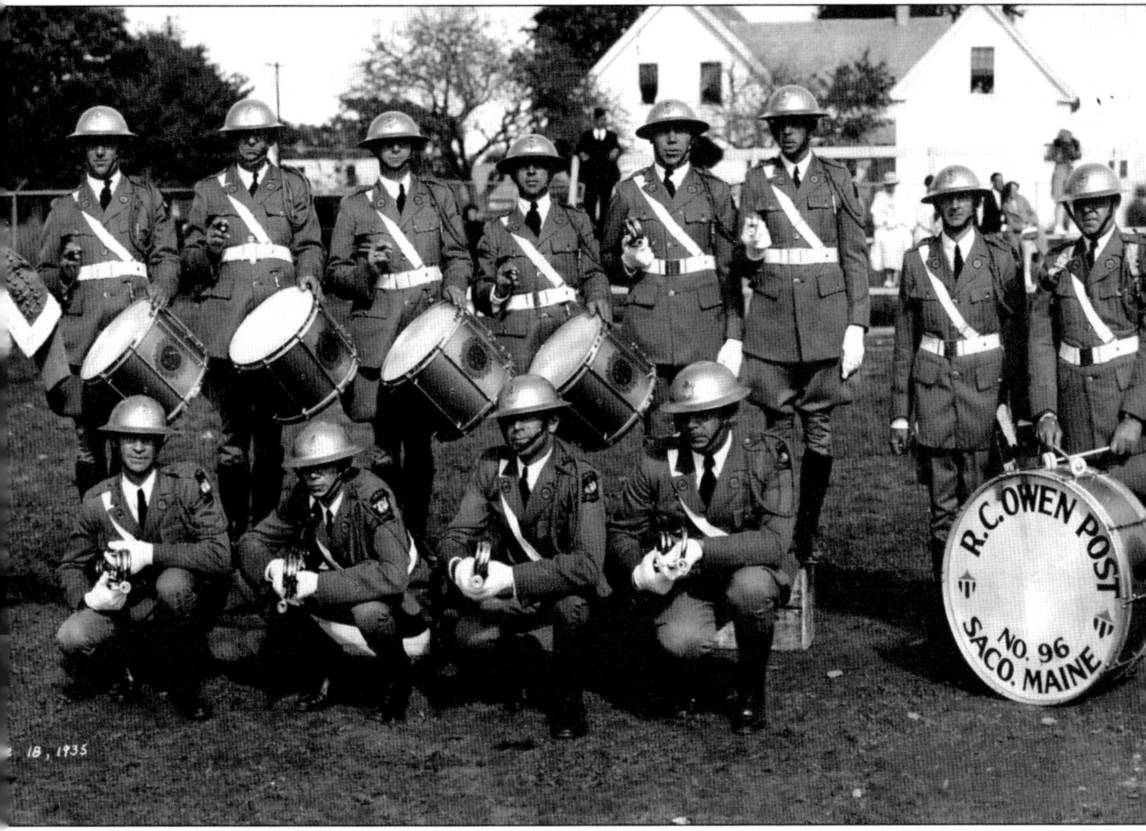

and Saco Drum Corps. This photograph was taken by Penobscot Studios of Stonington.

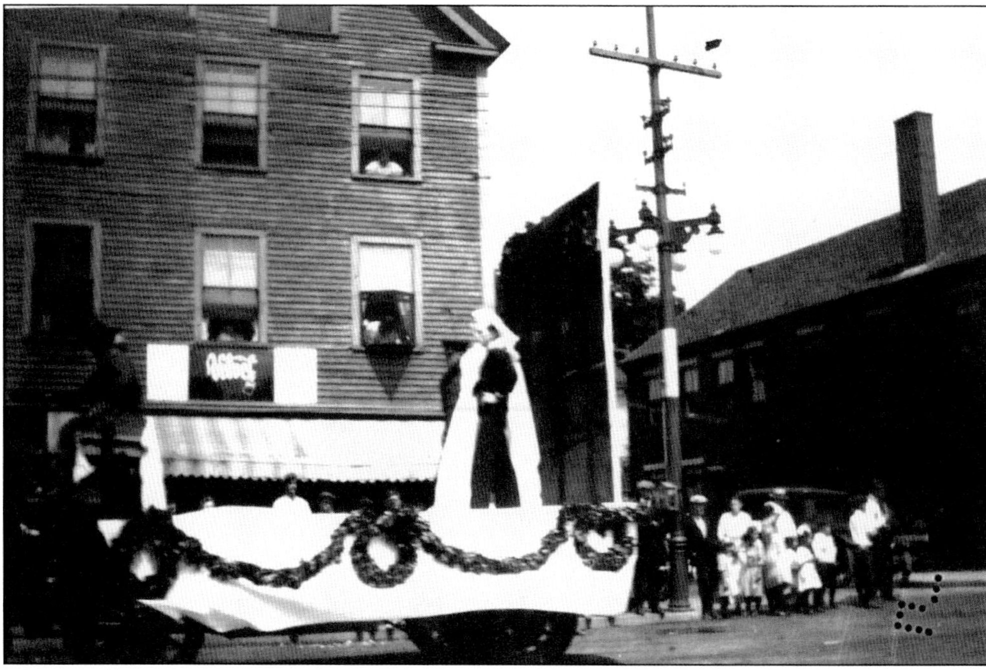

This World War I float passing in front of the D. F. Littlefield Fruit Store at the corner of Main and Storer Streets seems to be attracting a lot of attention from bystanders. The two soldiers appear to be flanking a very large person in a flowing white gown. The "velvet" advertised on the storefront was a cold, fruity drink popular at the time.

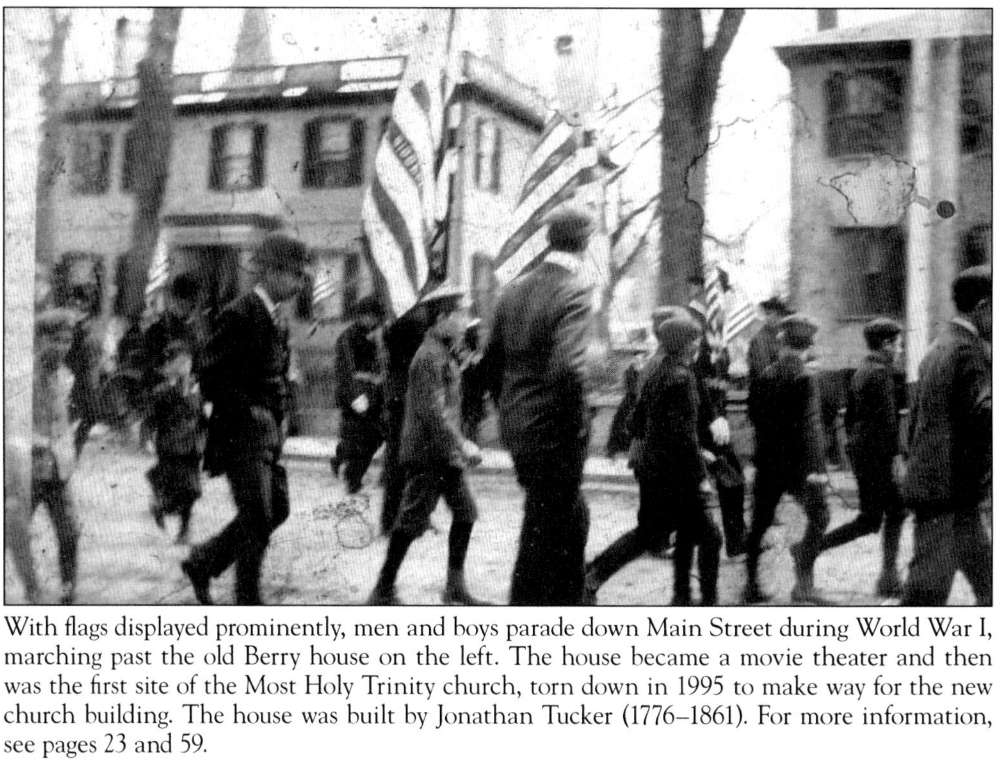

With flags displayed prominently, men and boys parade down Main Street during World War I, marching past the old Berry house on the left. The house became a movie theater and then was the first site of the Most Holy Trinity church, torn down in 1995 to make way for the new church building. The house was built by Jonathan Tucker (1776–1861). For more information, see pages 23 and 59.

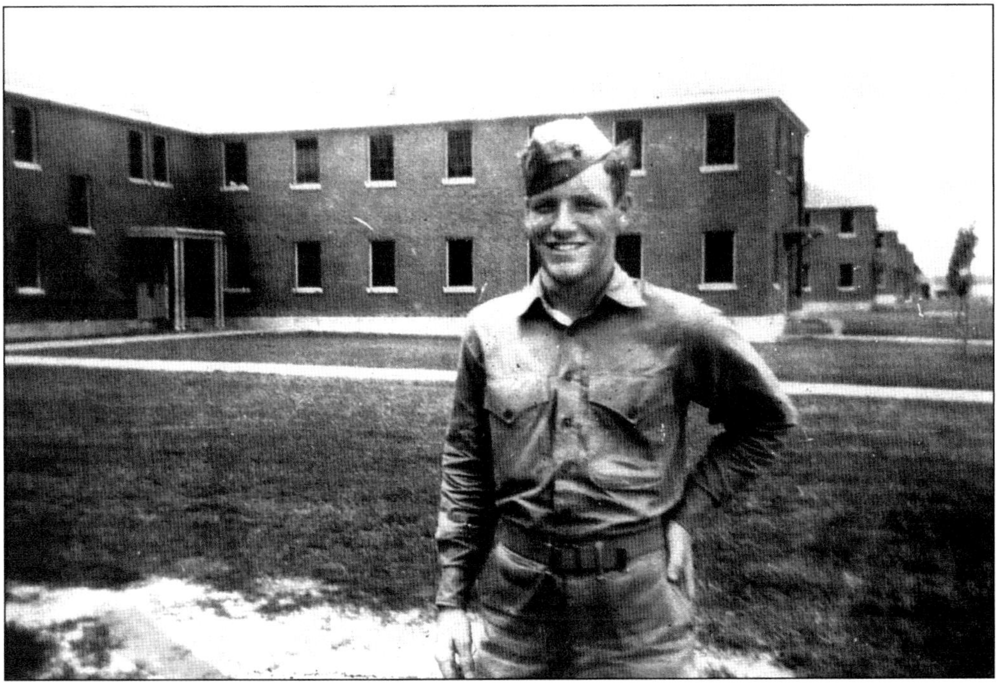

Pvt. Fred Clark of Saco poses at Camp Lejeune in North Carolina in the summer of 1946. He later rose to the rank of colonel in the United States Marine Corps and retired from the military in 1979; he subsequently became a volunteer in the Dyer Library archives. (Courtesy Fred Clark.)

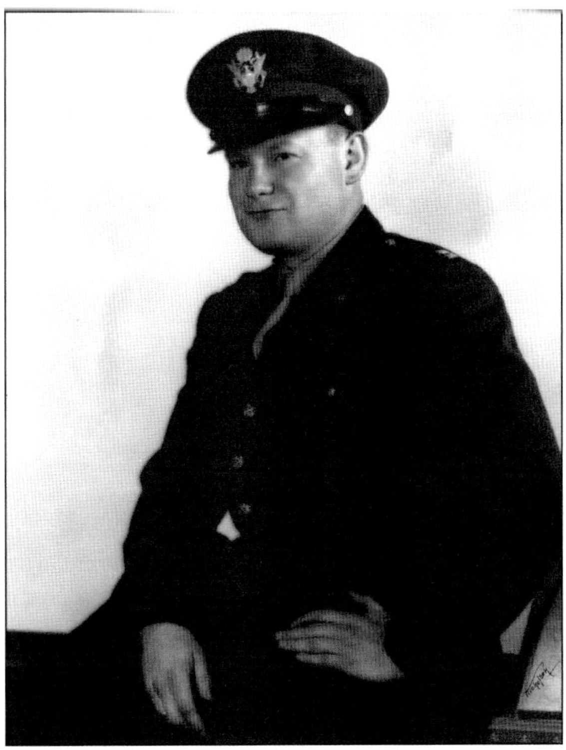

Paul S. Hill, from a family of Saco surgeons, served as personal physician to Gen. George S. Patton during World War II; he was one of the first doctors to be present at the liberation of a Nazi concentration camp. On May 3, 1945, he wrote to his wife from Dachau, "I am in the worst Hell hole on earth and that's putting it mildly."

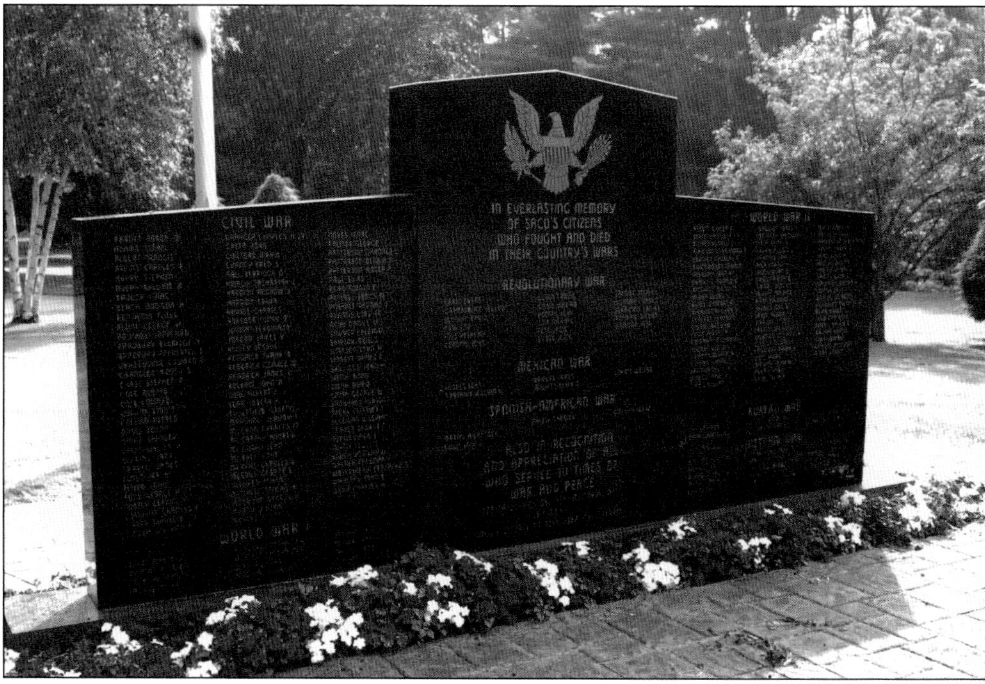

The melting pot of names on Laurel Hill's war memorial demonstrates that the period between the Civil War and World War II brought a wave of immigration to the cities on the Saco. English-speaking immigrants from Scotland and Ireland were followed by French Canadians, Greeks, Albanians, Jews, and others. (Photograph by Leslie Rounds.)

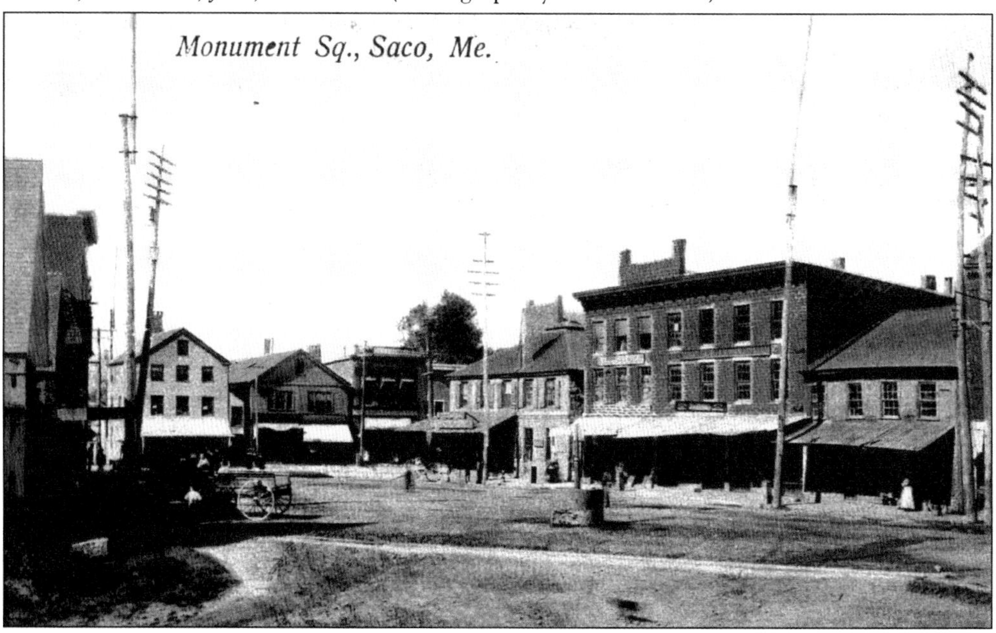

Mislabeled by the postcard company as Monument Square (note the absence of any monuments), Pepperell Square had always served as a busy mercantile center. The laundry operated by Chinese immigrant Seung Wong was located at 23½ Pepperell Square between 1900 and 1904; Wong lived in the rooms above. In 1904, he moved the laundry to 101½ Main Street.

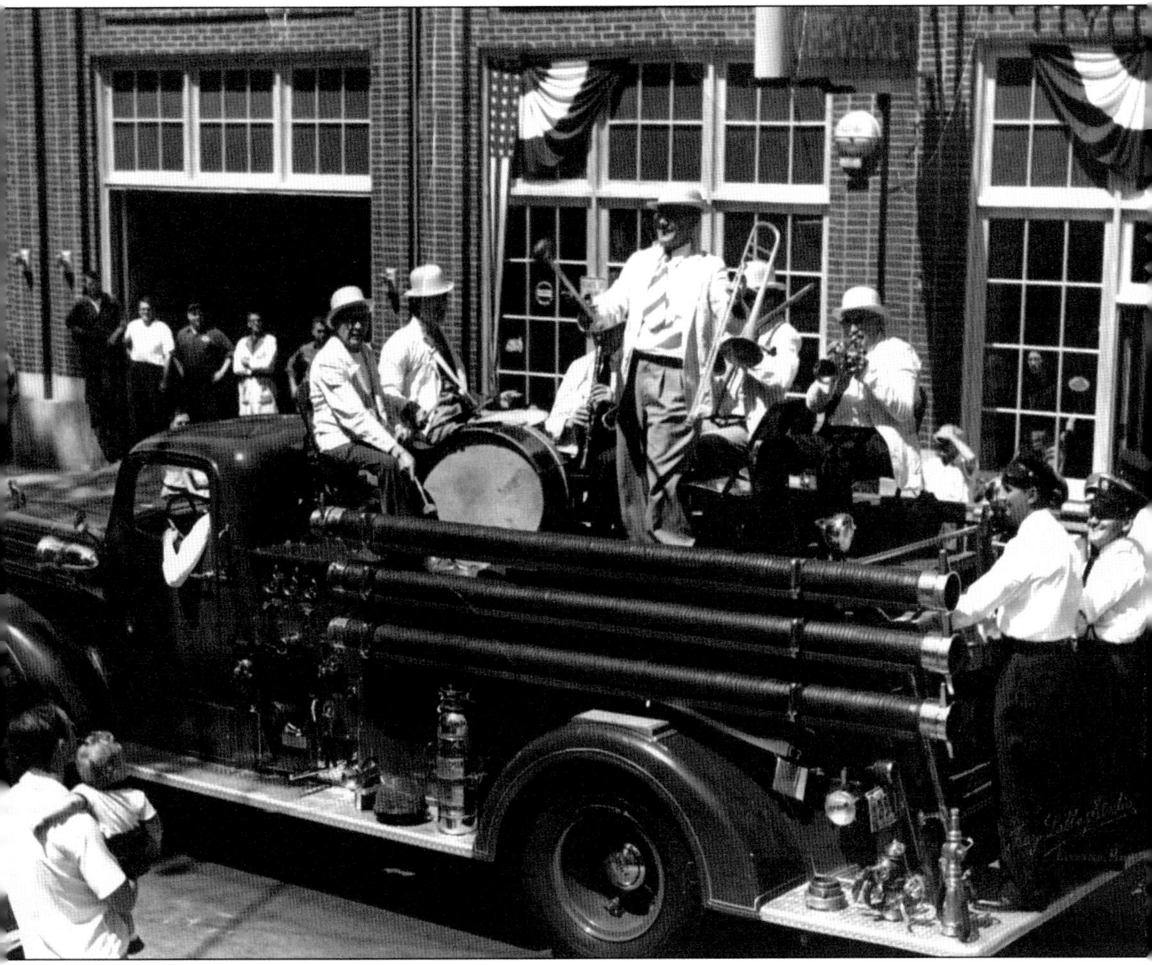

Laissez les bon temps rouler! Founded in 1870, Painchaud's Band still exists today. Canadian immigrant Pierre L. Painchaud founded La Fanfare Painchaud as an outgrowth of Biddeford's French-Canadian Institute, dedicated to protecting the heritage of the local French Canadian population. The band enjoyed popularity far beyond the French community, playing at concerts, celebrations, and fund-raisers all over southern Maine. The original band members were mostly Quebecois mill workers from Biddeford and Saco, but by the 1950s, when this photograph was taken at what appears to be a Fourth of July parade, members were from all ethnicities and walks of life. (Photograph by Ray Labbe Studios.)

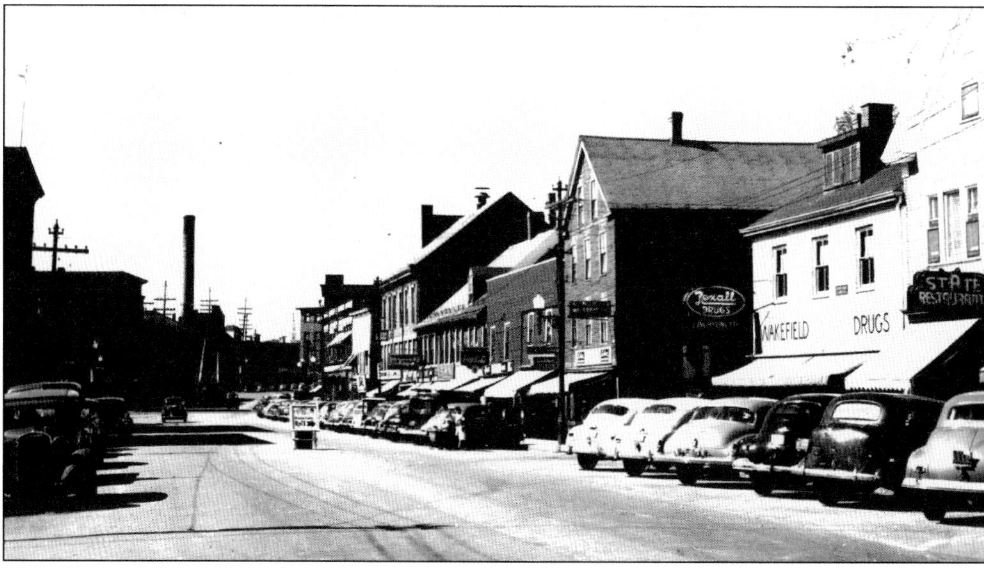

The Olympia Fruit Store, located in the ground floor of the tall, peak-roofed building in the center of the photograph, on the corner of Main and Storer Streets, was opened by Greek immigrant Efstratios (renamed "Sam" at Ellis Island) Anagnostis and his partner, Nick Janarous, after the men spent several years working in the textile mills. Anagnostis's son, John, born 1929, often helped in the store, and later became president of the Dyer Library Association. (Courtesy Jim and Edna Leary.)

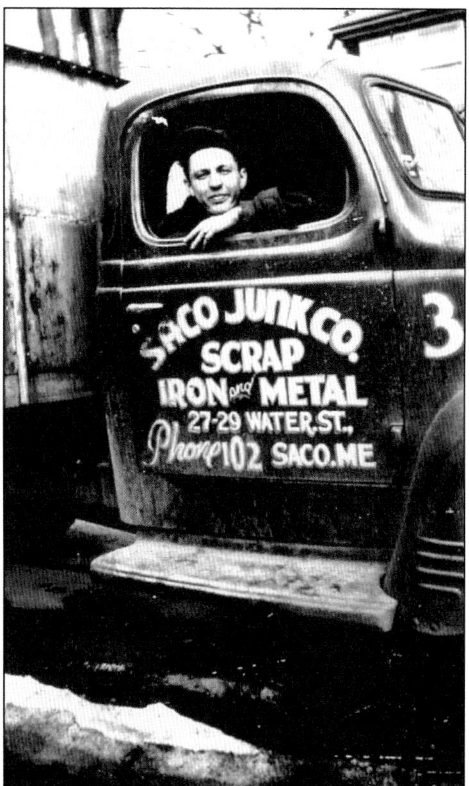

Harry Zaitlin is shown here in a Saco Junk Company truck around 1950. His father, a Jewish immigrant from Minsk, Belarus, founded the company in Saco in the early 20th century. It later became Saco Steel Company and was operated by three generations of the Zaitlin family. (Courtesy Michael Zaitlin.)

Five

Worthy of Imitation

The second half of the 20th century saw the close of many of Saco's mills and factories. This led to an economic downturn, with the empty, boarded-up mill buildings a reminder of the city's former strength. It was perhaps that visual reminder of how transient history can be that inspired citizens to begin historic preservation efforts in the 1970s. These efforts resulted in the development of a historic preservation ordinance and a downtown historic district in the 1990s.

Saco's architecture has not remained frozen in time, however. The evolution of the First Parish Congregational Church provides a compelling story of how Main Street has changed over time. Twice destroyed by fire, the church—rebuilt most recently in 2004—still proudly holds its street corner, and it remains an icon and a landmark in the community. Other efforts of the new millennium include the creative reuse of the old mill buildings as offices, apartments, shops and artist studios, and the construction of a new train station in 2009. With these projects, Saco citizens have found that there is indeed much in the city's proud past to revere and emulate.

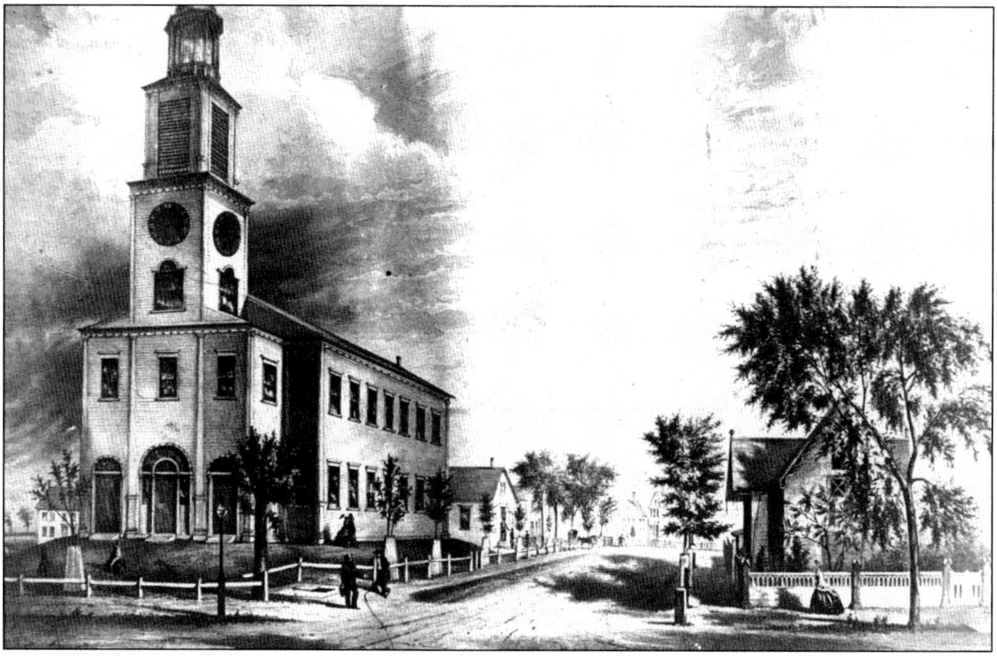

This lithograph shows the original First Parish Congregational Church of Saco, built in 1803 on the corner of Main and Beach Streets. The artist, Charles Henry Granger—himself an important icon of Saco arts and history—clearly made this print as a memorial after the church burned in 1860. The inscription on the original lithograph notes that the church was "Built 1803-DED-1806-Burnt July 8th 1860."

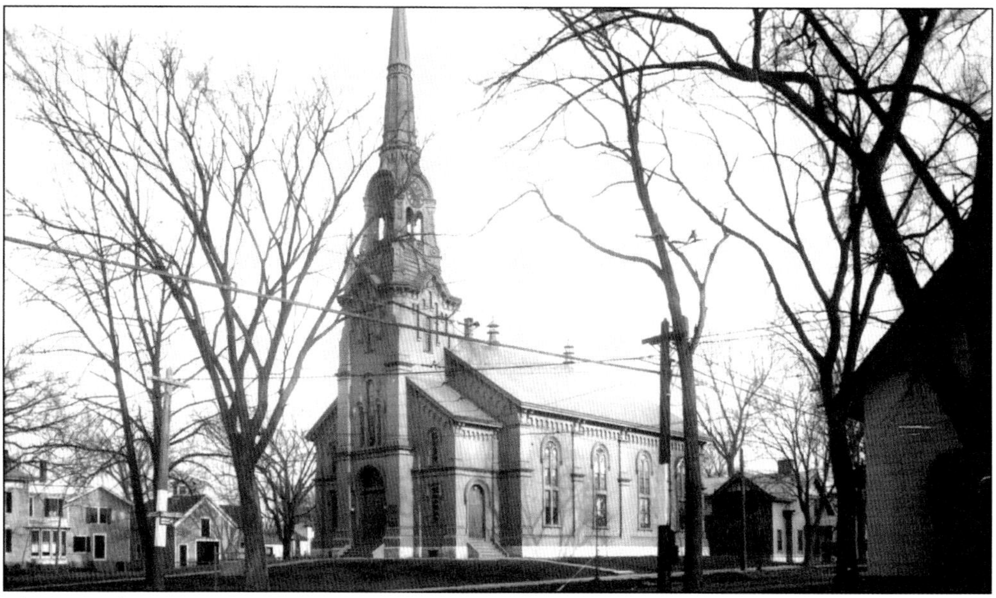

The second First Parish Congregational Church was built 1863 on the site of original church that had been destroyed by fire three years earlier. Seen here around 1896, it was designed by Boston architect John Stevens (not to be confused with Portland-based John Calvin Stevens, architect of the York Institute's 1926 building). Among its unique features were the 126-foot spire with a four-faced clock and a recast Paul Revere bell that had been in the original church.

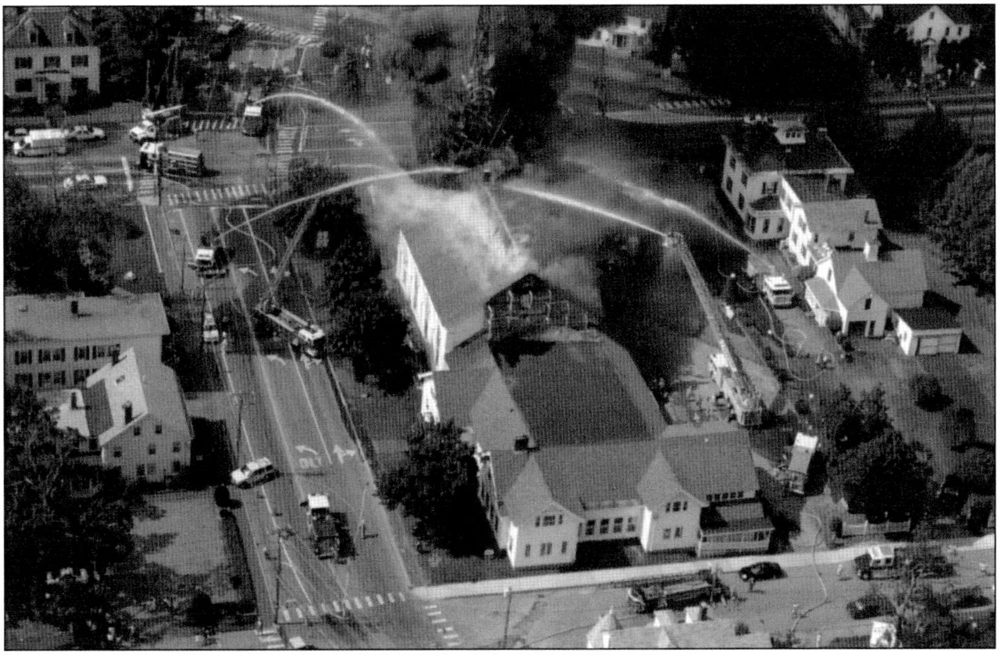

In 2000, the residents of Saco watched in horror as the landmark First Parish Congregational Church burned to the ground. The 1863 building was undergoing restoration when a cigarette from one of the workers ignited some nearby flammable materials. Although emergency workers responded quickly, the blaze was unstoppable, and the church was completely destroyed. As Charles Henry Granger did in 1860, citizens were moved immediately to memorialize the lost church. Surviving fragments of the building soon entered the collection of the Saco Museum.

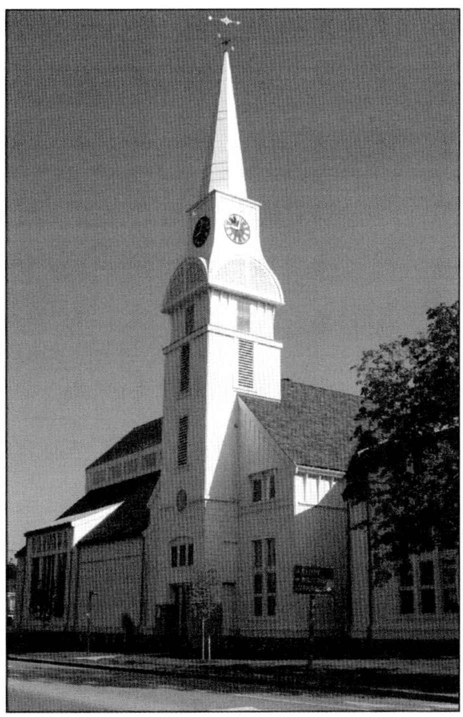

On December 5, 2004, the doors were opened to a new First Parish Congregational Church, which stands today on the original site on the corner of Main and Beach Streets. Remnants of the original 1803 Paul Revere bell were again recast for the bell of this church building. Although its physical presence has changed over the years, the church remains a pillar of the community. (Photograph by Leslie Rounds.)

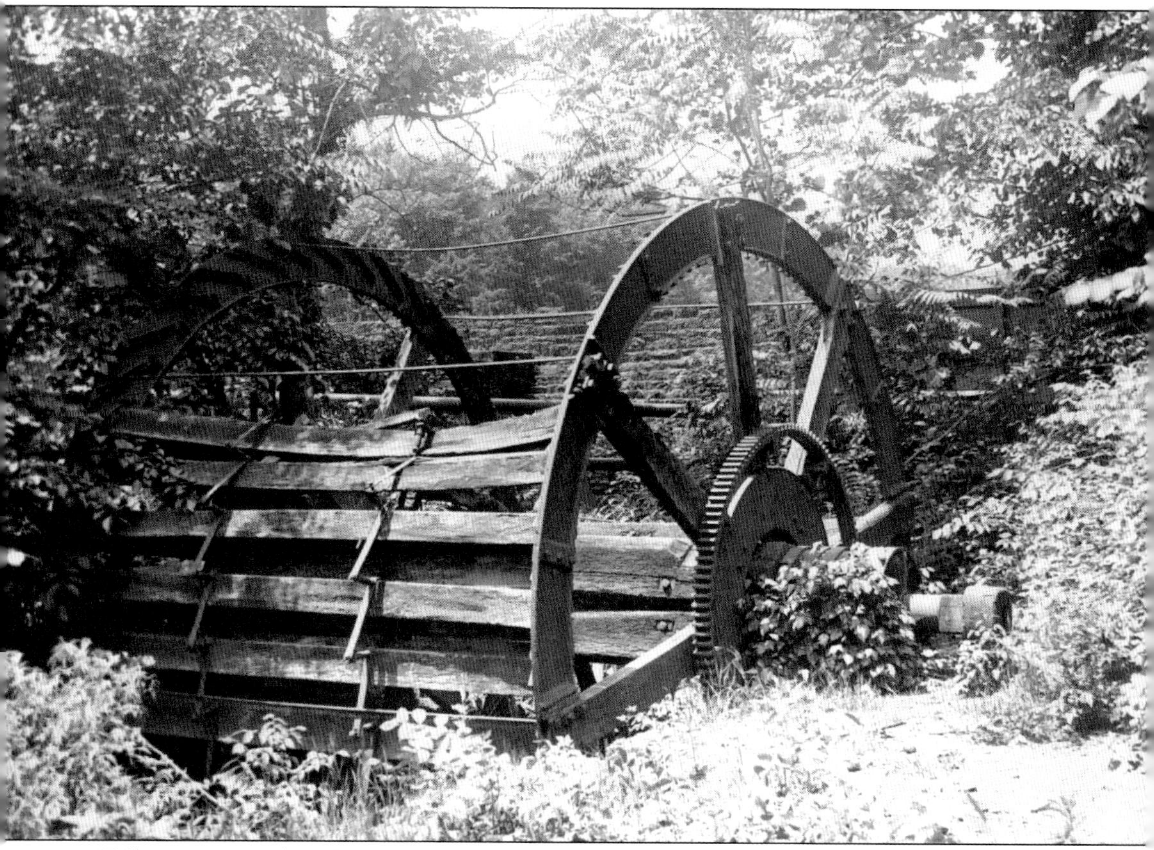

Fallen into ruin, this old, wooden waterwheel demonstrates how use of the river's power changed dramatically by the early 20th century. The wheel captured the power of the river in a modest way that was clearly a precursor to the dynamic forces that led to the explosive development of textile mills on the Saco River and the resulting dramatic changes in life for local inhabitants. (Photograph by Charles Moody; courtesy McArthur Public Library.)

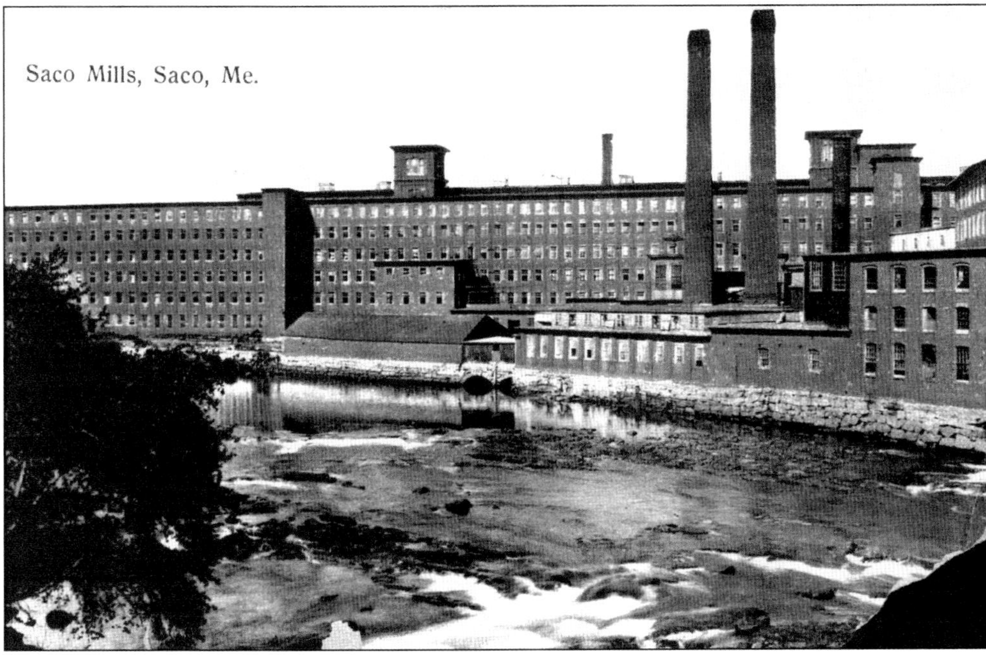

By the late 19th and early 20th centuries, the formidable mill district had completely transformed the landscape of the Saco River and falls as it rushed toward the sea. What had been a picturesque natural landscape had become a dynamic industrial one filled not only with the mills but also with throngs of workers.

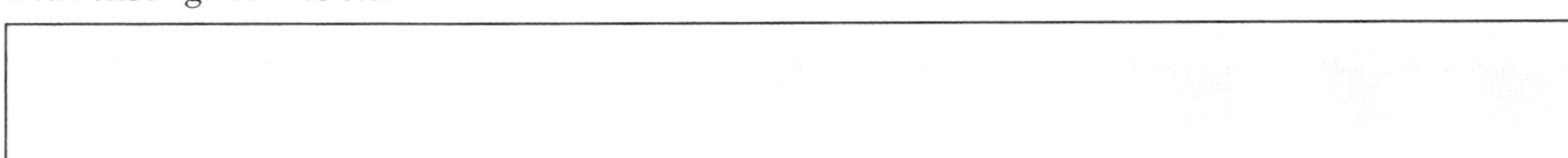

No longer used for large-scale textile manufacturing, the mills on Factory Island (now also known as Saco Island) have lost most of their giant smokestacks and other industrial features. Apartments, artists' studios, restaurants, and athletic facilities now make good use of the soaring spaces and plentiful light of the mills' interiors. The windmill used to power the 2009 train station is visible above the buildings. (Photograph by Leslie Rounds.)

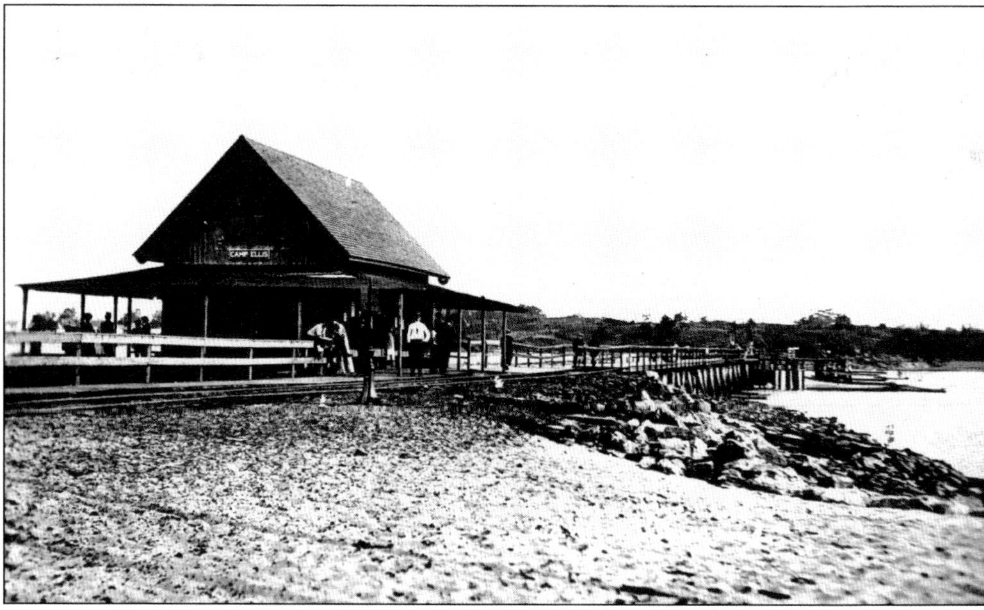

Tourists gather at the train station for the dummy railroad at Camp Ellis. This view of the old station represents what was at the time a modern way for getting from place to place. Although the dummy's route from Camp Ellis to Old Orchard Beach was short and simple, railways extending throughout the northeast and beyond made it possible to get from Saco to almost anywhere else in the country and vice versa.

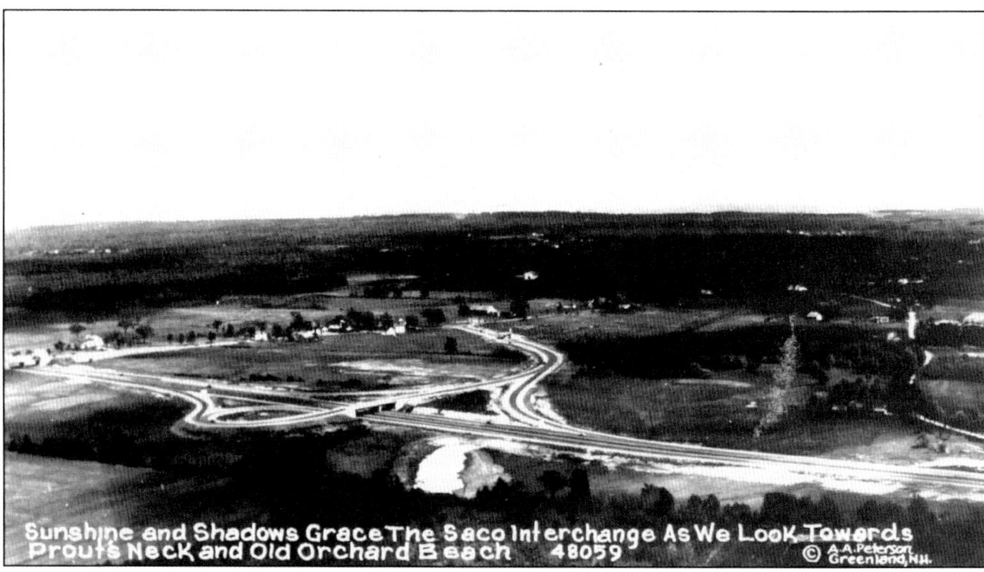

Prior to the completion of Interstate 95 in 1947, tourists came to the Saco Bay area first by train, then by surprisingly extensive interstate trolley routes, and later by automobile along Route 1 with its numerous traffic lights. The completion of the Saco highway interchange put southern Maine within convenient reach of many more potential tourists and had a dramatic impact on life in the Saco Bay area.

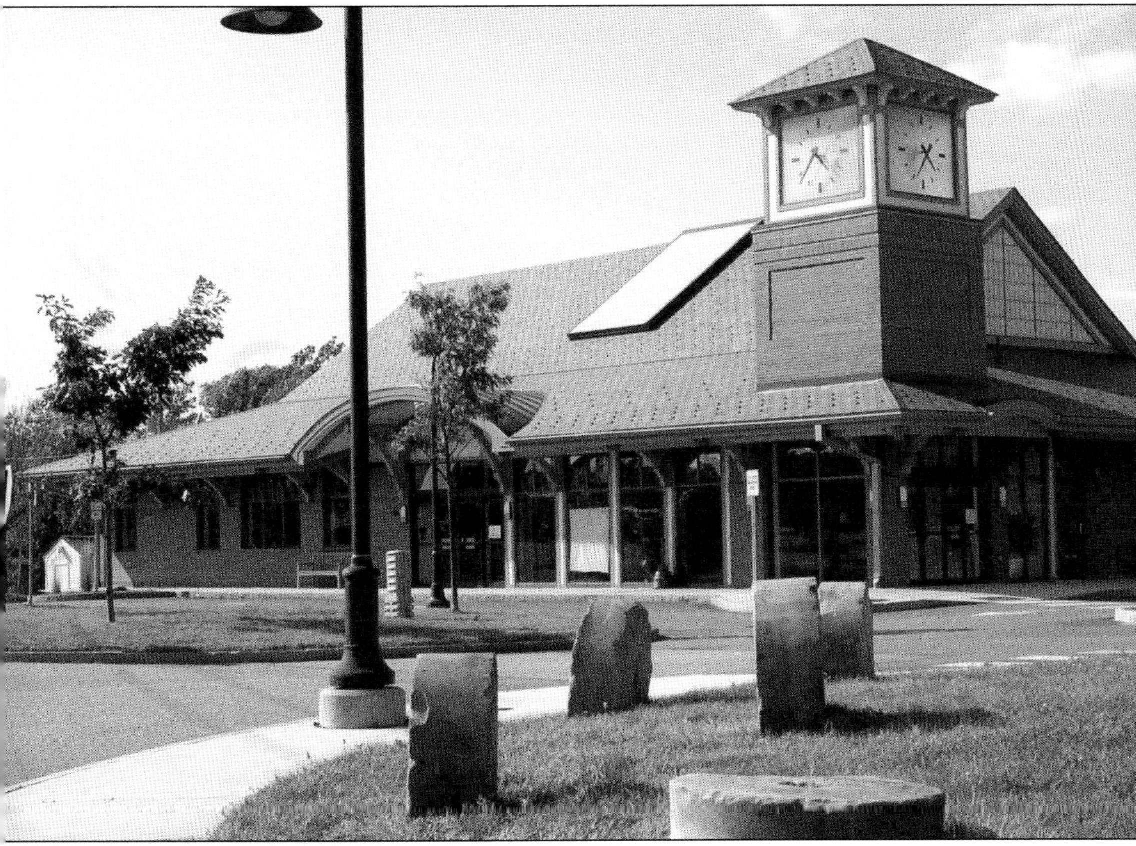

Opened on February 27, 2009, the Saco Transportation Center has once again made Saco a railway hub between Boston and the rest of Maine. The new building also broke new ground as the first "green" train station in the country. Just as the mills took advantage of the natural resource of waterpower, the train station employs a windmill just outside the main building to supply electricity; various architectural elements also work to harness and conserve energy. The stone grinding wheels arrayed outside, once used for grinding grain into flour at local gristmills, symbolically connect the transportation center back to the earliest buildings powered by nature's forces. (Photograph by Leslie Rounds.)

Bibliography

Anagnostis, John. *49 Storer Street*. Portland, ME: Walch Printing, 2007.

Deering, Frank C. *A Short Story on Saco River White Pine*. Biddeford, ME: 1901.

De Wolfe, Elizabeth A. *The Murder of Mary Bean and Other Stories*. Kent, OH: The Kent State University Press, 2007.

Downs, Jacques. *The Cities on the Saco: A Pictorial History*. Norfolk, VA: The Donning Company Publishers, 1985.

Fairfield, Roy P. *Sands, Spindles, and Steeples: A History of Saco, Maine*. Portland, ME: House of Falmouth, 1956.

———. *New Compass Points: 20th-century Saco*. Saco, ME: Bastille Books, 1988.

———. *Survival at Work and Home: Saco-Lowell Shops in WWII*. Saco, ME: Bastille Books, 2009.

Folsom, George. *A History of Saco and Biddeford, With Notices of other Early Settlements, and of the Proprietary Governments, in Maine, Including the Province of New Somersetshire and Lygonia*. Saco, ME: Alex C. Putnam, 1830.

Gibb, George Sweet. *The Saco-Lowell Shops: Textile Machinery in New England, 1813–1949*. Cambridge, MA: Harvard University Press, 1950.

Hardiman, Tom. "Downtown History." www.sacomaine.org, July 28, 2009.

———. "A History of Factory Island." www.sacomaine.org, July 28, 2009.

———. "History and Significance of the Old Dyer Library Building." www.sacomaine.org, July 28, 2009.

———. "Walking Tour of Main Street." www.sacomaine.org, July 28, 2009.

Locke, J. S. *Shores of Saco Bay: A Historical Guide to Biddeford Pool, Old Orchard Beach, Pine Point, Prout's Neck*. Boston, MA: J. S Locke and Company Publishers, 1880.

Owen, Daniel E. *Old Times in Saco: A Brief Monograph on Local Events*. Saco, ME: Biddeford Times, 1891.

Scontras, Peter. *Saco: Then and Now: A Diverse Heritage*. Saco, ME: Scontras Publishing Company, 1994.

Scully, Jeffrey A. *Saco*. Augusta, ME: Alan Sutton, Inc., 1994

———. *It Happened Right Here! More than 365 Events that Shaped the Course of History in Biddeford, Saco, and Old Orchard Beach*. Saco, ME: Doodlebug Publishing, 1999.

Sprague, Laura Fecych, ed. *Agreeable Situations: Society, Commerce, and Art in Southern Maine, 1780–1830*. Boston, MA: Northeastern University, 1987.

About the Dyer Library and Saco Museum

Located side by side, the Dyer Library and Saco Museum serve as a lively center of culture and education for Saco and surrounding communities. Since 1881, Dyer Library has served the changing educational and cultural needs of the Saco area. In addition to maintaining a strong and growing collection of books, periodicals, and reference materials, the Dyer Library offers extensive archives and a wide array of community programs. The Saco Museum, founded as the York Institute in 1866, boasts an exemplary collection of more than 10,000 artifacts, including superb collections of documented local furniture, clocks, and other decorative arts such as silver, ceramics, textiles, and costumes. The museum is well known for its rich collection of paintings from the Saco River region, including the finest and largest collection of portraits by the renowned deaf artist John Brewster Jr. (1766–1854). Historical collections and exhibits are augmented with exhibitions of contemporary local art and engaging, fun-filled programs and events for all ages.

In 2005, the pioneering One Card, Two Doors program debuted, offering unlimited free admission to the Saco Museum for all Dyer Library cardholders and their guests. In this way, the Saco Museum remains absolutely free to all residents of Saco, allowing the library and museum to fulfill their mission to "promote life-long learning and appreciation of culture; preservation of the past; and state-of-the-art services and resources for all."

The Dyer Library and Saco Museum are located at 371 Main Street, U.S. Route 1, in the heart of Saco's historic downtown. Nearby attractions include beaches, restaurants, theaters, and amusement parks. Both the library and museum are open year-round. Please call (207) 283-3861 or visit the Web site at www.dyerlibrarysacomuseum.org for hours, admission, and information about exhibitions and programs.